ACKNOWLEDGEMENTS

I would like to thank the wide variety of people who helped initiate and organise this book and the original series in *New Society*. I am particularly indebted to Michael Williams, editor of *Society Today*, who initiated, nay inspired, the original idea for this series, and to his successor, Caroline St John Brooks who 'mothered' it through its last year. Thanks too to David Lipsey, editor of *New Society*, for permission to reprint the Great Ideas series in this form. Finally, many thanks to Honor Dines for the time, effort and care she put into typing the manuscript.

I wish to dedicate this book to my father and to the memory of my mother for all they did and have done for me.

Martin Slattery

The author and publishers wish to thank the following for permission to use copyright material:

The Associated Examining Board, Joint Matriculation Board, University of Cambridge Local Examinations Syndicate, University of London School Examinations Board, University of Oxford Delegacy of Local Examinations and the Welsh Joint Education Committee for questions from past examination papers.

They also acknowledge the following photographic sources:

Camera Press, The Communist Party of Great Britain, Mary Evans Picture Library, Harvard University, Hulton Picture Company, Mansell Collection, Museum of London, Popperfoto, Topham Picture Library, University of Kent, University of Liverpool.

Every effort has been made to trace all the copyright holders but if any have been inadvertently overlooked the publishers will be pleased to make the necessary arrangement at the first opportunity.

CONTENTS

	Acknowledgements	iii
	List of Ideas	vii
	Introduction	ix
	History of Sociological Ideas	xi
1	Louis Althusser *and* structural Marxism	1
2	Howard Becker *and* labelling theory	9
3	Daniel Bell *and* post-industrial society	16
4	Basil Bernstein *and* linguistic codes	23
5	Harry Braverman *and* deskilling	31
6	Manuel Castells *and* collective consumption	39
7	Auguste Comte *and* positivism	44
8	Ralf Dahrendorf *and* conflict theory	50
9	Emile Durkheim *and* social solidarity	55
10	Emile Durkheim *and* anomie	63
11	Friedrich Engels *and* historical materialism	67
12	Feminists *and* patriarchy	77
13	Feminists *and* gender	86
14	Andre Gunder Frank *and* dependency theory	94
15	The Frankfurt School *and* critical theory	101
16	Harold Garfinkel *and* ethnomethodology	111
17	Erving Goffman *and* stigma	116
18	John Goldthorpe, David Lockwood *et al. and* embourgeoisement	120
19	Antonio Gramsci *and* hegemony	125
20	Jürgen Habermas *and* legitimation crisis	131
21	Edmund Husserl, Alfred Schutz *and* phenomenology	140
22	Ivan Illich *and* deschooling	149

23   Clark Kerr *et al. and* convergence thesis   156
24   Thomas S. Kuhn *and* paradigms   162
25   Oscar Lewis *and* culture of poverty   169
26   Karl Mannheim *and* ideology   176
27   Karl Marx *and* alienation   180
28   Elton Mayo *and* human relations   186
29   George Herbert Mead *and* symbolic interactionism   191
30   Robert K. Merton *and* sociology of science   196
31   Robert Michels *and* iron law of oligarchy   205
32   C. Wright Mills *and* power elite   210
33   Raymond E. Pahl *and* urban managerialism   215
34   Raymond E. Pahl, Jack Winkler *and* corporatism   220
35   Vilfredo Pareto, Gaetano Mosca *and* elite theory   227
36   Robert E. Park *and* human ecology   234
37   Talcott Parsons *and* structural functionalism   240
38   Karl Popper *and* falsification   247
39   Nicos Poulantzas *and* relative autonomy   252
40   John Rex, Robert Moore *and* housing classes   258
41   Robert Rosenthal, Leone Jacobson *and*
        self-fulfilling prophecy   265
42   Walt Whitman Rostow *and* modernisation theory   269
43   Georg Simmel *and* formal sociology   276
44   Herbert Spencer *and* social Darwinism   282
45   Frederick Winslow Taylor *and* scientific management   287
46   Ferdinand Tönnies *and gemeinschaft–gesellschaft*   292
47   Max Weber *and* Protestant ethic   297
48   Max Weber *and* bureaucracy   303
49   Bryan Wilson *and* secularisation   310
50   Louis Wirth *and* urbanism   315
     Bibliography   320

LIST OF IDEAS

ALIENATION   Karl Marx
ANOMIE   Emile Durkheim
BUREAUCRACY   Max Weber
COLLECTIVE CONSUMPTION
    Manuel Castells
CONFLICT THEORY
    Ralf Dahrendorf
CONVERGENCE THESIS
    Clark Kerr *et al*
CORPORATISM   Raymond E.
Pahl, Jack Winkler
CRITICAL THEORY
    Frankfurt School
CULTURE OF POVERTY
    Oscar Lewis
DEPENDENCY THEORY
    Andre Gunder Frank
DESCHOOLING   Ivan Illich
DESKILLING   Harry Braverman
ELITE THEORY   Vilfredo Pareto,
    Gaetano Mosca
EMBOURGEOISEMENT
    John Goldthorpe,
    David Lockwood *et al*
ETHNOMETHODOLOGY
    Harold Garfinkel
FALSIFICATION   Karl Popper
FORMAL SOCIOLOGY
    Georg Simmel

GEMEINSCHAFT–GESELLSCHAFT
    Ferdinand Tönnies
GENDER   Feminists
HEGEMONY   Antonio Gramsci
HISTORICAL MATERIALISM
    Friedrich Engels
HOUSING CLASSES   John Rex,
    Robert Moore
HUMAN ECOLOGY
    Robert E. Park
HUMAN RELATIONS
    Elton Mayo
IDEOLOGY   Karl Mannheim
IRON LAW OF OLIGARCHY
    Robert Michels
LABELLING THEORY
    Howard Becker
LEGITIMATION CRISIS
    Jurgen Habermas
LINGUISTIC CODES
    Basil Bernstein
MODERNISATION THEORY
    Walt Whitman Rostow
PARADIGMS   Thomas S. Kuhn
PATRIARCHY   Feminists
PHENOMENOLOGY
    Edmund Husserl,
    Alfred Schutz
POSITIVISM   Auguste Comte

vii

POST-INDUSTRIAL SOCIETY
  Daniel Bell
POWER ELITE   C. Wright Mills
PROTESTANT ETHIC
  Max Weber
RELATIVE AUTONOMY
  Nicos Poulantzas
SCIENTIFIC MANAGEMENT
  Frederick Winslow Taylor
SECULARISATION
  Bryan Wilson
SELF-FULFILLING PROPHECY
  Robert Rosenthal,
  Leone Jacobson
SOCIAL DARWINISM
  Herbert Spencer

SOCIAL SOLIDARITY
  Emile Durkheim
SOCIOLOGY OF SCIENCE
  Robert K. Merton
STIGMA   Erving Goffman
STRUCTURAL FUNCTIONALISM
  Talcott Parsons
STRUCTURAL MARXISM
  Louis Althusser
SYMBOLIC INTERACTIONISM
  George Herbert Mead
URBANISM   Louis Wirth
URBAN MANAGERIALISM
  Raymond E. Pahl

INTRODUCTION

This book is the complete series of Great Ideas run by the magazine *New Society* in their schools' supplement 'Society Today' between November 1984 until the magazine's 'marriage' with *New Statesman* in 1988.

The aim of the series was to provide short, sharp summaries of some of the 'great' sociological ideas of the past hundred years or so. The series was aimed at students taking 'A' Level or introductory courses in sociology or any of the related social sciences, such as social anthropology, politics, social policy, offering them brief but readable outlines of some of the major ideas and key thinkers that they were likely to come across or needed to study.

The aim of this book is essentially the same. It is simply more comprehensive, offering:

- Fifty instead of the original thirty-two published ideas
- More detail in terms of outline and analysis
- More guidance and suggestions for follow-up in terms of reading and examination questions.

The structure of this book is as follows:
1 The author – the man or woman who initiated a particular idea. This brief biographical introduction is intended to help readers understand more about the person behind a particular sociological idea, his/her own background and general theoretical aims. Where, as for example in the case of the feminists, no single author can be clearly identified, then some theoretical background is provided.
2 The idea – each idea is outlined in detail, in a fairly clear and structured way, using sociological terminology only when really necessary.

3 The idea in action – an evaluation of each idea in terms of its reception, criticisms and continued use within sociological theory and research.

Each idea is accompanied by:

A photograph/drawing of the author involved, where available.

Cross-referencing with other ideas where appropriate.

Suggested reading to enable students to follow up on a particular idea or author in more detail. The books suggested are those that are most appropriate for 'A' Level and introductory students (i.e. they are short, relatively easy to read and reasonably easy to get hold of).

Further reading giving the author's own work and criticisms of it which will enable the students to give a deep level of understanding.

Examination questions from all the major 'A' Level Boards to illustrate the way that each idea can be used to help with essays, exams and revision. Please note that no one idea can fully answer any questions and use the see also section for other ideas that should contribute to your essay or coursework.

In addition there is:

A brief history of sociological ideas showing how the fifty in this book fit into developments in social theory.

A List of Ideas complementing the 'Contents by Author'.

A Bibliography at the end to enable students to follow up references in the text.

This book is, therefore, an accessible introduction to social theory, particularly for 'A' Level students. The fifty ideas cover a wide range of sociological concepts and topics. It does not provide comprehensive review of social theory – other suitable textbooks are suggested – but it does provide fairly detailed explanations and reviews of many key sociological ideas. Social theory is now a virtually compulsory part of any 'A' Level or introductory course in sociology. It is probably the hardest part of such courses – and made that much harder by the abstract theoretical language sociologists often use. However, it is a vital foundation for properly understanding modern sociology as a source of ideas about our social world today and as a way of both understanding and examining it. This book will at least start you on the road to sociological enlightenment, help you begin to understand the great men and women who have produced ideas that, even today, inspire debate, research and further sociological thinking.

HISTORY OF SOCIOLOGICAL IDEAS

Though the history of social thought can be traced back to the earliest of civilisations, to the Greeks, Romans and Chinese, the history of sociological ideas as a distinct academic discipline is quite short – barely spanning the 150 years since Auguste Comte first coined the term 'Sociology' (or, as he initially called it, Social Physics). Sociology as a subject emerged from the great ideas of its three founding fathers – Emile Durkheim, Max Weber and Karl Marx. The grand theories of this 'holy trinity' have laid the foundation for sociological thought and research ever since. They sought to discover the inner workings of society at large. They tried to explain what society is, what the relationship between society and the individual is, what the dominant forces on social and historical change are.

■ All three saw society as an entity in its own right.
■ All three saw economic, political and ideological factors as crucial to social order and social change, though they differed radically in their interpretations of which factor(s) was the most important.
■ All three sought to unravel that most complex of issues, the relationship between man and society – is society more than the sum of its members? Does it have a reality of its own and the ability to control the lives and destinies of those living within its structure? Or, is man a free agent, capable of controlling his own future?

They identified the key issues for sociological analysis – issues such as social order and change, power and social control, inequality and social stratification – and laid down the foundations for sociology as a scientific discipline.

Durkheim, Weber and Marx, however, were not simply academics or armchair theorists. They honestly, and in Marx's case at least, passionately, believed that social analysis could change the world, that a science of society was not just a philosophical enterprise, but had the potential to improve society in the future. They, like many sociologists since, were inspired by the times they lived in. The eighteenth and nineteenth centuries in Western Europe experienced some of the great social, economic and political upheavals in human history, upheavals that were to change the face of western society as three great 'revolutions' broke forth almost simultaneously – the economic, the political and the ideological:

■ The great Industrial, Agrarian and Urban Revolutions of the seventeenth century onwards which transformed Britain and then Europe from rural agricultural societies into advanced industrial economies based on urban structures.
■ The great political revolutions of the late eighteenth and nineteenth centuries which began with the French Revolution, swept away the old feudal power structures and unleashed the forces of democracy, equality and freedom.
■ The great Scientific Revolution of the seventeenth century which, though less explosive, nevertheless transformed western thought and introduced 'science' as we know it today as a way of analysing and controlling the world about us.

Whilst we today are used to rapid change and accept it as part of modern life, to the men and women of the eighteenth and nineteenth centuries life was in turmoil and society seemed to be in the grip of forces beyond man's control. Traditional life, the very moral fabric and community spirit of the old order was being overturned and all the future seemed to offer was chaos and anarchy. It was against this background that the grand theories of Durkheim, Weber and Marx must be understood and appreciated. They had no modern computers or research teams, nothing but brilliant minds and profound social insight. Their true legacy is the fact that, even today, a hundred years later, all three are major schools of thought within sociology, still inspire intense debate and detailed research.

This book can only offer a taste of their ideas and the key thinkers that followed, but it does highlight some of their chief concerns and the context within which their ideas evolved.

Durkheim's concept of social solidarity and Marx and Engels' theory of historical materialism were both major attempts to explain social order and change, whilst both the concept of anomie and that of alienation attempted to analyse the individual caught up in forces beyond his control. Though Weber also saw industrialisation as progressive, he too feared that modern man would soon be trapped in an 'iron cage', one created not by the underlying economic or social forces within society, but by its inner logic of thought and organisation, the techno-rationality that infused both the protestant ethic as the spirit of capitalism and bureaucracy as the major form of organisation in advanced societies.

These three great thinkers were not, however, the only important social theorists of the late nineteenth and early twentieth centuries. They simply laid the foundations of three of the major theoretical perspectives within modern sociology. Many other social theorists provided crucial insights and laid the foundations for what have become key disciplines within sociology.

■ August Comte founded the positivist idea of sociology as a science.
■ Ferdinand Tönnies evoked the concepts of *gemeinschaft–gesellschaft* to express his fears about the 'loss of community in industrial society' and so founded the sociological tradition of community studies which evolved into present-day urban sociology.
■ Mosca, Pareto and Michels established the sociology of power, especially of elite power, as a central focus of modern sociology.
■ George Herbert Mead laid the foundations of symbolic interactionism.
■ F.W. Taylor, though a businessman rather than an academic, preached the virtues of scientific management which has become a key concept and source of debate in industrial sociology.

All these classical thinkers took as the focus of their analyses issues of central concern to western society at the turn of the century – society at large, the individual in modern society, the causes and effects of social change. All helped establish and spread the new discipline of sociology, though more amongst fellow academics than society at large. It is interesting to note the preponderance of European, especially German, thinkers in this age of grand theory. American and especially British sociology has always been more empirical and practical, more directed to factual evidence and social policy than abstract theory.

In the twentieth century, sociological thought has become more professional and technical, more specifically academic, specialist and university-based. Whilst brilliant individuals like Marx and Weber, with encyclopaedic knowledge and an enormous breadth of vision and practical insight, do still exist and come to the fore, modern sociology is primarily an academic profession conducted in universities and divided into specialist sub-disciplines concentrating on such 'sociologies'

as education, development, deviance and so on. Whilst some continue
to develop abstract theory, others using modern computer techniques
and quantitative analysis have opened up whole areas of social life to
surveys and other forms of empirical research. Schools of sociology and
research programmes characterise modern sociology more than outstanding individual thinkers.

Similarly, the grand theories of the founding fathers which sought to
take in and explain every aspect of modern society have tended to give
way to what Robert Merton has called 'theories of the middle-range' –
more limited concepts or theoretical explanations of one particular
area or topic in sociology. Examples of this approach include Basil
Bernstein's idea of linguistic codes in education and Ray Pahl's analysis
of urban managerialism. The Chicago School in America and the
Frankfurt School in Germany exemplified the team approach whereby
a team of sociologists using a similar theoretical framework sought to
analyse a wide range of contemporary social issues.

The great exception to this decline of grand theory is Talcott Parsons' idea of structural functionalism. As its title so clearly shows, this
was a highly technical and very abstract theory of social order and
change. Though inspired by such European thinkers as Simmel, Weber
and, especially, Durkheim, Parsons' schema reflected the emergence of
American sociology on to the western scene and, like much else American in this period, dominated Anglo-American sociology to the point
that most sociology in the 1940s and 1950s was structural-functional-
ist in perspective. The rise of 'new', more radical sociologies in the
1960s was in part inspired by a desire to throw off the theoretical
'shackles' of structural functionalism and to revive sociology by turning back to the great ideas of Marx and Weber.

Just as the nineteenth century was the age of the Industrial Revolution, so the twentieth century has been one of major economic, political and social changes, upheavals and crises – two World Wars, the
Russian Revolution and the spread of communism, Germany, Italy and
Spain and the rise of fascism, Hitler, Stalin and the growth of the
totalitarian state, the Cold War and the Nuclear Arms Race, the Great
Crash and the economic depressions of the 1930s and 1970s, the
collapse of the great European empires, the spread of nationalism and
emergence of Third World nations into world politics and the world
economy. Issues like these have inspired and informed many sociological theories such as A. Gunder Frank's concern with the relationship of dependency that exists between First and Third World nations,
and C.W. Mills' and Winkler and Pahl's concern with the 'corporate'
power of the modern state. Underlying many of these ideas is a con-

cern, even fear, for the individual in modern mass society – a fear that he is oppressed, alienated and manipulated – a fear epitomised by the Frankfurt School's 'Critical Theory' and by the Chicago School's urban sociology as it sought to plot the plight of urban man. Similarly, many of the ideas of the 1960s were directly inspired by, and also acted as inspirations for, the student revolutions in Britain, America and Europe in the 1960s, revolutions which reflected a growing concern about civil rights and the rights and freedoms of 'minority and oppressed' groups, whether of Blacks, women or gays, new 'underclasses' which have replaced or joined the working class as the basis of new radical theories of social reform, be they Manuel Castell's notion of collective consumption or feminists' assaults on patriarchy.

The best way, however, to view much modern sociology is as a debate – a debate either with contemporary theorists or with the founding fathers, a debate about how sociology generally, or a single sub-discipline in particular, should progresss. For example: whilst western sociology in general, and Anglo-American sociology in particular, in the 1930s and immediate post-war years, reflected the dominance of structural functionalism, the late 1960s and early 1970s saw a theoretical revolution which affected sociology everywhere. Younger, more radical sociologists threw off the conservative mantle of structural functionalism in search of more exciting theories which could explain more clearly the growth of violence, conflict and group struggle in western society as student revolution, Black power, women's rights and environmental groups poured on to the streets in protest. Some turned to the conflict-based ideas of Marx and Weber (e.g. Castells, Rex & More, Pahl), others used phenomenology in its varied forms (symbolic interactionism, ethnomethodology) to challenge the sociological establishment and the dominance of functionalism and positivism. Hence the emergence of labelling theory, the sociology of development, urban sociology, neo-Marxism and neo-Weberian ideas. Hence the renewed debate about sociology as a science and a renewed focus in theory and research on the individual, small groups and personal relationships. This challenge, however, was not just of new against old, but also female against male as the feminist assault on the male establishment grew in force and numbers. Just as sociologists never refer to 'founding mothers', so feminists highlighted the invisibility of half the human race from virtually all sociological perspectives. It was simply taken for granted that male sociologists were capable of representing women as well as their own sex. Feminists have forced the issues of gender and patriarchy on to the sociological agenda and established 'women's studies' as an accepted sub-discipline of sociology. How far male sociologists have incorporated gender issues into their analyses is still highly debatable.

These debates raged across the whole of sociology and within particular sub-disciplines. Hence, for example, the secularisation debate between Bryan Wilson and David Martin in the field of religion, the Rostow–Frank debate on development in the Third World and T.S. Kuhn's critique of traditional views of science and knowledge. What is significant throughout all these discussions is the extent to which, in this research for new ideas, younger sociologists turned again to the founding fathers for inspiration. Durkheim, Weber and, in particular, Marx are now again at the centre of sociological thought and debate. No one theoretical perspective dominates in the way structural functionalism did in the 1930 to 1960 period, but Marxist ideas have certainly proliferated in the 1970s and early 1980s. Marxism never was restricted solely to sociological thought, but has influenced thinking throughout the social sciences, humanities, and has even extended into such fields as literature, art and science. Equally, it never has been a single creed with only one orthodoxy, but always the subject of intense, often bitter, debate and re-interpretation. Even in his own time Marx had to disclaim the way some of this followers interpreted his ideas, even to the point of declaring, 'As for me, I am not a Marxist'. The incomplete and very complex nature of his writings, their popular interpretation by Engels and the ever-changing nature of the real world have all added fuel to the argument about the validity of Marx's theory which is as strong today as ever it was a hundred years ago. Follow the ideas of Marx and Engels, the Frankfurt School, Antonio Gramsci, Louis Althusser, Harry Braverman and Jurgen Habermas to get some idea of the ebb and flow of this Marxist debate as the western working class has failed to rise up in revolution and fulfil their historic mission of liberation, equality and fraternity.

This, then, is a very brief overview of the fifty sociological ideas covered in this book. It is incomplete and sketchy and any serious appreciation of the value and excitement of theoretical ideas can only come by follow-up reading using the references below. Social theory, however, is never easy, and often made all the more difficult by abstract language in which it is written. It does require real effort, imagination and careful thought if you are really to get to grips with it. Make that effort, read as much as you can and you will find it extremely rewarding. It will help make sense of sociology in general, but, more important, help you understand the society you live in. These fifty ideas are just a start. Hopefully they will inspire you to read further and deeper in a field of fascinating insights and ideas.

SUGGESTED READING

Anderson R.J. and Sharrock W.W. *Teaching Papers in Sociology* Longman including: Pettil P. 'The Philosophies of Social Science', Morgan D. 'Gender', Jessop B. 'Varieties of Marxism', Halfpenny P. 'Principles of Method'

Brown C.H. *Understanding Society*, John Murray, 1979

Craib I. *Modern Social Theory*, Wheatsheaf, 1984

Cuff E.C. and Payne G.C.F. *Perspectives in Sociology*, George Allen & Unwin, 1979, 1984

Hamilton P. ed. Key Sociologists series and Key Ideas series, Tavistock

Jones P. *Theory and Method in Sociology*, University Tutorial Press, 1985

Maynard M. *Sociological Theory*, Longman, 1989

Slattery M. *ABC of Sociology*, Macmillan, 1985

Williams M. ed. *Society Today*, Macmillan, 1986 – a collection of the *New Society/Society Today* series

Worsley P. *Modern Sociology. Introductory Readings*, Penguin, 1970

1

LOUIS ALTHUSSER *and*

STRUCTURAL MARXISM

THE AUTHOR

Louis Althusser (1918–   ) was born in Algeria and educated in Algiers, Marseilles and Lyons. As a soldier in the French army, he was captured by the Germans in 1940 and spent five years in a concentration camp. After the war he studied, and later lectured, at the Ecole Normale Supérieure in Paris. Althusser suffered from bouts of manic depression and occasionally spent time in mental hospitals. In November 1980 his wife Hélène was found strangled. Althusser confessed, but was too delirious to be charged, so he was sent to an asylum where he remains today.

Althusser was a French intellectual and Marxist philosopher. He was a leading figure in the French-based structuralist movement and his writings had a great influence on western Marxists after the student revolutions of the 1960s, particularly that in Paris in May 1968. His structural version of Marxism has not only influenced philosophers and sociologists, but anthropologists, historians and literary critics.

Althusser's key works include:

- *For Marx* (1965)
- *Reading Capital* (1965)
- *Lenin and Philosophy* (1969)
- *Essays in Self-Criticism* (1976)

(It is important to read Marx and Engels on historical materialism before attempting to understand Althusser's idea of structural Marxism.)

THE IDEA

Althusser's idea of structural Marxism arose in the 1960s out of the fervent and often bitter debates amongst western Marxists about the role of theory and the true interpretation of what Marx said (and meant). This radical reassessment was not only stimulated by such pre-war events as the Bolshevik Revolution, the rise of fascism and the failure of working-class revolutions, but by such contemporary events as the rise of Communist China, the student revolutions of the 1960s, particularly in Paris (May 1968) and, most especially, by Khruschev's denunciation of Stalin's rule in Soviet Russia in 1956. The inhuman atrocities, authoritarianism and oppression of Stalin's rule, justified in the name of Marxism, forced western intellectuals to reassess whether orthodox Marxism as propounded by the Soviet Communist Party was the only true interpretation of what the Master said. Many in the West looked back to the writings of the young or early Marx, particularly his emphasis on the individual acting on history and his concept of aliena-tion, and began developing a **humanist** interpretation of Marxism (e.g. Critical Theory, page 101).

   Althusser rejected both crude Marxism and Humanism with equal contempt, arguing that the only true Marxism was reflected in the scientific writings of the late Marx, writings which put the structure of society first and reduced the role of the individual to insignificance. Structural Marxism, therefore, rests on the notion of 'history without a subject'. Within the dynamic of historical change and the structures of society, human beings are merely puppets or props. For Althusser, Marxism was neither a world view nor an ideology, but a revolu-tionary science of history conceived as class struggle, offering both scientific knowledge of the world and a political strategy for promoting working-class revolution. His aim was to outline the mechanics of such a scientific and dialectical materialism, using the following key concepts.

SOCIAL STRUCTURES AND PRACTICES

Althusser identified three key social structures in any society (or, as he called it, 'social formation') – the economic, the political and the ideological. Within each of these structures, certain practices and rela-tionships take place.

RELATIVE AUTONOMY

Whilst crude Marxism saw everything in society as being determined by the economy, Althusser argued that each of his three social structures had some independence or relative autonomy. Each is capable of developing in its own way (up to a certain point) and its relationships to the other two levels of society may vary considerably according to the particular stage of historical development. To explain this inter-relationship, Ian Craib (1984) has suggested using the analogy of a multi-storey building. Whilst we cannot say that the ground floor 'causes' things to happen in the first and second floors, it does form their foundation, and all three do have some sort of relationship. None of the floors is independent, but equally none directly determines what goes on in the other two. They are both relatively dependent and relatively autonomous. Althusser goes further to suggest that the political and ideological levels may affect the economic – up to a certain point! Ultimately, 'the economic is determinant in the last instance', though 'the last instance never comes'. Thus Althusser is able to still give the economic substructure ultimate priority and yet recognise the independent and causal influences of political and ideological factors without being accused of being as deterministic as crude Marxism, nor as unscientific as humanism. It allowed Althusser to encourage the French Communist Party and his own students to take political action without compromising his belief that human action has little if any influence on history in the long term.

He went on to develop the concept of 'structure in dominance', the idea that within each social formation, one level may be dominant, may determine the other two (to a certain extent). For example, in feudal societies it was the political and ideological levels that were dominant, in early capitalist society the economic. Ultimately, however, it is the economic level which determines which level dominates, and when.

OVERDETERMINATION

By this concept Althusser meant that, with all three levels causing and determining change, society faces a mass of internal conflicts and contradictions. Moreover, each level also contains its own contradictions – the economic level, for example, is riven by the contradiction between the ability of capitalism to produce massive wealth, yet its inability to distribute this wealth equally and fairly because it is appropriated by the powerful few who own the means of production. This conflict of ownership and distribution not only sets up the dynamic of recurrent economic crises, but a class conflict. The conflicts within each level ultimately meet and reinforce each other, producing a potentially revolutionary situation as happened in Tsarist Russia, where not only were the peasants and landlords in conflict, but also the reactionaries and reformers within the Tsarist government.

MODE OF PRODUCTION

This term refers to a particular economic epoch or stage, distinguished by a particular set of forces and relations of production. Althusser's colleague Etienne Balibar outlined four main modes of production:

- Feudalism
- A transitional mode between feudalism and capitalism
- Capitalism
- Socialism

In contrast to crude historical materialism, structuralism saw the relationship both within and between modes of production as varied, complex and only indirectly determined. This allowed Althusser to overcome a major problem with crude Marxism of trying to explain how some societies, like the Chinese and even the Russian, jump or deviate from certain stages in historical materialism and so may adopt alternative paths to communism.

CLASS CONFLICT

Althusser, and his colleague Nicos Poulantzas, also developed a more complex analysis of modern class structures. In contrast to the basic two-class division of orthodox Marxism in any one mode of production (MOP), Poulantzas identified

- sub-classes such as the 'petit bourgeoisie' (managers, accountants, etc. who serve the owners of means of production) and such 'social categories' as state bureaucrats and the military who serve the state.
- class 'fragments' such as land-owners, industrialists and financiers, all of whom belong to the bourgeoisie in the capitalist mode of production but all of whom have separate interests and views, and so often conflict. The role of the state is to unify such fragments of the capitalist class and represent the interests of the capitalist system at large. To do this, it has to have relative autonomy (see page 252).

Althusser himself used the idea of ideological state apparatuses (ISAs) to highlight the complex correlation of political and ideological forces with the economy. Althusser's concept of the state is much broader than the normal view. It extends beyond the government bureaucracy, courts, police, and army to include the education system, media, church, trade unions and even the family – in fact any social institution that helps perpetuate the capitalist system. He thus placed the state as the head of the political system, at the heart of the capitalist social formation. State power, he argued, is two-fold. In the last instance the physical force of the police and army – the repressive state apparatus – will be used, but in advanced capitalist societies this is usually unnecessary due to the efficiency of the ideological state apparatus in gaining popular assent and controlling the masses ideologically.

The structuralist model of class conflict and state power was, therefore, far more sophisticated and flexible than that of orthodox Marxism, but still left analysis at the structural level and the economy pre-eminent. Political and ideological factors were important but subordinate, and the human actor had yet to make an appearance! Althusser confirmed the limited role of human action in his system of historical materialism by his final concept.

DEATH OF THE SUBJECT

Using concepts borrowed from the French psychoanalyst Jacques Lacan, particularly that of the unconscious, Althusser argued that we do not live in a real world but an ideological one created by the ideological apparatus of each social formation. By this means history ensures that we fulfil the roles and behaviour it has assigned to us. We may believe that we are in control of our own lives, that we are authors of our own actions, but this is, in fact, an illusion created by the socialisation process. We are but puppets on the strings of historical destiny and such a mystified, ideological existence will continue even under communism. Thus Althusser was able to totally reject the humanist idea of history as the embodiment and gradual emancipation of the human spirit.

THE IDEA IN ACTION

Althusser's structuralist interpretation of Marxism stimulated international recognition and widespread enthusiasm in the late 1960s and

1970s as a major challenge to both orthodox and humanist Marxism. It inspired intellectuals and students on both sides of the Atlantic, and has generated important empirical research, both within and outside the social sciences. His work attempts to tackle an inherent paradox in Marxism as to whether the ultimate driving forces in historical change are the impersonal ones of underlying economic forces or the revolutionary action of exploited and oppressed people united as social classes. Althusser's sophisticated analysis of scientific Marxism comes down firmly in favour of the former view, but by allowing the political level 'dominance' in the late capitalist stage, is able to continue encouraging contemporary political action by students, revolutionaries and the Communist Party. His division of Marx's writings into 'early' and 'late' and his key concepts, particularly 'mode of production', 'ISA' and 'death of the subject', inspired intense debate and research, and structuralism spread into an international movement which included Paul Hirst and Barry Hindess in Britain and Pierre Bourdieu in France.

However, Althusser's work also inspired extensive criticism, often bitter and even personal. He was accused of distorting Marx, of reviving Stalinism and simply of producing pretentious rubbish. Althusser's own manner and style of writing only helped fuel such ferment. His writings are very difficult to read, full of jargon, polemic, dogmatism and even abuse. He does not claim just to be interpreting Marx, but to be actually speaking for him. He would, therefore, not tolerate criticism or opposition and dismissed mainstream sociology as merely bourgeois and unscientific.

Criticisms highlighted important weaknesses in his key concepts.

MODE OF PRODUCTION

Structuralists only identified four modes, but others such as the Asiatic, identified by Marx, are also evident.

This concept is useful as a description of historical–economic stages, but fails to explain the mechanisms of social change – how one MOP evolves into another.

RELATIVE AUTONOMY

Whilst this concept helps give political and ideological factors some force in history, Althusser failed to specify clearly their limits – at what point the economic level steps in and takes charge.

CLASS CONFLICT

Neither Althusser nor Poulantzas clearly explain where class conflict originates from. It cannot come from the political or ideological apparatuses since they are designed to keep the system free from conflict. If they come from the economic sub-structure then we are back to crude economism. Althusser's notion of subjectivity leaves human beings merely acting out predetermined historical scripts. Why, then, bother taking political action? Why rebel against the system when the future is already predetermined? Surely the system cannot work, let alone change, without human action?

It is this problem of causality of what makes the system change – whether it is people or the class conflict – that is a central criticism of structuralism. It seems to depict the capitalist system as working itself by its own inherent contradictions and conflicts. The very structure of Althusser's model, its highly scientific notion of interlocking systems, make it seem both mechanical and inhuman. It leaves people out, disclaims human action and so lacks the appeal of humanist Marxism.

Finally, his claim to structuralism as a scientific theory of history and knowledge ends up being self-defeating. Althusser rejected the empiricist idea that the ultimate test of all theories and ideas is the real world, in favour of the claim that every theory is its own judge; every theory has its own framework of thought (what he called problematic) and so can only be judged on its own terms. Whilst it may make sense to argue that we cannot judge all theories against facts in the so-called real world – we cannot, for example, actually see a mode of production or a social class but we can still usefully use such concepts to make sense of the world – it does not make sense to say that we have no way of judging between theories or of criticising them except in their own terms. If this were true, how could Althusser himself claim that structuralism was superior to crude Marxism or humanism? Surely his writings were just as ideological as all others? Althusser sought to overcome this problem by claiming that structuralism was outside ideology, a sort of super-science. Such claims to intellectual superiority, to being above criticism, were swiftly decimated by other academics.

Althusser revised his work in the light of such criticisms, but in so doing lost much of the originality, verve and passion of his initial ideas. Though Althusserianism is still influential in philosophy and social science, its impact today is more indirect than dominant.

SEE ALSO

☐ **Historical materialism** as an outline of what Marx and Engels actually said.
☐ **Relative autonomy** as an example of structural Marxism by one of Althusser's collaborators Nicos Poulantzas.
☐ **Critical theory** as a very different humanist approach in modern Marxism.

SUGGESTED READING

Callinicos A. *Althusser's Marxism*, Pluto Press, 1976

FURTHER READING

Althusser L. *For Marx*, Penguin, 1965
Althusser L. *Reading Capital*, New Left Books, 1965
Althusser L. *Lenin and Philosophy*, New Left Books, 1969
Althusser L. *Essays in Self-criticism*, New Left Books, 1976

EXAMINATION QUESTIONS

1 'Marx's concept of class may have been adequate for understanding nine-teenth-century industrial capitalism but is inadequate for comprehending contemporary industrial society.' Discuss. (WJEC June 1986)
2 What have sociologists identified as the role of the state in advanced industrial societies? (AEB June 1985)

2

HOWARD BECKER *and*
LABELLING THEORY

THE AUTHOR

Howard Becker (1928–   ) is an American sociologist who was born in Chicago, Illinois in 1928. He was educated at the University of Chicago and, after a variety of research posts including a Ford Foundation fellowship and an assistant professorship at Stanford University, he was made Professor of Sociology and Urban Affairs at North-Western University, Evanston, Illinois.

Heavily influenced by such writers as W.I. Thomas, Herbert Blumer and Everett Hughes, Becker became a leading figure in the Symbolic Interactionist Movement of the 1950s and 60s particularly through his contributions to the study of deviancy and his advocacy of participant observation as a key technique of sociological research. At the age of fifteen he became a professional musician and later used his inside knowledge of the 'Jazz World' as a key source of ideas about deviancy, labelling and sub-cultural or 'underworld' ways of life. He is also a keen photographer and this has led to his studies of the 'Art World' and of the contribution of photography to sociology.

Howard Becker was not the founder of the idea of labelling – this distinction is usually attributed to Frank Tannenbaum and Edwin Lemert and to the concepts developed by such symbolic interactionists as G.H. Mead, W.I. Thomas and Charles Cooley. Nor has Becker been the only figure in the idea's development and refinement (Lemert, Schur, Goffman and others can claim equal credit). Becker's contribution was more in refining labelling's key concepts and stages into a systematic statement or theory and popularising it via his book *Outsiders* (1963).

THE IDEA

Traditional or positivist criminology tended to explain deviancy either as an innate characteristic in the make-up of certain criminal or anti-social types or as a result of poor home background, environment or socialisation.

Labelling theorists like Howard Becker, however, attempted to shift the focus of attention away from simply the deviant himself onto the way deviancy and crime are defined and the way society and in particular its agents of social control (the police, courts, teachers, parents, media, churches, etc.) *react* to deviant behaviour. From the labelling perspective it is this 'social reaction', particularly when symbolised by public labelling, that in a sense creates or at least amplifies deviant behaviour, not only by isolating and segregating deviant groups but by significantly altering the individual's perception of himself. It is the symbolic interactionist concern with the way social behaviour is largely created by interaction and negotiation, by such social symbols as public labels and rituals, and by people's perceptions of their own public images and statuses, that is at the heart of labelling theory.

In his key contribution *Outsiders* (1963) Becker argued that there is no such thing as deviancy *per se*. Rather, a particular form of behaviour only becomes deviant when others so define it:

Social groups create deviance by making rules whose infractions constitute deviance, and by applying those rules to particular people and labelling them as outsiders. From this point of view, deviance is not a quality of the act a person commits, but rather a consequence of the application by others of rules and sanctions to an 'offender'. The deviant is one to whom the label has successfully been applied; deviant behaviour is behaviour that people so label.

Nor are such definitions and labels consistently applied. They not only vary according to the situation, time or place involved but according to who does it and his or her power to resist labelling. Thus, for example, there is nothing intrinsically wrong or abnormal about nudity or hysterical behaviour; it all depends on where it takes place. Even killing someone is not necessarily wrong and in fact is justified if it occurs in self-defence or wartime. What is crucial is the reaction of those involved, particularly those in authority. But even this varies. Consider for ex-ample the likely police treatment of a doctor's son and a black youth from Brixton both caught speeding. Thus argued Becker, 'Deviance is not a quality that lies in behaviour itself but in the interaction between the person who commits an act and those who respond to it' – in particular the agencies of social control and their public labelling of deviant individuals.

The label deviant, be it as a criminal, drug addict or prostitute, tends to override all other statuses held by an individual as a father, friend, worker, neighbour. It becomes a 'master' status that not only profoundly affects the way other people respond to him thereafter – by isolating, snubbing or castigating him and reinterpreting their previous image of him – but equally affects the individual's own self-image. Socially rejected and stigmatised, the individual increasingly begins to 'live up' to his label, even to adopt a deviant career as he progresses through a series of stages towards a sort of self-fulfilling prophecy.

■ The initial public labelling as a delinquent, queer or loony; a labelling process that often includes a public ceremony and official definition be it by a judge at a trial or a doctor at a medical examination.
■ Subsequent rejection by family, friends and employer.
■ The gradual development of a deviant 'career' involving the withdrawal into a deviant sub-culture of criminals or drug addicts as a result of such social rejection. Within such groups and lifestyles the individual finds acceptance, support and legitimisation for his deviancy and a solidification of his self-image as a deviant to the point where such an identification becomes the 'controlling one'.

Thus, argues Becker, society's reaction to deviant behaviour causes or at least contributes to its creation and development by stigmatising, isolating and negating individuals for particular acts of anti-social behaviour. Such a process is not inevitable (ex-convicts do get jobs and drug addicts do give up the habit) but it takes a strong character to resist and overcome the pressures of public labelling especially if it is accompanied by being shut away in a prison or mental hospital.
Other labelling theorists have expanded on and refined such themes.

■ Edwin Lemert, for example, has made the key distinction between primary and secondary deviance, between deviant acts *before* they are publically labelled (and if they are) and the effect of societal reaction on an individual's personal self-concept and status *after* being labelled. In Lemert's view most people at some time or another commit deviant acts but only a few are caught and publicly labelled, so much primary deviance has little effect on their self-image or daily life. Therefore, delving deeply into the backgrounds of criminals for the 'causes' of crime, as traditional criminology does, is irrelevant. Rather, the cause of deviance is public labelling and its effect on the individual (secondary deviance).
■ In his study of the way police and juvenile officers handle potential deliquents in California (1976) Aaron Cicourel outlined the key stages in such criminal labelling – the way both policemen and juvenile officers are guided by a stereotyped picture of a typical deliquent as

male, black and from a poor home background and district, in their
search for criminal types and how they are influenced by the individual's
ability to negotiate and resist arrest and prosecution. Thus in Cicourel's
view 'justice is negotiable' and, far from reflecting the reality of crime,
official statistics are more a reflection of police stereotypes in interaction with relatively powerless social groups. Hence the inclusion of
young, working-class and black males and the exclusion of white
middle-class youngsters and girls.

■ Erving Goffman has revealed (1968) how such total institutions as
prisons, mental hospitals and reform schools seek to destroy inmates'
self-identity and individuality and reduce them to an institutional
number, cell and status by a process of mortification – stripping new
entrants of their clothes, hair and personal possessions, putting them
into uniforms and making the daily routine of the institution so controlled that the inmates have no freedom, involvement or initiative. Far
from reforming them such institutional organisation only confirms
their deviant identity, makes re-entry to normal society even more
difficult and so significantly increases their chances of reverting back to
crime and, eventually, to the sanctuary of prison.

THE IDEA IN ACTION

Such a dramatic reanalysis of crime and deviance, shifting the focus of
attention from the individual to societal reaction and the agencies of
social control, has had a major impact on the sociology of deviance. It
has stimulated a wealth of studies modifying and extending the idea of
labelling, not only in the field of criminology, but in the study of
medicine, race, education and feminism. Like its parent perspective
symbolic interactionism, labelling became one of the new sociologies of
the 1960s and, for a period, dominated the sociology of deviance. It
even influenced social policy and the practices of such institutions as
prisons and asylums.

   However, it equally inspired a growing flood of criticism over the
vagueness of its theory and its lack of empirical evidence:

■ Labelling theory fails to explain the 'origins' of deviance, what
motivates certain individuals to break society's norms and laws whilst
the majority conform and obey the law.

■ It seems to put all the blame for crime and deviance on the labellers
and to portray deviants as innocent victims. As Ronald Akers has so

succinctly put it: 'One sometimes gets the impression from reading the literature that people go about minding their own business and then – "wham" – bad society comes along and stops them with a stigmatized label.' Those who take drugs or steal are fully aware that they are breaking the law and often are even proud of their defiance, yet labelling theory tends to portray deviants as passive, as unaware of the deviant nature of their acts until arrested. Rather, the individual commits a murder, an act of vandalism or truants from school, and then and only then does society and its agents of social control react.

■ It does not fully explain 'societal reaction' – why the police, teachers, etc. react in the way that they do, where they get their attitudes and stereotypes from, why they label some individuals and not others. More important, it does not explain who makes the rules that define deviance. For Marxists and other radical writers it is this failure to analyse the *power* of rule-making and in particular to show the 'class' basis of such power that is the key weakness of labelling theory. Becker and Lemert fully recognise that certain groups have the power to impose rules and labels on other, weaker sections of society (the old on the young, men on women, the middle class on the working class) but they fail to extend such an insight into a detailed analysis of the social system at large. Instead labelling studies tend to concentrate on the 'underdog', on the hippies, delinquents and homosexuals who are labelled, rather than on those who enforce the laws on labels and in particular those who make them – politicians, top businessmen, media magnates, etc. Such an analysis has been left to Marxist writers who have developed a full-blown critique of crime and deviance in capitalist societies and so replaced labelling theory as the dominant influence on the sociology of deviance.

■ Finally, it has equally come under strong criticism from more traditional perspectives for the weakness of its concepts and its lack of detailed evidence. There tends to be a wide array of labelling definitions, some of which overlap and even conflict. Some theorists like Becker and Lemert even reject the idea that labelling is a theory, arguing instead that it is merely a sensitising concept designed to stimulate more detailed analysis. Moreover, as Walter Gove (1976) and his colleagues argue, actual studies tend to refute many of the claims of labelling theory, showing that at most it is a marginal influence compared to personal or background factors and in particular that 'the available evidence indicates that deviant labels are primarily a *consequence* of deviant behaviour and that deviant labels are not the prime *cause* of deviant careers'.

Thus labelling theory has contributed enormously to the development of the sociology of deviance, redirecting attention from rule-breakers to rule-makers, from an acceptance that the norms and laws of society are natural and given, to a recognition of their relative nature. It has led to a recognition that far from deviance being a minority activity it is in fact quite widespread. What is abnormal, as official statistics show, is to get caught and be publicly labelled. What labelling theorists like Howard Becker have failed to do though is to develop this powerful insight into a full-blown theory of crime and deviance. Hence their replacement in this field by the more powerful theories of radical and Marxist writers.

SEE ALSO

☐ **Symbolic interactionism** as the philosophical source for this idea.
☐ **Stigma** as an example of this theory in practice.

SUGGESTED READING

Becker H.S. *Outsiders*, Free Press, 1963
    Becker's own study is readable and stimulating whilst the following are some examples of sociologists using this theory.
Box S. *Deviance Reality and Society*, Rinehart & Winston, 1971
Cohen S. ed. *Images of Deviance*, Penguin, 1971
Keddie N. *Tinker Tailor: The Myth of Cultural Deprivation*, Penguin, 1973
    A short article on Howard Becker in *Social Studies Review* (Nov 1988) offers a useful overview and assessment.

FURTHER READING

Cicourel A. *The Social Organisation of Juvenile Justice*, Heineman, 1976
Gove W.R. *The Labelling of Deviance*, Sage, 1975
Hargreaves D.H. *et al. Deviance in Classrooms*, Routledge & Kegan Paul, 1975

EXAMINATION QUESTIONS

1 What is 'labelling theory'? Critically assess its contribution to the socio-logical understanding of crime and deviance. (Cambridge Local Examinations Syndicate June 1987)

2 Analyse the contribution of labelling theory to our understanding of criminal activity and reactions to it. (WJEC June 1987)

3 'Deviant behaviour is behaviour that is so labelled.' How adequate is this view as a way of understanding **either** crime **or** mental illness? (Cambridge Local Examinations Syndicate June 1986)

4 Evaluate the contribution made by the labelling approach to our understanding of differential educational achievement. (AEB November 1985)

5 By examining the social significance of deviance in any *two* societies, compare and contrast *two* theoretical perspectives on deviancy. (London University June 1986)

3

DANIEL BELL *and*

POST-INDUSTRIAL SOCIETY

THE AUTHOR

Daniel Bell (1919–   ) was born in New York, educated at City College, New York and Columbia University. Originally he was a journalist, working for *The New Leader* (1939–44) in New York and then acting as managing editor of *Common Sense* and Labour Editor of *Fortune Magazine* (1945–58). He then took up an academic career, initially as an instructor at the University of Chicago and then as a lecturer and professor of social science, first at Columbia (1969–80) and, ever since, at Harvard University (1980–   ).

A key feature of Bell's sociology has been his efforts to identify and draw out the chief characteristics of post-industrial society. In *The End of Ideology* (1960), for example, Bell predicted that an increasingly similar post-industrial social structure would emerge, cutting across ideological differences of socialist and capitalist societies, and in his work for the American Commission on the Year 2000 he has attempted to sketch out possible structural changes in future world society (for examples of such social forecasting, see *New Society*, 18 December 1987).

Daniel Bell is considered by many today as the 'world's greatest living sociologist' (*New Society*, 18 December 1987). He is a prolific writer and is noted for holding both liberal and independent views politically. His range of non-academic interests have included membership of Presidential Commissions on Technology, Automation and Economic Progress and the American Civil Liberties Union.

He edited the academic journals *Daedalus* and *Public Interest* and has produced an enormous amount and range of publications which have included:

- *End of Ideology* (1960)
- *Towards the Year 2000* (ed.) (1969)
- *The Coming of Post-Industrial Society* (1974)
- *The Crisis in Economic Theory* (co-ed.) (1981)

THE IDEA

Daniel Bell is seen as one of the leading exponents of the idea of a post-industrial society, a term he developed from David Riesman and attributed to Arthur Penty, a follower of William Morris in the 1890s.

In *The Coming of Post-Industrial Society* (1974) Bell set out five key components of a post-industrial society:

■ Economically, the change from a goods-producing to a service economy.

■ Occupationally, the pre-eminence of the professional and technical class, of white-collar over traditional industrial blue-collar workers.

■ Politically, the creation of a new knowledge class, capable of challenging the traditional power structure of businessmen and politicians.

■ Culturally, the centrality of theoretical knowledge as the key source of innovation and policy formation.

■ Finally a 'future orientation' concerning the control of technology and technological assessment.

Whilst stressing that these components were only the key features of some abstract notion of what a post-industrial society might look like, he did predict that by the year 2000 many of today's advanced industrial societies, including Japan, USSR and western Europe, would be entering a post-industrial phase and he cited America as the leading example.

. . . the first and simplest characteristic of a post-industrial society is that the majority of the labour force is no longer engaged in agriculture or manufacturing but in services, which are defined, residually, as trade, finance, transport, health, recreation, research, education and government.

The United States today is the first service economy, the first nation in which the major proportion of the population is engaged in neither agrarian or industrial pursuits. Today about 60% of the U.S. labor force is engaged in services; by 1980 the figure will have risen to 70%. (p. 15)

Whilst the growth of the service sector, and with it the rise in the proportion of professional and technical occupations, is a significant feature of a post-industrial society, the decisive characteristic is the growth of a new intelligentsia centred on the expansion of the universities, professions and government; a new 'knowledge class'.

The life-blood of a post-industrial society is not money but knowledge, in particular theoretical, or as Bell called it, 'codified' knowledge.

Such knowledge is fundamentally different in nature and type from that 'discovered' by such 'leading lights' of the Industrial Revolution as Watt and Edison. Post-industrial knowledge is not generated by personal experience but by massive research programmes funded by the government or major corporations and conducted in the research laboratories of big business or the major universities. Science and technology, he argued, are increasingly interrelated with abstract theory increasingly directing practical application, and with decision-making, whether industrial or political, dependent on computer-based simulations. At the heart of this explosion in knowledge use is the modern university. Hence the rise in status and resources of universities such as Massachusetts Institute of Technology in America and of Bath and Salford in the U.K.

The rise of this new knowledge class has a fundamental effect on the traditional balances of power and privilege. The new professional and technical classes represent a new form of power, that based on knowledge and expertise rather than wealth or property. Such a shift in social stratification raises the possibility of the knowledge class becoming a new ruling class, leading the post-industrial society towards a more rational, harmonious future, free of ideology and political conflict. Whilst Bell considers this a possibility (Chapter 6) he finally rejects it. Whilst the new intelligentsia may work with, even compete with, politicians for control of decision-making, ultimately 'the relationship of knowledge to power is essentially a subservient one'.

The rise in a service economy and the rise of a new knowledge class are likely to produce a significant shift in the dominant values, norms, and culture of a post-industrial society. The traditional work ethic is likely to be superseded by a greater emphasis on individual freedom and pleasure-seeking; market forces and the profit motive are likely to be controlled or at least subdued by the increased stress on social, economic and welfare planning. Issues such as the environment, health and education may well rate higher on the political agenda than the traditional class-based conflicts over the distribution of wealth and property.

As Bell concluded, the key feature of a post-industrial society is the central role of scientific and technical knowledge and the way such modes of thought penetrate and profoundly influence not only the political and industrial process of decision-making but every other aspect of social culture from the aesthetic to the literary.

THE IDEA IN ACTION

The idea of a post-industrial society has had a major impact on post-war sociology. Whilst writers like Alaine Touraine (1971) have postulated their own versions of this concept, Daniel Bell's has probably had the greatest influence. He offered an ideal-type of future society which like Weber's notion of bureaucracy contained the key features of modern development without actually depicting all known societies. It was designed as a 'logical construct', a skeleton outline of post-industrial society to stimulate debate and research.

The concept of post-industrial society is an analytical construct, not a picture of a specific or concrete society. It is a paradigm or social framework that identifies new axes of social organization and new axes of social stratification in advanced Western society. Social structures do not change overnight, and it may often take a century for a complete revolution to take place.

It was not an attempt to describe in detail all advanced industrial societies, though that is how some readers have perceived it.

Inevitably such an attempt at futurology inspired much comment and criticism.

1   The view that the post-industrial order is a social and economic structure radically different from that in the past is severely criticised by writers such as Kumar (1978) and Williams (1985). They claim that the shift towards a service-based economy is not a new order but merely the extension of an existing trend that dates back to the beginning of industrialism itself. As Anthony Giddens (1989) explains:

. . . from the early 1800s onwards manufacture and services BOTH expanded at the expense of agriculture, with the service sector consistently showing a faster rate of increase than manufacture. . . . Easily the most important change has not been from industrial to service work, but from farm employment to all other types of occupation.

Moreover, the notion of a service sector itself needs more careful and detailed analysis. It is very heterogeneous occupational sector, covering an enormous range of jobs and occupations, some of which might be classified as white-collar (finance officers, economists and scientists) whilst others are essentially manual and even unskilled (e.g. petrol station attendants). Even amongst those service occupations that are white-collar, most involve little specialised knowledge and many are increasingly subject to mechanisation. This is evident in most lower level office work involving secretarial or clerical duties.

Secondly, as Jonathan Gershuny (1978) argues, more than half the existing service occupations are in fact part of, or at least contribute to, the manufacturing process. The engineer, technician or computer programmer working for an industrial concern is in fact part of the manufacturing sector not a member of a distinct and separate occupational class.

Finally, no-one can be certain of the long-term impact and use of the new technologies, in particular microprocessing and electronic communications systems. At present they are part of modern manufacturing rather than displace it.

The decline in the proportion of production workers and the proportionate rise in service occupations may not therefore represent decline of the manufacturing sector but simply its restructuring. Manufacturers are replacing industrial workers with automation and new technologies, transferring production to the Third World where labour is cheap and creating a wide variety of new white-collar occupations to 'service' – not replace – the manufacturing process.

2 The notion of codified knowledge and the idea that information is becoming the main basis of the economic system are similarly debatable. As huge multinationals have increasingly dominated the world economy so the growth in theoretical knowledge, in research and development, has reflected the changing nature of big business and world markets. Radical writers see the growth in collaboration between universities and big business not as a Brave New World where rational thought and intellectual harmony will reign supreme but as an extension of the traditional pursuits of profit and power. New knowledge can be used to develop new products and new markets and even the increase in government spending on research is primarily in the fields of defence and space rather than health, education or welfare. Neither big business nor government, they claim, aims to create knowledge for knowledge's sake; neither has any intention of allowing society to be run by the planners or technocrats. Rather, both intend to use such experts to perpetuate the existing industrial and political order, not to overthrow it.

3 Bell portrayed the United States as a key example of a post-industrial society, but as Giddens (1989) argues, it may well be that America is the exception rather than the rule. 'The American economy has long been different from that of other industrialised countries; throughout this century, a higher relative proportion of workers has been in service

occupations in the United States . . . it is not clear that other countries will ever become as service-based as the U.S.A.' America may not therefore be the best basis for generalising about world society.

4   Finally, Bell's thesis is often associated with convergence theory and as such is criticised for exaggerating the importance of economic factors in producing social change. This represents a distorted view of his writings. He in fact rejected the idea that all advanced industrial societies are 'converging' towards some common social, economic and political system ('As a social system, post-industrial society does not "succeed" capitalism or socialism but, like bureaucratization, cuts across both') and dismissed any idea that the post-industrial society was some sort of 'sub-structure initiating changes in a superstructure'. Post-industrialism, he argued, is but one (important) 'dimension of a society whose changes pose management problems for the political system' to resolve.

Daniel Bell's vision of a post-industrial society may therefore represent a continuation of existing social, economic and political tendencies rather than a radical new social order. Even if this is true, his idea has stimulated a major and ongoing debate in sociology about the structure and character of future society, a debate to which he still contributes, as always, with the most powerful and challenging of observations (see *New Society* 18 December 1987).

SEE ALSO

☐ **Convergence thesis** as a prediction about future trends in industrial development.
☐ **Corporatism** as an example of 'converging' political trends.

SUGGESTED READING

Bell, D. 'Future Society', *New Society* 18 December 1987 – reflects his recent thinking on industrial and social trends
Giddens, A. *Sociology*, Polity Press, 1989
Kumar, K. *Prophesy and Progress – the Sociology of Industrial and Post-Industrial Society*, Penguin, 1985

FURTHER READING

Bell, D. *The End of Ideology*, Free Press, 1960
Bell, D. ed. *Towards the Year 2000*, Houghton Mifflin, 1969
Bell, D. *The Coming of the Post-Industrial Society*, Heinemann, 1974
Bell, D. co-ed. *The Crisis in Economic Theory*, Basic Books, 1981
Gershung, J. *After Industrial Society*, Macmillan, 1978
Schumacher, E.E. *Small is Beautiful*, Abacus Books, 1973
Touraine, A. *The Post-Industrial Society*, Random House, 1969

EXAMINATION QUESTION

What do you understand by the term 'post-industrial society'? (WJEC June 1986)

4

BASIL BERNSTEIN *and*
LINGUISTIC CODES

THE AUTHOR

Basil Bernstein (1924–   ) came from a very working-class part of East London and after gaining a B.A. from the London School of Economics and his Ph.D. at University College London, went back to teach there at City Day College Shoreditch for six years. Sensitised to the social class basis of language by his predominantly working-class students, he developed his early ideas on linguistic codes until he obtained a Research Assistantship at University College London in 1960. His rise to academic eminence was then meteoric. Within seven years he had risen to Professor of the Sociology of Education and Director of the London Institute of Education Sociological Research Unit, gained a series of academic accolades and became world famous for the concept of linguistic codes. His initial ideas were outlined in a series of publications in the early 1960s. They were then expanded and developed in Bernstein's key works *Class, Codes and Control* published in three volumes between 1971 and 1975 and recently (1990) updated in Volume IV.

THE IDEA

Basil Bernstein's theory of linguistic codes, which he himself now agrees should have been called 'sociolinguistic' codes, is one of the most quoted and least understood concepts in the sociology of education. Every year thousands of 'O' level Sociology candidates used to trot out garbled versions of elaborated and restricted codes arguing not only that working-class children are linguistically deprived (they can't speak proper) but that they are even 'depraved'.

Bernstein's theory is both more elaborate and complex. It derives from both of the two main traditions in the post-war British sociology of education.

■ The attempt in the 1950s and 1960s to explain the great differences in educational achievement between middle- and working-class children in terms of home background.

■ The attempt of the 'new' sociology of education in the 1970s to reveal how knowledge is an integral part of class inequalities, reproduction and social control in a capitalist society.

Bernstein's thesis attempted to bridge both traditions and to link what went on in the home and school with the overall structure of power and inequality by showing that the way people speak gives them access to, or excludes them from, not only educational knowledge and success, but positions of power and privilege. His aim has been to crack the linguistic and cultural codes that he believes control the distribution of wealth and power in advanced capitalist societies.

His early work centred on outlining the key characteristics of middle- and working-class speech patterns which he initially termed formal and public but later elaborate and restricted codes. Whilst the middle classes have access to both codes the working class tends to be limited to restricted speech patterns, to 'short grammatically simple, often unfinished sentences' with limited and repetitive vocabulary and an extensive use of gesture and voice intonation. Since those using this form of communication have much in common, much is taken for granted, meaning is implicit and particularistic, limited to a particular situation or relationship, and so it is difficult for an outsider to understand what is being said.

Elaborate codes are far more grammatically accurate, logical and descriptive. Meaning is made explicit by a wider vocabulary, greater use of detail and an individualistic explanation selected to fit the needs and knowledge of a particular listener. Elaborate codes are therefore universalistic, they can be understood by anybody, they do not depend on existing knowledge of a particular context or social group.

Bernstein explains the origins of these social class speech codes in terms of family relationships, socialisation practices and the nature of manual and non-manual occupations. In working-class families relationships and authority are clear cut and distinct; what Bernstein calls positional. The father asserts his authority merely by a command ('shut-up') rather than by discussion. In middle-class families relationships are more personal and less rigid. Communication is more elaborate and fluid, decisions are discussed and rules negotiated. Such class-family differences in turn reflect the different work situations of the middle and working classes, the manual skills of the blue collar worker where conversation is limited to a few direct instructions compared to the verbal skills of the white collar worker where decision making, negotiation and the development of ideas are the very essence of his job. Thus their respective children are socialised into both a particular form of communication and a structure of authority.

Such an analysis even links up with Durkheim's idea of mechanical and organic forms of solidarity whereby in working-class communities relationships are more face-to-face (mechanical) and so a lot of meaning can be left out. The middle-class 'world', in contrast, is much more mobile, impersonal and individualistic so communication has to be more formal and explicit (organic). Thus Bernstein suggested that if we look into the work relationships of this particular group, its community relationships, its family role systems, 'it is reasonable to argue that the genes of social class may well be carried less through a genetic code but far more through a communication code that social class itself promotes'.

Bernstein used these codes initially to explain social class differences in educational attainment. Schools are very middle-class institutions based on 'universalistic orders of meaning'. Teachers are essentially middle class and communicate primarily in an elaborate code. So, whilst the middle-class child feels 'at home' at school, the working-class child feels in an alien environment faced by a 'foreign' language. Moreover their restricted style of speech not only hinders the learning of school-type knowledge – abstract ideas and concepts from textbooks and teachers – but it gets them into trouble (and the lower streams). Their 'slang' language is downgraded and discouraged by teachers. They are constantly being corrected and their limited vocabulary interpreted as both ignorance and rudeness. They are therefore more likely to be labelled, more likely to be punished. They cannot relate to the teachers in the way the middle-class child can but comes to see them purely as authority figures. As Bernstein puts it 'this may well lead to a situation where pupil and teacher disvalue each other's world and communication becomes a means of asserting differences'. The working-class child is therefore more likely to end up in a lower stream, excluded from the fullness of academic knowledge (and the resultant qualifications), made to feel inferior and so socialised into future subordination at work.

Linguistic codes therefore function as a form of class reproduction providing a means of creating and maintaining the identity and unity of the middle class which excludes the working class from power and privilege.

Bernstein and his colleagues at the London Institute have conducted numerous experiments to try and identify exactly how linguistic codes operate in a variety of contexts – in the description of pictures, the playing of games, in a theft situation and even in the different modes of control used by middle- and working-class mothers. But Bernstein himself has moved on from this to an analysis of educational know-ledge as a key form of class control and reproduction. Whoever con-trols the school curriculum not only has better access to it but can actually control what is defined as knowledge. Schools and teachers promote academic knowledge which requires an elaborate code to gain access to it, to do well in our examination system and so get into top jobs. The middle class therefore have an inbuilt advantage and so can be sure that their children maintain their existing class dominance. Equally, working-class children fail in our school system not, as was implied in Bernstein's earlier work, through their own inadequacies, their restricted speech and language, but because the system makes sure they fail by selecting out the middle class on the basis of middle-class knowledge and speech codes. Thus, far from schools being 'classless' institutions processing pupils purely on the basis of merit, they are an integral part of a system of class reproduction and inequality operating under the guise of equal opportunity.

Bernstein's overall aim now is to explain 'how power relationships penetrate the organisation, distribution and evaluation of knowledge through the social context'. Whilst Durkheim and Mead influenced his early work on linguistic codes, Marxism is predominant in his more recent analyses. By this intermingling of interpretative and structural ideas what he is attempting is nothing less than a complete theory of the cycle of class reproduction.

THE IDEA IN ACTION

Basil Bernstein's idea of linguistic codes had a major impact on British sociology of education. It inspired a host of empirical studies and added a new dimension to the perennial debate about educational achievement.

However, it also inspired a number of quite fervent criticisms, some of which are due to exaggerated or distorted versions of his thesis.

■ Although Bernstein never said working-class speech patterns were either inferior or inadequate, never said that because 'the working class don't speak proper, they can't think clever thoughts', he did imply it and other writers like Carl Bereiter have used this theory to argue that low income groups and Blacks fail in the American educational system because their speech patterns retard their intellectual development and make it difficult for them to understand abstract ideas. Harold Rosen (1974) and William Labov (in Keddie 1973) launched furious attacks on such claims. Rosen argued that Bernstein's definitions of social class were so vague as to be useless – at times Bernstein lumps together all non-manual workers as middle class and all manual as working class, at other times he refers only to the lower working class – and his evidence of such codes is so sparse and weak at times that it can in no way meet the claim of middle-class superiority. Labov's analysis of Black American speech patterns show that far from being incoherent, ungrammatical or illogical they are as rich and rational as the elaborate code, just as rule-bound and capable of handling complex ideas. It is simply that the middle class have the social power to claim that their form of English is superior.

Bernstein himself described working-class language as warm and vital, simple and direct:

'My own view has always been that code restriction where it does exist, does not constitute linguistic or cultural deprivation, for there is a delicacy and variety in cultural and imaginative form'.

Moreover in an article entitled 'Education Cannot Compensate for Society' (1970) he attacked the concept of compensatory education, of attempts like Education Priority Areas to overcome the educational deficiencies of the poor working class, because it blamed parents rather than asking why schools failed such children.

He argued that there was nothing in the 'working class dialect as such' to prevent a child from learning the elaborate code, though not having it does put such children at a considerable disadvantage in our education system. He similarly distinguished linguistic codes from regional dialects, though, again, speaking in a Scouse or Cockney accent rather than standard middle-class English can often be a handicap and be labelled a sign of unintelligence and inferiority.

■ Other writers have criticised certain ambiguities in Bernstein's definition of linguistic codes, in his presentation of them as polar opposites when in fact speech seems more a continuum from slang to fluent exposition, and, most important, that his experiments do not provide enough evidence to prove conclusively that such codes are the key to social class differences and relations. His colleagues are using this concept less in their experiments and even Bernstein now puts more emphasis on 'modes of control' than sociolinguistic codes. Moreover studies like David Hargreaves *et al.* (1975), show that schools do not necessarily use only the elaborate code but also rely heavily on 'im-plicit' understanding and short sharp commands, which should, according to Bernstein's theory, make working-class pupils feel more at home in school!

■ Despite his recent use of a Marxist framework, radical writers like Rachel Sharpe see Bernstein's work as essentially functionalist or Weberian. In her view he fails to provide a proper Marxist definition of class, make proper use of a dialectical analysis or clearly relate such codes to the underlying relations of production in a capitalist society. Research (by Pap also and Pleh (1974) shows that elaborate and restricted codes exist even in such apparently classless societies as Hungary. As Karabel and Halsey (1977) argue, whilst Bernstein's thesis makes a lot of sense in an obviously class-based society like Britain it would be difficult to apply to, for example, America or the USSR.

Since the original exposition of this idea in the 1960s and 70s, Bernstein and his colleagues have moved on from analysing educa-tional achievement in particular to using the notion of linguistic codes to explain the structures and processes of power and control in a class-based society. In particular they are keen to identify the processes by which power and control in society at large operates at the institutional and personal level; how through linguistic codes the social relations of a capitalist society are transmitted and reproduced within the family, in schools and at work to the point of influencing, if not determining, individual behaviour and relationships. He aims to define more pre-cisely the concept of linguistic codes and to identify the principles behind them: how they are created and how they help legitimise and promote inequality. He argues that, whilst relatively simple divisions of labour give rise to 'restricted' linguistic codes and relationships, the more complex the social division of labour and the more impersonal the relations of production between employer and worker, the more elaborate becomes the linguistic code of communication and control.

In *Class, Codes and Control* (Vol. IV Chapter 3), Bernstein cites the example of the relationship between a peasant working on a sugarcane plantation and the *patron* who owns it. Whilst the peasant works within a social division of labour that is relatively simple – he has a direct and personal relationship with his employer – the *patron* is part of a more complex set of economic relationships: with other plantation owners, the local sugarcane market, the financial system, and ulti-mately the market forces of the sugar industry at national and international levels. Whilst the peasant need communicate just on a restricted and personal basis, the *patron* requires a more elaborate code to communicate with the complex and impersonal world of international trade and finance. Through such elaborate codes the *patron* has access to local and national power structures through which his class is able to control and exploit the rural working class. The key to gaining access to such elaborate codes and controls is the education system.

Thus, whilst linguistic codes operate in the economic sphere, they originate in the symbolic sphere – in the religious systems of simple societies, in the cultural systems of complex ones. Moreover, whilst such codes are an essential mechanism of class control and reproduction, they can also generate 'oppositional' codes both in school (for example, pupil subcultures) and at work (trade unions). They can also induce internal class conflicts, such as between different 'fractions' of the bourgeoisie competing for profits, markets or state aid. Thus, whilst some writers have criticised Bernstein's theory as highly deterministic – for example, R. Gibson states that 'codes make people mere tools or puppets in the hands of absent structures which create and govern them' (in *Class, Codes and Control*, Vol. IV, p. 182) – his notion of oppositional codes highlights the potential for resistance by oppressed classes and even internal contradictions and conflict within ruling classes. Code controls are not established in a passive manner; they involve a continuous interaction – even struggle – between 'transmitters' and acquirers'. Ultimately the theory perceives man's potential for resisting and even revolting against class controls, be they symbolic, economic or political.

Bernstein's theory of linguistic codes has thus moved on to a much broader and deeper analysis. Whilst it still has its roots in education, it is now more explicitly focused on analysing power, control and communication in a class society.

SUGGESTED READING

Bernstein B.B. 'A Sociolinguistic Approach to Social Learning', in Worsley P. *Modern Sociology Introductory Readings*, Penguin, 1970 – Bernstein outlines his own ideas
Labov W. 'The Logic of Non-standard English', in Keddie N. *Tinker Tailor . . . The Myth of Cultural Deprivation*, Penguin, 1973
Rosen H. *Language and Class*, Falling Wall Press, 1974 – both provide criticisms of Bernstein's ideas

FURTHER READING

Bernstein B.B. 'Social Class and Linguistic Development – A Theory of Social Learning' in Halsey *et al. Education, Economy and Society*, Free Press, 1961

Bernstein B.B. *Class, Codes and Control* Vols 1–3, Routledge & Kegan Paul, 1971–5

Hargreaves D.H. *et al. Deviance in Classrooms*, Routledge & Kegan Paul, 1975

Karabel J. and Halsey A.H. eds. *Power and Ideology in Education*, OUP, 1977

Sharpe R. *Knowledge, Ideology and the Politics of Schooling*, Routledge & Kegan Paul, 1980

EXAMINATION QUESTION

How important are differences in 'linguistic codes' in explaining social class differences in educational achievement? (Oxford Delegacy May 1985 P1)

5

HARRY BRAVERMAN *and*
DESKILLING

THE AUTHOR

Harry Braverman (1920–76) was an American Marxist who began his working life as a coppersmith in a New York naval yard and progressed from there through a wide variety of associated crafts – sheet metal worker, pipefitter, steel worker, freight-car repair man – across a variety of American states. During the 1950s he moved into socialist journalism and publishing, becoming co-editor of *American Socialist*, a monthly magazine, and later director of the left-wing *Monthly Review Press*.

It was this experience of both manual and non-manual craftwork, of traditional labour processes, that both inspired and informed his major publication, *Labor and Monopoly Capital* (1974) which he sub-titled 'The Degradation of Work in the Twentieth Century'. As he himself recognised, technological change is both necessary and inevitable, even in the most venerable of crafts. What he objected to was 'the manner in which these [changes] are used as weapons of domination in the creation, perpetuation and deepening of a gulf between classes in society'.

I had the opportunity of seeing at first hand, during those years, not only the transformation of industrial processes, but the manner in which these processes are reorganized; how the worker, systematically robbed of a craft heritage, is given little or nothing to take its place. Like all craftsmen, even the most inarticulate, I always resented this, and as I reread these pages, I find in them a sense not only of social outrage, which was intended, but also perhaps of personal affront.

THE IDEA

A wide variety of writers have speculated on the likely effects of advanced industrial technology, whether it would liberate or eliminate the traditional working class, whether it would reskill or deskill the

craft worker, whether it would lead to an improvement or deterioration in the quality of modern working life. Braverman's contribution to
this debate has not only been to explain in detail how deskilling takes
place in both manual and non-manual occupations, but to link such
changes in the labour process to an updated Marxist analysis of class,
of the system of social control and exploitation in today's capitalist
society. From his initial thesis of deskilling he went on to contribute to
the 'proletarianization thesis': the thesis that modern capitalist labour
processes are creating an expanding proletariat, increasingly exploited,
oppressed and class conscious.

According to Braverman, the primary aim of the capitalist mode of
production is to increase efficiency, and so, profits. There is an essential antagonism between those who own the means of production and
those with only their labour to sell. Within the capitalist work system,
the worker is not a human being with needs, feelings and potential. He
is simply a unit of production, a source of surplus value or profit. The
purpose of new technology, however, argues Braverman, is not only to
increase productivity, but to increase management's control of the
work force. It is a system of class control as well as of class exploitation. *Labor and Monopoly Capital* is a detailed outline of how the
capitalist labour process actually works.

The traditional craftsman of the early Industrial Revolution was, in
a sense, self-employed and independent. He owned his own tools and
place of work, bought his own raw materials and sold the finished
product direct to the consumer. He alone possessed the necessary skill
and knowledge required for the whole production process, from conception through to execution. He had a certain status and power in
relation to his employer. However, such a system of production was
not only expensive and inefficient, but difficult to control. Though
centralising the workforce within the factory system improved managerial control, the workgangs still had considerable autonomy and independence. According to Braverman, the introduction of F.W. Taylor's
techniques of scientific management in the early twentieth century (see
page 287) provided both the method and the philosophy for destroying
worker power, for extracting from the workers their skill and knowledge, centralising such information in the hands of management, as
the means for a full-scale exploitation and control of the workforce.
This managerial revolution involved three key principles.

■ The dissociation of the labour process from the skills of the workers,
i.e. management henceforth gathers together all the traditional know-

ledge previously possessed by the workmen, and reduces it to 'rules, laws and formulae'.

■ The separation of conception from execution, of mental from manual work. Henceforth, the initiation and planning of the work process is controlled by management. Work tasks are divided and sub-divided, simplified and fragmented, the worker divorced from overall planning and understanding and reduced to a cog in a massive assembly-line process.

■ The use of the monopoly over knowledge to control each step of the labour process and its mode of execution. Henceforth, every work-task is planned in minute detail by management and the role of the worker is reduced to simply executing these written instructions.

Through scientific management, argues Braverman, the knowledge and skills of the traditional workers were sucked up into the hands of management and the work force subsequently reduced to highly-controlled and manipulable units of labour – alienated, isolated, powerless and easily replaced. Such total control from above, such fragmentation of the work force, was epitomised in Henry Ford's giant assembly-line plants; and new technologies ever since, be they automation, computers or robots, have simply extended this process of control by deskilling.

Braverman goes on to argue that such a process of deskilling is not restricted to the factory or shop floor, but is evident in all areas of work, not least the modern office. From being a person of some importance, knowledge and power, the clerk today is merely a small cog in an assembly line of paper controlled by senior management or Head Office via computers and telecommunications. With the introduction of time and motion studies, open-plan offices and new technology, even non-manual workers have lost their skills, status and control of the work process. They too have been degraded, routinised and re-placed. They are left unskilled, powerless and alienated, subject to external controls whilst undertaking meaningless and mindless tasks, devoid of any intrinsic job satisfaction. Consider the effect, and purpose, of automated cash points and the like on the traditional role, status and numbers of the bank cashier. Consider how easily both the modern factory and office worker is now replaced by new machinery or unskilled and semi-skilled labour.

Braverman goes on to link this process of deskilling to the Marxist thesis of proletarianisation, to link changes in the labour process to changes in the class structure of advanced capitalist societies. Braverman claims that relations of production in capitalist societies are essentially those of dominance and subordinacy, so creating the two main classes, the bourgeoisie and the proletariat. The proletariat is the class that, 'possessing nothing but its power to labour, sells that power in return for its subsistence'. As the process of deskilling has infiltrated every area of work, so claims Braverman, 'almost all the population has been transformed into employees of capital', whether it be in the form of private firms or its agent the state. Using this definition, Braverman calculates that some 70 per cent of the American labour force can now be categorised as proletarian and that even the 15 to 20 per cent who constitute the intermediate classes as lower level managers, technicians and state employees, whilst receiving 'its petty share in the prerogatives and rewards of capital . . . also bear the mark of the proletarian condition'. Eventually they, too, will be deskilled and fully proletarianised as monopoly capital continues its relentless pursuit of profit. Such intensified pressure of deskilling, decontrolling and degrading the mass of the population through control of the labour process, through new machinery and technology, will ultimately create the conditions for a proletarian uprising – though Braverman is careful not to predict when. As he sums up:

'The mass of humanity is subjected to the labor process for the purposes of those who control it rather than for any general purposes of 'humanity' as such. In thus acquiring concrete form, the control of humans over the labor process turns into its opposite and becomes the control of the labor process over the mass of humans. Machinery comes into the world not as the servant of 'humanity', but as the instrument of those to whom the accumulation of capital gives them ownership of the machines. The capacity of humans to control the labor process through machinery is seized upon by management from the beginning of capitalism as the prime means whereby production may be controlled not by the direct producer but by the owners and representatives of capital. Thus, in addition to its technical function of increasing the productivity of labor – which would be a mark of machinery under any social system – machinery also has in the capitalist system the function of divesting the mass of workers of their control over their own labor.

Whilst recognising that similar processes are occurring in socialist countries, Braverman argues that these are transitional, created by the imitation and use of western technology. The essential difference is that the ultimate aim is not relentless profit nor the degradation of the worker. Where the means of production are in common ownership then new work techniques will be used to enrich the work experience and extend worker control. Braverman is not against technical advance, only against its misuses as a form of exploitation.

THE IDEA IN ACTION

Labor and Monopoly Capital has been hailed as a classic, as a major advance in Marxist analysis of class and the labour process: 'one of the two most important works of Marxist political economy to have appeared in English in the last decade' (Rowthorn 1976). It offered a radical, forceful and passionate critique of the prevailing liberal claims that modern work techniques were enriching and reskilling the work experience, yet fragmenting and defusing the working class. It inspired a wealth of studies into the work process on all levels and in all occupations (examples below). It provided the focus for a major debate on the labour process and even led to what Graeme Salaman (1986) has called 'Bravermania'. Research into many of the new, non-manual occupations showed little improvement in the level of skill, control and job satisfaction: 'The chemical operator is singled out time and time again as the outstanding beneficiary of automation . . . yet few have stopped to think whether it is harder to learn to read a dial than tell time' (Braverman, 1974). Braverman's thesis offered a major theoretical explanation for various workers' attempts to resist deskilling, not least the 1985 printers' dispute. It revived the Marxist analysis of class formation and class relations and restored it to the centre of radical analysis.

However, once the initial flush of academic and left wing enthusiasm subsided so the criticisms of the deskilling thesis began.

DEFINITIONS

Firstly, the very term skill is ambiguous. It can refer to real attributes of knowledge and/or manual dexterity, or to labels used by management or workers to up- or down-grade a particular job. Skills may be technical or personal and often a job is labelled 'skilled' even though the work involved is largely unskilled. Jobs may be deskilled but workers not – they may be reskilled or redeployed. Such ambiguous definitions make an analysis of 'deskilling' highly problematic.

Secondly, Braverman's definition of the proletarian class has been heavily criticised as too simple, too broad. He tries to include all 'classes' of worker in it.

STRATEGIES

Braverman has been accused of both overestimating the resources, knowledge and will of capitalists to so relentlessly pursue a strategy of deskilling and controlling the work force and underestimating the ability of many work groups to resist such a process. Whilst some managers have sought to improve the work situation by, say, job rotation or human relations approaches, others have used alternative strategies to deskilling and Taylorism for controlling the work force. Equally, historical research shows how many unions, especially craft unions, have successfully resisted, or at least, manipulated deskilling attempts. By solely concentrating on scientific management, Braverman ignores different management strategies, different industrial relations as, for example, in Sweden. As Graham Winch (1983) and David Knights *et al.* (1985) have argued, employers are not simply motivated by a desire to control their workforces. They face stiff competition from rival firms and have to adopt new technology to survive.

ANALYSIS OF CLERICAL WORK AND CLERICAL WORKERS

Whilst studies like Crompton and Jones (1984) and Goldthorpe (1980) support Braverman's view that most clerical work is routine and involves little skill, control or satisfaction, many groups of office workers welcome new technology as relieving them of the most boring tasks and freeing them to develop and expand their skills and authority (National Economic Development Office Study, 1983). Moreover, office workers do not constitute 'a large proletariat in a new form', but rather are stratified by age, qualification, gender and level of post. Like most non-manual workers, they are highly mobile and can (and do) move up into more intermediate positions. They have greater self-control, are more organised to resist deskilling and a loss of job status. They are less class conscious than the working class. White-collar workers may have become more unionised in the 1970s, but this was to protect their class/status differences with manual workers, not eliminate them. They still identify with the capitalist class, not the proletariat; with those in authority rather than with their subordinates.

MARXIST CRITICISMS

Marxist writers have criticised Braverman's analysis of class firstly for failing to analyse the modern working class in terms of class consciousness as well as class position, and secondly for failing to place such an analysis within the framework of a broader analysis of other forms of political domination and of the class struggle. By only analysing the modern working class as a class 'in itself', not 'for itself', Braverman ignores all the subjective elements of class consciousness, portrays the working class as essentially passive, unable to resist control from above. Such a deterministic picture fails to put the class struggle and class conflict at the heart of what is supposed to be a Marxist analysis, fails to offer any glimpse of the underlying dialectical process and struggle for control.

FEMINIST CRITICISMS

Feminists have applauded Braverman for including female labour in his analysis, for highlighting their role in monopoly capital as a reserve army of labour used to replace men and so reduce the status, skill and cost of many jobs. At last sexual stratification has been used in a class analysis. However, they too criticise him for failing to take a broader perspective, for failing to include the domestic division of labour, women's unpaid work in the family, the degradation of housework, in his analysis of the labour process. Equally, his analysis of class fails to give sufficient weight to differentiations and cleavages within the working class other than those of gender.

HISTORIANS' CRITICISMS

Historians have criticised Braverman's account for:

■ being historically inaccurate, particularly about the timing, extent and pace of deskilling;
■ glamourising the traditional craft worker and postulating a sort of 'golden age of work' in pre-industrial societies. Work in the past was often far more onerous, exploitative and oppressive than even the twentieth-century factory Braverman describes.

Though Braverman's deskilling thesis is now considered somewhat dated in the light of recent research and new developments in the work place, it has rightly been acclaimed as a major contribution to this sociological and radical debate and still informs, even fifteen years later, much of modern analysis of the nature of work and the labour process.

SEE ALSO

☐ **Scientific management** as the target of Braverman's critique.

SUGGESTED READING

Braverman H. *Labor and Monopoly Capital*, Monthly Review Press, 1974
   Try Braverman's own study as it is well worth the effort.

FURTHER READING

Crompton R. and Jones G. *White Collar Proletariat*, Macmillan, 1984
Goldthorpe J.H., Lockwood D. *et al. Social Mobility and Class Structure in
   Modern Britain*, Clarendon Press, 1980
Knights D. *et al.* eds., *Job Redesign*, cited in *Society Today/New Society*,
   8 Nov. 1985
Lockwood D. *The Black Coated Workers*, Allen & Unwin, 1958
Salaman G. *Work*, Tavistock, 1986

EXAMINATION QUESTIONS

1 'The major effect of technological change is to increase the skill of a small
number of jobs, whilst reducing the skill level of a large number of jobs.'
Discuss. (Oxford Delegacy May 1985)
2 Does technological change inevitably result in 'de-skilling' jobs? (Oxford
Delegacy May 1986)
3 Examine the relationship between technology and work satisfaction in
advanced industrial societies. (AEB June 1983)
4 'The class positions of clerical workers and skilled manual workers are now
almost identical.' Discuss (AEB June 1988)
5 Examine the view that advanced industrial societies require ever increasing
skill levels from their workforce. (AEB November 1984)
6 'Increasingly, the position of white-collar workers resembles that of manual
workers.' Examine this view and its implications for white-collar workers.
(AEB June 1989 Paper 1)

6

MANUEL CASTELLS *and*
COLLECTIVE CONSUMPTION

THE AUTHOR

Manuel Castells (1942–   ) was born in Spain. He received his Ph.D. in sociology from the University of Paris in 1967. He taught sociology there for twelve years, directing a seminar in urban sociology at the Ecole des Hautes Etudes en Sciences Sociales. He has also been Visiting Professor at the Universities of Montreal, Chile, Wisconsin, Copenhagen, Boston, Mexico, Hong Kong, Southern California and Madrid. He is at present Professor of City and Regional Planning at the University of California, Berkeley, a position he has held since 1979. Castells has published twelve books, the best known of which are:

- *The Urban Question* (1977)
- *City, Class and Power* (1978)
- *The City and the Grassroots* (1983) which earned him the 1983 C. Wright Mills Award.

THE IDEA

In the late 1960s the cities of America and Western Europe exploded in orgies of violence, destruction and rebellion. The Blacks of America vented their frustration with the American Dream, their anger with their poverty, decay and racism, on the ghetto environments of Harlem, Watts and Detroit; women, students and ecology groups marched in protest over Vietnam, civil rights and the pollution of the urban environment; urban guerillas took the class and race war onto the streets of West Germany, Japan and the USA. The student and worker revolution in Paris in May 1968 climaxed in the resignation of President Charles de Gaulle. The city had become the focal point, the battleground of social unrest and political protest, but the traditional perspectives in urban sociology could not explain such conflict and confrontation so academics turned to the more radical theories of

Marx and Weber. Traditional Marxism however saw events in industrial cities merely as a reflection of the broader forces underlying
advanced capitalism; Marx and Engels did not make detailed analyses
of urban life. More important, the enormous variety of protest groups
in the 1960s and 1970s, ranging from women and Blacks to such
middle-class groups as students, tenants and ecologists did not neatly
fit traditional Marxist analyses of social revolution as essentially a class
struggle.

By his concept of collective consumption Manuel Castells sought to
update modern Marxism, to integrate urban protest into a class analysis and to harness the revolutionary potential of such varied urban
groups into a unified and radical protest movement capable of ultimately undermining or even overthrowing modern capitalism. As a
professor in Paris during the May revolution he was uniquely posi-
tioned to both observe and influence the students and workers of 1968.
His book *The Urban Question* became a theoretical bible for radical
and student groups of this period and Castells' writings inspired a
whole new tradition of urban Marxism.

Castells contemptuously dismissed all previous theories of the city as
bourgeois ideology because they failed to perceive such 'social problems' as crime, poverty and pollution as direct reflections of the underlying capitalist system and its relentless pursuit of profit. In his view the
modern city is a key centre in modern capitalism, not as a place of
production (modern factories are mainly located outside the city) but
as a control centre in the world capitalist system. It houses the head-
quarters and financial institutions of today's multinational corporations and, most importantly, acts as a centre of collective consumption
and worker reproduction. By 'collective consumption', Castells was referring to those goods and services such as health, education, housing,
transport and leisure provided by the modern welfare state in order to
ensure that the modern worker is healthy, happy and materially satisfied with capitalism, willing to continue working for the bourgeoisie
and unlikely to challenge their power and privilege. Welfare therefore
in Castells' view is a form of class control and such 'collectively
consumed goods' as education and housing are primarily distributed
through local, especially city, governments because the bulk of the
working population live in towns and cities.

The state in capitalist society both national and local, therefore, has
a key role in controlling the working class through its welfare provisions. However in the late 1960s and 1970s, western societies faced a
major economic crisis, a fall in profits and a massive growth in bank-
ruptcies and in unemployment. Governments had to cut public spend-

ing at the very time when the need for goods of collective consumption was increasing. An 'urban crisis' thus developed as local government revenue and services were drastically cut and western cities fell into disrepair – roads were not repaired, houses built or schools maintained. Some, like New York, even went bankrupt (1975). In response a wide variety of pressure groups emerged – the poor, Blacks, tenants, women, the working and the middle classes – all directing their protests against the local state. Unable any longer to buy off such urban protest, the capitalist state has to show its true face and resort to repression. Increasingly demonstrations and marches are suppressed by the use of force: the police and, in extreme cases, the army. The use of such force, however, only increases the militancy and class consciousness of ordinary people, leading to an increase in urban protest and conflict. Castells' hope was that if such disparate urban protests could be fused under the leadership of the Communist Party into full 'social movements', such power on the city streets might generate an urban crisis of such proportions that western capitalism might begin to collapse from within: 'A spectre haunts the world; will the urban crisis become an urban revolution?'

THE IDEA IN ACTION

The concept of collective consumption and such a radical re-analysis of urban conflict dramatically reopened the urban question both as a sub-discipline within sociology and as a topic of analysis for neo-Marxism. Castells' critique offered modern Marxists the vision of the city making a significant contribution to the downfall of capitalism and enabled them to include all forms of urban protest within their class analysis. Castells' writings gained particular support from militant groups because they both justified their actions and offered theoretical guidelines for the future.

However, Castells' thesis also sparked off widespread criticism not only of the often obscure language he used and the contemptuous way he dismissed all other 'urban' theories, but, more important, of his concepts and their applicability to all forms of urban protest in all capitalist cities.

Concepts like collective consumption and protest movements were criticised as vague and ill-defined. As R.E. Pahl argued (1977), it was not clear whether Castells' idea of collective consumption referred to goods and services provided by the welfare state or simply to those collectively consumed. Does the term, for example, include all forms of housing, both private and public or only that provided by the government? How do you define a privately owned car using a public highway? Moreover, such welfare goods are also provided in socialist cities and have been a source of urban protest there too – so does that mean socialist societies are about to collapse too? Similarly Castells' definition of protest movements was so broad that it included under its banner such disparate and non-revolutionary groups as one-parent families and the Women's League. Far from such varied pressure groups merging into one revolutionary force, they remained distinctly separate and often simply died out.

Ironically, the very research Castells' thesis inspired – detailed analyses of cities throughout the world – increasingly undermined his claim that his ideas applied to all cities, that all capitalist cities were undergoing similar crises. Rather they revealed that Castells' analysis was more true of French cities than cities everywhere.

Fellow-Marxists were particularly scathing of a radical critique that focused on consumption rather than the mode of production, on the city rather than the workplace as the battlefield for class struggles. Castells highlighted urban conflicts over housing and ignored those over plant closures and redundancies, analysed the role of the capitalist state but ignored that of the police.

Nevertheless Castells' thesis was a major breakthrough and revitalised both modern urban sociology and neo-Marxism. The idea of collective consumption inspired a wealth of research and is still the basis of such recent analyses of class voting as that by Patrick Dunleary (1980) and the local state by Cynthia Cockburn (1977). Castells himself has now adopted a more mature and less revolutionary viewpoint and, in his most recent study, *The City and the Grassroots* (1983) dramatically re-analysed his earlier claims, made detailed studies of specific urban protest movements and accepted that such struggles are unlikely to bring down capitalism on their own but that they do give local life more meaning and possibly nurture the embryos of tomorrow's social movements.

SEE ALSO

The various other theories of urban development that both enraged and stimulated Castells:

☐ **Urbanism**
☐ **Human ecology**

☐ Housing classes
☐ Urban managerialism

SUGGESTED READING

Castells M. *The City and the Grassroots*, Edward Arnold, 1983 – his most recent and readable work. His other works, listed below under Further Reading are extremely dense and difficult to read.
Saunders P. *Urban Politics*, Penguin, 1979
Saunders P. *Social Theory and the Urban Question*, Hutchinson, 1981 – two very good summaries of urban politics and sociology
Slattery M. 'Urban Sociology' in Haralambos M. ed. *Sociology New Directories*, Causeway Press, 1985 – a short overview of urban sociology

FURTHER READING

Castells M. *The Urban Question*, Edward Arnold, 1977
Castells M. *City, Class and Power*, Macmillan, 1978
Cockburn C. *The Local State*, Pluto, 1977
Dunleavy P. *Urban Political Analysis*, Macmillan, 1980
Pahl R.E. 'Collective Consumption' in Scase R. ed. *Industrial Society: Class, Cleavage and Control*, Allen & Unwin, 1977

EXAMINATION QUESTIONS

1 What social problems have been associated with urbanisation, **either** in the 'advanced' **or** in the 'developing' nations? (Cambridge Local Examinations Syndicate June 1986)
2 To what extent are British cities residentially segregated on the basis of social class? (Oxford Delegacy May 1985 P2)

7

THE AUTHOR

Auguste Comte (1798–1857) was born in Montpelier, Southern France, the son of an aristocratic and conservative family. He was educated at the progressive Ecole Polytechnique in Paris. From 1817 to 1824 he worked as secretary to the radical prophet of utopian socialism, Henri de Saint-Simon. However, their collaboration broke down amid some acrimony and Comte turned to teaching mathematics. In 1848 he established the Positivist Society, and the rest of his life was taken up with expanding and expounding positivism as a search for 'order and progress' amid the chaos of the times he lived in – the Industrial, Agrarian and Political Revolutions, particularly those in his own home country, France.

Comte's writings fall into two main phases, both of which form part of a single unified vision of knowledge and society. In his first phase – of which the major work is the six-volume *Cours de Philosophie Positive* (1830–42) – he sought to outline his views on science, both natural and social. His later writings, particularly *Système de Politique Positive* (1848–54) set out his blueprint for a new social order and a new religion of humanity. Comte is generally regarded as one of the founding fathers of both positivist philosophy and of sociology. He invented both the terms, 'positivism' and 'sociology'.

THE IDEA

Positivism can be defined as the philosophical view that 'empirical science is the only valid form of human knowledge'. Many different forms of positivism have been developed. Within sociology, this perspective is based on the fundamental assumption that the social world is essentially the same as the natural world, that both have an objective reality which can best be studied by using the 'scientific method' developed by natural scientists. Such a perspective rejects abstract philosophising, the metaphysical study of supernatural forces in favour of the observation, categorisation and measurement of hard facts from which can be deduced by logical reasoning, testable hypotheses, cause and effect relationships and ultimately laws of causation and evolution comparable to the laws of nature discovered by physicists, chemists and biologists. From this point of view, only observable phenomena have any scientific reality and the true facts about society can only be discovered and scientifically analysed by the researcher being as objective, impartial and unbiased as possible. Subjective feelings, interpretations and emotions have no place in a positivist perspective, not least because they cannot be observed and measured, but especially because they might distort any objective analysis.

Comte's contribution was to initiate positivism as a major form of sociological research and theorising. Having seen in his own time the advances in knowledge achieved by the natural sciences, his overriding aim was to establish the foundations of a comparable 'science of society' which he initially called social physics, but later re-named sociology (1838). Comte himself gave various meanings to the term 'positive'. Scientific inquiry should concern itself only with what is real, useful, certain, precise and constructive, not with imaginary, idle, uncertain, vague and destructive or critical questions. The whole emphasis in this new philosophy was to be on the positive, on discovering constructive, useful and reliable knowledge as a basis for improving society. It represented a repudiation of both pre-positive and revolutionary modes of thought. It was essentially a conservative philosophy, designed to help restore order through scientific analysis and progress, through practical policy. It sought to establish positivism as a science. Thereafter, whatever could not be known scientifically could not be known.

In his first phase, Comte set out his famous Law of Three Stages, an historical analysis of the evolution both of society and of human thought. He identified three key stages of intellectual development and thought:

■ The Theological Stage, during which all natural phenomena and social events were explained in terms of supernatural forces and deities, culminating in the Christian theory of one almighty God;

■ The Metaphysical Stage, during which abstract and even supernatural forces were still the main source of explanation but they were
more consistent and systematic than the capricious gods of the past;
■ The Positivist Stage, during which thought and explanation are
based on science not speculation, empirical experimentation not abstract philosophising. Only then will the world be de-mystified and
reality truly exposed.

According to Comte, all branches of human knowledge have evolved
through these three stages, but not simultaneously. The lower, more
basic sciences adopted the positivist spirit of inquiry first; the higher,
more complex disciplines later because they depended on the ground-
work in the lower sciences for their development. Thus astronomy and
mathematics preceded physics, which laid the foundations for chemistry and, in turn, biology, and finally sociology. Chemistry and the
lower sciences constitute 'analytical' disciplines because they deal with
fundamental laws and the most elementary components of natural
phenomena. Biology and sociology Comte referred to as 'synthetic'
sciences because they deal with complete organisms and offer an overall picture.

Moreover, these very varied scientific disciplines form a natural
hierarchy, rising from generality to complexity, from autonomy to
interdependence and culminating in sociology as the ultimate explanation of human and social development.

According to Comte's thesis, human society has followed similar
stages of evolution, and each stage has been associated with one
particular mode of thought (a view he later modified as he sought to
explain the emergence of each new stage as a struggle between traditional and progressive ideas). Using an organic analogy, he argued that
through the division of labour, society has become more complex,
differentiated and specialised. A social solidarity has evolved based on
an underlying consensus, and the increasing interdependence of its
constituent parts – the family, education and all the other institutions
which comprise the social system and all the aspects of culture and
language which provide its fabric. The role of sociology is to provide an
overview, to analyse both the statics (laws governing social order) and
dynamics (laws governing social change) of society.

Comte's sociology increasingly developed into a search for the essential principles of both social order and social change, and came to
reflect an underlying tension between traditional conservatism's opposition to science, reform and revolution, and radicalism's belief in a
new golden age based on science and industry. Comte became increas-

ingly sympathetic to the conservative view of social order as requiring an underlying set of common moral values. Accepting the view that, through the decline of traditional religion and rise of revolutionary philosophies, Europe was undergoing a moral as well as a social crisis, Comte sought to offer positivism as a means towards creating a new moral consensus as the basis of his new social order, even going on to outline a new 'religion of humanity'.

This concern with values equally underlies Comte's view of social theory and research. He rejected pure empiricism, the simplistic collection and measurement of social facts for their own sake. Unlike many later positivists, he argued for the inter-relationship of facts and theory. He equally recognised that social research could never imitate the methods of natural science in all their purity, could not conduct pure experiments. Nevertheless, he proposed indirect or natural social experiments and identified such scientific principles as observation, analysis and, in particular, comparison, as the foundations of his new science of society.

Though Comte's search for underlying laws of social development implies historical fatalism – that even if it is possible to understand how society is developing, it is not possible to change it – his ultimate aim was to provide policy makers with the knowledge and ideas to control and improve social conditions. Just as scientific method had provided natural scientists with the tools for mastering as well as understanding nature, so, believed Comte, positivist sociology would enable man to become master of his social and political destiny.

THE IDEA IN ACTION

Comte's idea of positivism has had a considerable impact both on philosophy and on sociology. It laid the foundations for the French tradition of positivism, influenced such leading English philosophers as J.S. Mill and Herbert Spencer, and pre-dated the Vienna School of Logical Positivism in the 1920s. It attracted considerable attention in Europe, Latin America and the USA. Comte's motto, 'Order and Progress' is emblazoned on the national flag of Brazil. It stimulated the notion of positive economics that is still influential in economics today.

Comte's influence within sociology has been even more profound. He founded the positivist tradition which has so dominated British, European and American sociology right up to the present day. His use of organic analogy, his use of such concepts as social consensus and social statics laid the basis for functionalism as proclaimed by Emile

Durkheim and American structural functionalists. His emphasis on scientific method still influences both sociological and anthropological research. His faith in scientific knowledge as the basis for a more rational, just and stable society pre-dates many modern theories of post-industrial society. However, his own attempts to outline an ideal society were somewhat less successful, even somewhat absurd. Comte envisaged a 'sociocracy', a society run by sociologists, and a sociolatry – a series of festivals paying homage to a new religion of humanity. Such extremes lost Comte many supporters, and even Durkheim denied that he was a positivist.

Positivism's dominance over western sociology, however, came under increasing attack in the late 1960s. Marxists criticised its conservative bias and failure to acknowledge the class conflict underlying capitalist societies. Phenomenologists went deeper and attacked its very foundations, its belief in a social reality above and beyond any group of individuals, its faith in scientific method and objective analysis for uncovering the truth about the fundamental laws governing social structure, social change and human behaviour. In contrast, phenomenologists argued that social reality is fundamentally different from nature, that it is no more than the interpretations and meanings given by people to their everyday lives. From such a perspective, objective analysis becomes impossible and scientific method a distortion. Rather the aim of sociological research should be to discover the very subjective factors so totally rejected by scientific sociology – meaning, feeling and interpretation. Such a relative view of knowledge, even of physical knowledge, received increasing support from philosophers and even from historians of science such as T.S. Kuhn (see page 162).

This fall from both philosophical and sociological grace was partly due to the way the term positivism had been both used and abused, especially when used to justify a narrow concentration on quantification, an obsessive faith in social facts to the exclusion of human values and meaning. Comte, in contrast, actually emphasised the inter-relationship of fact and value, the need for moral evaluation in conducting social research. Thus, though now considered arcane by many sociologists and philosophers, positivism continues to draw strength from its scientific status, continues to influence, though no longer dominate, mainstream sociology.

SEE ALSO

☐ **Structural functionalism** as a more modern version of Comte's sociology and the following as criticisms of his whole approach.

☐ **Phenomenology**
☐ **Paradigms**
☐ **Critical theory**
☐ **Falsification** – Karl Popper's idea is in a sense an attempt to update positivism.

SUGGESTED READING

Bryant C. 'What is Positivism?', *Social Studies Review*, January 1986
Pettit P. 'The Philosophies of Social Science', in Anderson R.J. and Sharock
  W.W. *Teaching Papers in Sociology*, Longman

FURTHER READING

Comte A. *The Positive Philosophy of Auguste Comte*, Bell, 1838
Comte A. *Cours de Philosophie Positive*, Ballière & Sons, Paris 1877, 1830–42
Comte A. *Système de Politique Positive*, Longmans, Green & Co., London, 1875–77, 1848–54

EXAMINATION QUESTIONS

1 Examine the argument that the logic and methods of the natural sciences are applicable to the study of human society. (AEB June 1982)
2 Positivism, one of the main methodological approaches recognised in sociology, is based on the assumption that objective study of the social world is desirable and possible. Its most common research technique is the social survey which produces large scale quantifiable data from which variables can be statistically controlled in order to establish causal relationships. Criticisms of the explanations and theories produced in this way centre on the reliability of the techniques involved in carrying out the surveys and the validity of the type of data obtained from them.
  (a) Briefly define the following terms.
    (i)   objective
    (ii) quantifiable data
    (iii) causal relationship
  (b) Using at least **one** study with which you are familiar, demonstrate how social surveys can be used in the way indicated in the passage.
  (c) Outline **one** criticism of the reliability and **one** criticism of the validity of social surveys.
  (d) Explain and illustrate how the choice of methodological approach influences the type of results and explanations which sociologists arrive at. (JMB June 1987)

8

RALPH DAHRENDORF *and*

CONFLICT THEORY

THE AUTHOR

Ralph Dahrendorf (1929–   ) was born in Hamburg, the son of a German politician. He was imprisoned in a concentration camp in 1944–5 and then educated at Hamburg University (1947–52) where he studied philosophy and philology. He went on to postgraduate work in sociology at the London School of Economics (1952–4) where he was influenced by Karl Popper's ideas. After doing research work at the Centre for Advanced Study at Palo Alto, Dahrendorf went on to lecture at the universities of Saarland, Hamburg, Tübingen and Constance. He became involved in German politics, joined the Free Democratic Party and became a member of the Baden Württemberg Landtag (1968–70) and of the Bundestag (1969–70). He held a series of leading political posts including those of Parliamentary State Secretary for Foreign Affairs and Member of the EEC Commission. In 1974 he was appointed Director of the London School of Economics. In the following year he gave a series of Reith Lectures on 'The New Liberty' and in 1982 was awarded an honorary knighthood.

Dahrendorf's sociological interests have been very varied and diverse, ranging from democracy in Germany to world modernisation and concentrating in particular on class and conflict theory and role theory.

Dahrendorf's major works to date have been:

- *Class and Class Conflict in an Industrial Society* (1959)
- *Society and Democracy in Germany* (1967)
- *The New Liberty* (1975)
- *Life Chances* (1979)

THE IDEA

Dahrendorf's concept of conflict theory was based on the ideas of both Marx and, in particular, Weber. It was developed as a direct alternative to the consensus theories of Talcott Parsons and the Functionalist School of sociology. Where such writers argued that sociological analysis should concentrate on explaining social solidarity and value consensus, Dahrendorf argued for an analysis based on conflict and change. Like Marx and Weber, he saw class conflict as the key dynamism for social change. However, where Marx based his analysis of class on the ownership and non-ownership of the economic 'means of production', Dahrendorf saw participation in and exclusion from power (in particular authority) as the key dialectic and motive force of historical and social change – and, ironically, social integration.

In any organisation there are those who hold power, who make decisions, hire and fire, allocate resources. Such power is not personal but depends on the position one holds. Such office-holders have authority – what Weber called 'legitimated power'. Whilst those in power seek to maintain their position, authority and control, those without power or authority strive to attain it – or at least to resist it, especially if they disagree with the way it is being used. Thus, even in a stable, democratic society, there is a constant underlying power struggle going on in which even those in authority – be they headmasters or prime ministers – have to face constant resistance – be it from staff and pupils or opposition politicians and voters. This power struggle takes place at all levels of society from the Cabinet and Houses of Parliament through to the rivalries and conflicts in the local tennis club – and in the home!

This interminable contest between those in and out of power only erupts into class conflict when individuals find that the only way to protect or promote their own interests is by collective action. Such group conflict develops in degrees and takes a variety of forms from trade unions going on strike to pressure groups demonstrating. Only in the most extreme situations does collective action explode into class conflict or revolution. However, according to Dahrendorf, such class solidarity may equally disintegrate into competition between individuals when opportunities for individual advancement improve, as, say, during periods of economic prosperity. Thus, whilst Marx predicted that as industrialisation advanced in capitalist societies, so would class solidarity and class conflict, Dahrendorf predicted the opposite – that with technological development the working class would become increasingly heterogeneous and fragmented, 'increasingly complex machines require increasingly qualified designers, builders, maintenance and repair men'. With such increasing specialisation, the working class becomes highly differentiated, divided rather than united by differences of pay, status and skill. Competition between the different levels of the working class – skilled, semi-skilled and unskilled – is likely to become even more intense than that between the middle and working classes. Dahrendorf even went on to claim that 'it has become doubtful whether speaking of the working class still makes much sense'. Dahrendorf's picture of society is thus one of the interminable conflict at the personal, group, organisational and class level. It is chaotic and apparently random conflict between those in and out of power, between the dominant and the subordinate. Yet such conflict has a purpose.

■ Firstly, it holds society together. For Dahrendorf, the basis of social integration is not, as Parsons argues, consensus, but coercion, the power of those in authority to force the masses to obey them. Though, in his view, social conflict is endemic to all societies, for the majority of time it is confined within boundaries based on some general agreement, or at least acceptance, of basic values and institutions. It rarely spreads across the whole of society, rarely explodes into violent revolution. For example, trade unions go on strike over economic and industrial disputes; for them to directly enter the political arena would be seen as illegitimate.

■ Secondly, it is a key mechanism in a democracy for preventing tyranny and the abuse of power, for promoting individual rights and the rule of law and keeping a check on those in power.

THE IDEA IN ACTION

Amid the intense social and political conflicts of the 1960s and 1970s – student riots, strikes, industrial unrest and mass unemployment – Dahrendorf's analysis seemed inadequate compared to more radical and Marxist predictions of class upheavals and impending revolution. He was even accused of being reactionary. However, with the aid of hindsight, looking back from the late 1980s, it is clear that, in some ways, Dahrendorf's predictions have so far shown as much strength and accuracy as more radical ones.

Far from the conflicts of the 1970s paving the way for proletarian revolution and uniting the working class in defence of jobs and pay against new technology and big business, the last ten to fifteen years have seen the British working class fragment and divide. Even those most classic of working class struggles, the miners' dispute (1984), and that at Wapping (1985) when over 6000 printers were made redundant at a stroke, failed to unify the British working class or even get unswerving support from the trade unions. Rather, with the support of a powerful Conservative Government, new machinery was installed, manning-levels cut and the workers left defeated and dispirited, as capitalism marched on anew.

As Dahrendorf predicted, the prosperity of the 1980s has created greater economic and social opportunities for individual and group advancement, epitomised by that most upwardly mobile of social creatures, the 'Yuppie'. Traditional class formations are disintegrating and the working class in particular seems to be shrinking and fragmenting in the face of new technology, the growth of service industries, and the shift of population from the north to the south, the inner cities to the suburbs. New 'class' lines appear to have emerged based on employment/unemployment, private/public consumption of housing, education and health, private ownership and shareholding.

Dahrendorf's conflict theory has equally much to offer in explaining 'modern' conflicts which seem to be based more on civil rights, the environment, housing and welfare issues, nuclear power, etc. than on the traditional ones of ownership and non-ownership of the means of production. Bureaucracy as much as big business is now the target of protest. Dahrendorf's neo-Weberian analysis, however, only offers an explanation of social conflict and social division. It fails to provide:

■ Any detailed analysis of the basis of social conflict beyond competition for power and authority. Social order, therefore, seems to be more a matter of chance than organised structure.
■ Any programme of action, any solutions to social conflict in the way functionalism and even Marxism attempt to. Conflict is simply accepted as natural and inevitable.

Thus, whilst Dahrendorf's analysis appeared to offer a real alternative to Marxist ideas of social conflict and fragmentation in the 1960s, its lack of analytical depth has limited its sociological influence and use.

SEE ALSO

☐ **Structural functionalism** and **historical materialism** as two key ideas in influencing Dahrendorf in very different ways.
☐ **Housing classes** as an example of conflict theory at work.

SUGGESTED READING

Dahrendorf R. *Class and Class Conflict in an Industrial Society*, Routledge & Kegan Paul, 1959 – difficult but worth trying

FURTHER READING

Dahrendorf R. *Society and Democracy in Germany*, Routledge & Kegan Paul, London, 1967
Dahrendorf R. *The New Liberty*, Routledge & Kegan Paul, London, 1975
Dahrendorf R. *Life Chances*, Routledge & Kegan Paul, London, 1979

EXAMINATION QUESTION

What explanations do sociologists offer for social conflict and social change?
(AEB June 1985)

9

EMILE DURKHEIM *and*

SOCIAL SOLIDARITY

THE AUTHOR

Emile Durkheim (1858–1917) was probably the founding father of sociology in the sense that:

■ he in particular sought to establish sociology as an academic discipline in its own right. He occupied the first chair in sociology anywhere.
■ he helped establish one of the major perspectives in modern sociology, that of structural functionalism.

He was born in Epinal, Alsace-Lorraine, at that time part of Eastern France but partitioned by Prussia after the Franco-Prussian War of 1870. Possibly the national humiliation and social disorder that followed partly explains his lifelong interest in social solidarity. His father was a Jewish Rabbi and Durkheim considered following in his footsteps but in his teens he converted to Catholicism and later became an agnostic. At the elite Ecole Normale Supérieure he proved himself to be a brilliant student, graduating in 1882. He embarked on an academic career and during his time in Germany he was impressed not only by the ideas of republicanism but the advances in social science and psychology. In 1887 he was appointed to the first post in social science at a French University, that of Bourdeaux. There, between 1887 and 1902, Durkheim produced most of his key works and attracted to him a host of outstanding students eager to spread the word about the new 'science of society'. In 1902 Durkheim was recalled to Paris and eventually appointed Professor of Education and Social Science at the Sorbonne, the first chair in sociology. For many years he edited the journal *L'Année sociologue*, an annual collection of key writings by sociologists, through which the academic status of this new discipline was both expanded and promoted.

Durkheim lost his only son in the First World War and the subsequent grief undoubtedly contributed to a heart attack from which he died on 15 November 1917 at the age of fifty-nine.

Durkheim's key works were:

- *The Division of Labour in Society* (1893)
- *The Rules of Sociological Method* (1895)
- *Suicide: A Study in Sociology* (1897)
- *The Elementary Forms of Religious Life* (1912)

THE IDEA

One of the central issues of sociology, past and present, is that of social order – or as Durkheim called it, 'social solidarity'. For Durkheim this was an especially pertinent question, living as he did amidst the political turmoils and industrial/urban upheavals facing Europe and especially France, at the turn of the century. He was concerned to use the new science of sociology to analyse the very essence of social order – how it is established, maintained and, in particular, re-established after a period of severe and rapid social change; how do traditional societies evolve into modern ones, rural communities into mass industrial-urban ones? In particular, how, amid all this transitional change, are the individual rights and freedoms so characteristic of advanced industrial societies promoted and protected in the face of mass society's need for social order and control? The answer, argued Durkheim, lay in 'a transformation of social solidarity due to the growing development of the division of labour'.

Durkheim devoted his first major publication, *The Division of Labour in Society* (1893) to the topic of social solidarity and he drew up two ideal types of social order – mechanical and organic solidarity – as the basis for comparing and analysing the simple social structures of traditional societies with the complex divisions of labour of modern ones.

In traditional societies, communities or groups, relationships are essentially face to face (or mechanical), the division of labour very simple, with most people involved in essentially the same occupation, be it hunting or farming. There is a common lifestyle, a common set of beliefs, customs and rituals, known and practised by all. There is an underlying common consensus which Durkheim referred to as '*conscience collective*' – a term which, whether translated as 'common consciousness' or 'collective conscience', still evokes the same essential idea of a common morality or set of values upon which social solidarity is based and which guide and control individual behaviour. In mechanical societies, the *conscience collective* is all-dominant because within such simple social systems everyone is essentially the same. There is little individuality, social differences are few and far between, private property is almost unknown and so conformity is both 'natural' and easily established through socialisation and such key social controls as the family and religion. Deviations are severely and publicly punished.

However, as societies grow and modernise, adopt industrial economies and complex divisions of labour, and people move from the country to the city, so they outgrow mechanical solidarity. Similarity gives way to differentiation, homogeneity to heterogeneity, as a variety of occupations, lifestyles and sub-cultures proliferates and multiplies. Collectivism gives way to individualism, common ownership to private property, communal responsibility to individual rights, commonality to class and status differences. Face-to-face relationships and informal social controls are no longer enough to hold society together; power and authority have shifted from the family and the church to the law and the state. Just as in nature, such differentiation and complexity requires a new basis for social solidarity, an *organic* one that can successfully combine social order and individual freedom.

For Durkheim, the heart of organic solidarity is the complex division of labour that underpins the industrial economies of modern societies where everyone is interdependent. In today's advanced industrial-urban societies, no individual is totally self-sufficient (in contrast to the self-sufficiency often displayed by people in simple societies). Whilst we are all very different, we all depend on a complex economic system that requires us to specialise in a multiplicity of occupations and allows us the freedom to live very different lifestyles. It is the economic interdependency, this reciprocity and co-operation for mutual benefit, survival and prosperity, argued Durkheim, that forms the foundation of modern organic societies. However, he totally rejected the utilitarian arguments, particularly those of Herbert Spencer, that economic self-interest alone is enough to cement and stabilize a civilized society. In his view, self-interest alone would produce conflict and social chaos. Underlying the contracts and economic exchange of advanced industrial societies there has to be some form of morality, some ethical code of generally-agreed principles, norms and values upon which a system of trust and justice could be based. Man is as capable of altruism as of greed and the role of society is to encourage as much as to restrain such human traits according to its own particular stage of evolutionary development. Durkheim thus proposed the notion of the duality of human nature, the idea that we all have two consciences – a personal one and a social one, one based on self-interest, one on the interests of society. Moreover, whilst in mechanical societies the individual and collective conscience are virtually synonymous, in organic societies the two consciences are both distinct, separate, and often in conflict. Formal social controls, therefore, become more necessary in organic than mechanical societies.

But how, with the decline of traditional social controls – the family and the church – is social solidarity to be enforced and maintained in advanced societies? Durkheim put his faith in the state and the law at the societal level and in occupational and professional associations or guilds at the industrial level. Whilst the government and courts pro-mote the law as the fullest expression of the social consensus, Durkheim hoped that it would be the professional associations that would estab-lish and enforce the essential codes of ethics and behaviour of organic societies. Therefore, in contrast to many of his contemporaries, he did not see social change as a destructive force, as the demise of social order, traditional morality and civilized society. He was optimistic that the new industrial order would be a step forward, both progressive and liberating.

Having identified the two main types of social order and their underlying moralities, Durkheim now sought to monitor and measure scientifically the transition from mechanical to organic solidarity and the instrument he attempted to use was the law. Whilst moral phenom-ena do not easily lend themselves to precise observation, legal codes do provide an external and measurable index because they are a formal expression of moral values. In particular, all laws involve sanctions and Durkheim identified two contrasting types of sanction:

■ Repressive sanctions, which involve punishment and suffering, be it loss of liberty, or of life!
■ Restitutive sanctions as in civil or common law, which involve re-adjustment rather than punishment, restoring matters to their previous state prior to a transgression (e.g. returning goods or property).

Durkheim argued that legal codes based primarily on repressive sanctions reflected a strong underlying *conscience collective* of the type predominant in traditional societies whilst restitutive law reflected the 'organic' morality of more modern societies and their need for contrac-tual relationships. He was, therefore, able to draw up an index of social solidarity, a continuum for plotting society's evolutionary progress from religious to rational morality, from social regulation by the family to social direction by the state. In modern societies the state and its agencies, the police and the courts, embody an organic *conscience collective,* symbolise the people's will and moral values in the way that the church did in medieval Europe.

Durkheim saw modern morality, modern legal systems, as a superior basis for social order, justice and development than either mechanical solidarity or self-interest. However, he was deeply concerned that the transition from mechanical to organic solidarity was neither always successful nor painless. It often produced social strain, even social conflict, as the old order was replaced by the new. During this period of structural transition there is a severe danger of a period of normlessness – or as Durkheim called it, anomie (see page 63) – as the old morality and traditional social controls declined but the new social consensus was still in its infancy. Durkheim believed that many of the early capitalist societies in western Europe were undergoing just such a transition and were suffering the problems of anomie and of a forced or artificial division of labour: one imposed on the economic structure by the old ruling class as it struggled to stay in power rather than one that arose naturally to reflect the needs of industrialisation. This created unjust social inequalities and so led to an escalation of social conflict, and possibly, as in many nineteenth-century European countries, revolution.

Durkheim saw the role of social science as being that of identifying such problems and helping to overcome the problems of social transition by proposing effective solutions and social policies. However, by the end of *The Division of Labour in Society* he was showing doubts about the possibility of organic solidarity emerging automatically from an increasing division of labour. He accepted that it may require direct planning and control.

Mechanical and organic solidarity were, therefore, the two ideal types Durkheim used to explain scientifically his theory of social order and change. He was increasingly aware, however, of the inherent problems and potential sources of conflict produced by this transition from an old to a new division of labour, from traditional to modern society.

THE IDEA IN ACTION

The concept of social solidarity, this concern with social order and evolution has been at the heart of functionalist writings from Durkheim onwards. Durkheim's emphasis on morality and social consensus as the foundation of a successful social order has remained a central theme in modern sociology whilst his attempt to analyse scientifically and to monitor social change – its causes, effects and sources of strain – has inspired the whole positivist tradition within sociology and stimulated a mass of research into anomie, suicide and religion.

However, this concept and its use has also been the subject of extensive criticism:

■ Durkheim's use of an organic analogy and his belief that all societies would follow the same evolutionary path have been severely criticised as socially and historically inaccurate. In his defence, though, Durkheim was only using mechanical and organic solidarity as ideal types, useful for analytical purposes but not necessarily prescriptive. He fully recognised that not all societies neatly fitted these models and that societies may well evolve in different ways.

■ Whilst the concept of social solidarity offered a major framework for analysing social order, it lacked the depth for explaining social change and social conflict.

'Social solidarity' could explain gradual evolutionary development but not sudden or revolutionary change. It explained change in terms of social adaptation or the re-establishment of equilibrium but offered little explanation of class or political conflict save as a social problem (as in the concept of anomie). In contrast, Marxist and more radical writers have put the class struggle at the heart of their theories of social development. Durkheim tended to perceive class conflict as simply a symptom of the social strain created by an artificial division of labour and a perpetuation of existing social inequalities. In fact, he was very sympathetic to socialist ideas and, like St Simon, predicted the emergence of a classless society in the future based on organic solidarity and equality of opportunity. Recognising that such a mature society may not emerge naturally, he came to support the idea of state planning to create a more rational division of labour, a fairer system of social justice.

Whilst anthropological research tended to support Durkheim's concept of mechanical solidarity, his faith in economic reciprocity and occupational ethics as the basis of organic solidarity seemed somewhat optimistic, if not utopian. Recognising this criticism, Durkheim gradually shifted his analysis of the moral and social consensus of organic solidarity from economic interdependence to a re-creation of religious values in modern societies and to the rise of moral universalism represented by such social mores as nationalism and the power of education and citizenship to create the sense of common humanity needed to bind the individual to society. Unfortunately, the *conscience collective* of modern societies often seems too varied, changeable and superficial to support the organic solidarity required to stabilize and order advanced mass societies.

Durkheim has also been accused of exaggerating the contrast between repressive and restitutive law as a basis for measuring mechanical as opposed to organic solidarity. Critics have argued that many of the traditional societies he cited had forms of restitutive law whilst others, like the Trobriander Islanders, did not use repressive sanctions at all. Equally, many modern states have used highly repressive legal codes to enforce their authority and suppress individual rights, notably South Africa and many communist societies.

Despite all these criticisms, Durkheim's concept of social solidarity, his evolutionary theory of social change and his attempt to analyse and monitor social development have proved a major stimulus to sociological ideas and research ever since.

SEE ALSO

☐ **Structural functionalism** as an extension of Durkheim's ideas.
☐ **Historical materialism** as a very different theory of social order and social change.
☐ Anomie

SUGGESTED READING

Giddens A. *Durkheim*, Fontana, 1978
Lukes S. *Emile Durkheim: his Life and Work*, Allen & Unwin, 1972
Thompson K. *Emile Durkheim*, Tavistock, 1982
Any of the above offer concise, readable and authoritative outlines of Durkheim's life, work and ideas. Kenneth Thompson's book is especially good on the concept of social solidarity.

FURTHER READING

Durkheim E. *The Division of Labour in Society* (1893), Free Press, 1960
Durkheim E. *The Rules of Sociological Method* (1895), Free Press, 1958
Durkheim E. *Suicide: A Study in Sociology* (1897), Free Press, 1951
Durkheim E. *The Elementary Forms of Religious Life* (1912), Allen & Unwin, 1954

EXAMINATION QUESTION

How far is the distinction between 'traditional' and 'modern' a valid and useful way for the sociologist to classify societies? (WJEC June 1987)

10

EMILE DURKHEIM *and*

ANOMIE

THE IDEA

Durkheim's work rests on two main, interlinked themes

■ An analysis of the bases of social order and in particular of the effects of industrialisation as outlined in studies like *The Division of Labour in Society* (1893) and *The Elementary Forms of Religious Life* (1912).
■ An attempt to establish sociology as a respectable and 'scientific'. academic discipline, capable of not only diagnosing society's ills but recommending possible cures. (*The Rules of Sociological Method* (1895) and *Suicide* (1897))

To achieve both these aims, Durkheim adopted a functionalist model by which society is seen not merely as a collection of independent individuals but as an entity in itself. It functions like any other natural organism as a system of independent parts – the economy, the family, the government and so on – held together not by a central nervous system but by a central value system, a set of social guidelines called norms based on an underlying moral consensus, or collective consciousness. Such norms not only give society a basic framework and source of stability but are crucial in controlling and directing its individual members. In Durkheim's view, man's appetites are unlimited, insatiable, and if any form of social order or civilisation is to exist such desires must be controlled. Simply for his own personal wellbeing, the individual needs to keep his ambitions in check, needs moral guidelines, or else he will end up isolated and rootless. Thus, in Durkheim's view, there is always going to be an underlying conflict or tension between the individual's aspirations and society's needs for order and control.

An absence of norms or a fundamental conflict over society's basic values Durkheim called *anomie*, and he particularly feared that such a social 'sickness' would occur during periods of social upheaval or transition. In small-scale traditional societies, where relationships are personal and there is a limited division of labour, it is fairly easy for a general consensus as to the values and norms of society and of the rights and privileges of individual members to be established and upheld – especially if backed by the moral authority and sanctions of religion. Everyone knows their place and aspires no higher. However, in the transition from the mechanical solidarity of such societies to the organic solidarity of industrial ones where there is an extensive division of labour and where relationships are often highly impersonal, a break- down in social consensus and so of social controls over the individual is highly possible. Just such a situation faced Durkheim and his con- temporaries in the late nineteenth century as both political revolutions and industrialisation swept across Europe destroying not only tradi- tional communities but the very moral fabric of society. The new industrial division of labour seemed to be out-stripping existing moral values. Without the discipline of traditional social norms, Durkheim feared that individual ambitions would rise sky-high and so be very frustrated if the new social order was unable to fulfill its apparent promises. As people in the nineteenth century left their traditional roots in the village, their family and friends, for the bright lights and high wages of the new industrial cities, many soon found themselves disillu- sioned, isolated and friendless, creating in Durkheim's view an enormous potential for social disorder; as evidenced in the rampages of 'the mob' in many European cities at this time.

Durkheim, however, was not as pessimistic as such fellow writers as Ferdinand Tönnies. Beneath the social upheavals and demand for individual rights and liberties, he perceived the potential for a new social order based on the morality and ethics of the new professional guilds and associations.

The concept of anomie, however, as one of Durkheim's biographers Anthony Giddens (1978) argues, is not only an analysis of social disorder but an explanation of individual behaviour. The classic ex- ample of this is Durkheim's analysis of 'anomic' suicide, the type of suicide that occurs during periods of social instability such as economic booms and slumps. Those at the top of their profession, particularly in such fields as business and commerce, argued Durkheim, are particu- larly prone to anomic suicide because they are the ones with the greatest personal ambitions, the ones least restrained by traditional morality and social controls and the ones for whom personal failure is particularly devastating. Thus, whilst the suicide rate in America gen- erally shot up after the 1929 Wall Street Crash, it was businessmen and financiers who were most likely to throw themselves out of skyscraper windows.

THE IDEA IN ACTION

The concept of anomie has been adapted and reinterpreted in a variety of ways.

Some have used it to explain juvenile delinquency, the growth of crime and social unrest in advanced industrial societies and even the riots in America in the 1960s and Britain in the 1980s, arguing either in terms of inadequate socialisation, of parents failing to bring up their children properly or of the need for stricter social controls and for a stronger emphasis on traditional moral values via the family and the church. Others have used it to explain the collapse of social consensus and so order in societies such as Northern Ireland and the Lebanon.

The American sociologist, Robert Merton, however, emphasised the idea of norm conflict as the basis of the high rate of crime, deviancy and unrest in modern America. According to his analysis, there is a lack of fit between the unlimited ambitions of the American Dream that all youngsters in America are socialised into, and the limited opportunities available for achieving such wealth and fame. Not everyone can become a millionaire or President and for some groups like the Blacks the opportunities to rise are virtually non-existent. So how do people adapt to such failure? Merton outlined five forms of adaptation, four of which involved some form of deviance. Whilst a few reach the top legitimately by conforming – by promotion, luck or skill – others succeed by illegitimate means through crime. The rest adapt to failure by withdrawing into drugs, retreating to alternative societies such as communes or even rebelling against the whole idea of such materialism and competition by joining urban guerilla groups such as the Black Panthers or Minutemen. In the 1960s a whole range of programmes of 'positive discrimination', particularly the massive Headstart Programme, were instituted to try to increase opportunities for deprived groups especially Black youngsters and to socialise them into 'normal' social values, to overcome their 'culture of poverty' and draw them into mainstream society. However this approach had limited success and, as its critics argued, it left the basic inequalities of America society unaltered.

The concept of anomie has further suffered from the more general critique of the whole functionalist model, in particular the idea that societies rest on an underlying consensus and that all age groups in society accept the same norms and values. The idea that the ethics of professions such as doctors, accountants and lawyers could provide the moral basis for industrial societies is accepted by few writers today.

Nevertheless the concept of anomie has highlighted a key social problem of advanced industrial societies, that of rapid social change, and stressed the importance of moral guidelines for the wellbeing of both society at large and the individual in particular.

SEE ALSO

☐ **Alienation** as Karl Marx's theory of this modern malaise.
☐ **Social solidarity** as the background theory to this idea.

SUGGESTED READING

Giddens A. *Durkheim,* Fontana, 1978
Thompson K. *Emile Durkheim,* Tavistock, 1982
Lukes S. *Emile Durkheim: his Life and Work,* Allen & Unwin, 1972
The above offer concise, readable and authoritative outlines of Durkheim's
   life, work and ideas.

FURTHER READING

Durkheim E. *The Division of Labour in Society* (1893), Free Press, 1960
Durkheim E. *The Rules of Sociological Method* (1895), Free Press, 1958
Durkheim E. *Suicide: A Study in Sociology* (1897), Free Press, 1951
Durkheim E. *The Elementary Forms of Religious Life* (1912), Allen & Unwin,
   1954

EXAMINATION QUESTION

What is meant by the term 'increasing complexity of the division of labour'? Using comparative examples, what do you consider to be *either* the main causes *or* the main consequences of this? (London University January 1988 Paper 3)

11

FRIEDRICH ENGELS *and*
HISTORICAL MATERIALISM

THE AUTHOR

Friedrich Engels (1820–1895) was born in Barmen, Germany, the son of a prosperous textile manufacturer with factories in both Germany and England. Though brought up to take over the family business, Engels developed a taste for radical social criticism, became heavily involved with the radical German group, the Young Hegelians, and through them met and later befriended Karl Marx. In 1842 he was sent to the firm's Manchester factory. Whilst there he developed contacts with such English radicals as the Chartists and Owenites and wrote his vivid eye-witness account of *The Condition of the Working Class in England*, the birthplace of the Industrial Revolution. He was now convinced that the new industrial working class was the revolutionary force of the future. Marx had reached a similar conclusion and impressed by Engel's newspaper article 'Outlines of a Critique of Political Economy', collaborated with him on their first joint publications *The Holy Family* (1845) and *The German Ideology* (1845).

Between 1845 and 1850 Engels devoted himself to political work with Marx in Brussels and Paris as they sought to establish Marxism as both an intellectual theory and a revolutionary movement. Engels became very active in socialist politics, worked extensively for the Germany Social Democratic Party and helped establish the Communist League. He co-wrote the Communist Manifesto on the eve of the 1848 European Revolutions, was actively involved in the German revolution of that year and had to flee with Marx into exile when these revolutions collapsed. He rejoined the family firm in Manchester in 1850 and remained there for the next twenty years during which time he helped Marx and his family financially and began developing his own ideas about dialectical materialism.

Engels retired in 1870 and moved to London to help the ailing Marx with both his writing and his political work in running the First International. He began popularising Marxism, even writing articles for the New York *Daily Times* under Marx's name. Through such works as *Anti Dühring* (1878), *Socialism: Utopian and Scientific* (1892) and through Ludwig Feuerbach, Engels began developing the key themes of historical materialism. By the time of the Second International, Engels' philosophical and political reputation surpassed Marx's.

After Marx's death in 1883 Engels devoted himself to editing and publishing the second and third volumes of *Das Kapital* in 1885 and 1894. He had just began the fourth volume when he died of cancer in 1895.

Engels is always portrayed today as the junior member of the Marx–Engels partnership and, certainly in terms of theoretical analysis, this is true. Nevertheless he was a skilled journalist, social historian, military expert and natural scientist in his own right. He produced numerous articles and works of his own including 'Dialectics of Nature' (1925) and 'Origins of the Family' (1884), one of the earliest contributions to socialist feminism. In his later years he was the authority on Marx, the editor and executor of all his works and until the First World War the great propagandist of Marxism. It was not until the positivist strains in Engels' writings culminated in the adoption of Marxism as official orthodoxy by the Bolsheviks and especially Stalin that controversy about his scientific interpretation of Marxism grew and his reputation declined accordingly.

Though Engels always credited Marx with the idea of historical materialism, it was Engels who coined the phrase historical materialism, who fleshed out the key themes of what Marx saw as merely a 'guiding thread' into a law of historical development, and who popularised and spread this key idea.

THE IDEA

Traditionally history is seen as the progressive unfolding of man's social and economic development propelled forward by the political actions of certain key historical figures – Julius Caesar, Napoleon, Nelson – and certain outstanding kings and queens. Historical materialism similarly sees history as progressive but rejects the idea that it is the actions of individuals, however powerful, that is the key dynamic. Rather for Marxists the key dynamism is economic development. As Engels summed it up (*Socialism: Utopian and Scientific*) historical materialism 'designate[s] that view of the course of history which seeks the ultimate cause and the great moving power of all important historic events in the economic development of society, in the changes in the modes of production and exchange, in the consequent division of society into distinct classes, and in the struggle of these classes against one another'.

Historical materialism therefore is a theory of historical development through economic or material forces rather than political or social ones.

The term materialist is a philosophical concept which sees the *external* world as real, governed by its own laws of cause and effect and independent of human consciousness. This perspective contrasts with idealism which sees the external world, both natural and social, as ultimately determined by men's ideas and consciousness of it. The philosophical debate between these two views was at its height in mid-nineteenth-century Germany, with the great philosopher Hegel proclaiming that ideas were the dominant force in history, that history was simply the progressive unfolding of reason. Marx 'stood Hegel on his head', declaring that it was not ideas that determined historical development but the economic facts of life, not least man's need to produce food, shelter and water.

The simple fact [is] that human beings must have food, drink, clothing and shelter first of all, before they can interest themselves in politics, science, art, religion and the like. This implies that the production of the immediate material means of subsistence, and consequently the degree of economic development of a given people or epoch, form the foundation upon which the state institutions, the legal conceptions, the art, and even religious ideas are built up. It implies that these latter must be explained out of the former, whereas the former have usually been explained as issuing from the latter. (Engel's speech at the graveside of Karl Marx, 17 March 1883)

It is not the consciousness of men that determines their being, but, on the contrary, their being that determines their consciousness. (Karl Marx, Preface to *Critique of Political Economy*, 1859)

Historical materialism therefore is a theory of social structure and social change based on the following key concepts.

1   That society is a totality based on two key structures:

■ An economic substructure concerned with the production and distribution of goods and services.
■ A social, political and ideological superstructure comprising such key social institutions as the state, the law and the family.

2   The economic substructure forms the basic foundation of society. It determines not only the production of goods and services but all other major social institutions in the superstructure – even a society's way of life, form of government and the way it thinks. It can be broken down into two key elements:

■ The forces of production – the methods and tools of production including labour and machinery.
■ The relations of production that exist between the owners of the means of production and the workers. These will vary from one mode of production to another. Under feudalism they were those of master and serf, under capitalism, bourgeoisie and proletariat.

3. A mode of production refers to the economic system prevailing at any particular point in historical time. Thus, in the Middle Ages, feudalism was predominant, based on land as the chief means of production. In capitalist society industry and trade predominate. Besides socialism, Marx identified four major modes of production (MOP): Asiatic, Ancient, Feudalism, Capitalism. Each MOP is a progressive step forward in man's march forward towards socialism. The key mechanisms for such progressive social change are:

■ The underlying contradictions within the economic substructure resulting in a growing conflict and mismatch between the forces and relations of production as new economic methods start to outgrow their social and legal structure as, for example, when industry and commerce began to outgrow feudalism.
■ The growth of class conflict as the owners of the means of production begin to increase their exploitation of the workforce in order to maintain their privilege and profits. Social classes for Marxists arise simply from the ownership and non-ownership of the means of production, a relationship which at heart is antagonistic due to its exploitative nature and unequal distribution of wealth, be it between feudal lords and serfs or capitalists and workers.

For Marx and Engels 'the class struggle' was the heart of historical materialism, the dynamic of social change: 'the history of all hitherto existing society is the history of class struggle'. And though immediately destructive, ultimately such conflict is progressive: 'no antagonism, no progress', claimed Marx. Marx used these 'guiding threads' of historical materialism to outline in detail his analysis of his contemporary mode of production capitalism.

CAPITALISM

The key forces of production in capitalist society are industry and commerce, the factory and the mill; the key relations of production those of bourgeoisie and proletariat. Whilst the forces of production are governed by the market forces of supply and demand and by the capitalist search for continuous profit and investment, the binding tie of the capitalist–worker relation of production is the impersonal and solely self-interested one of the 'cash nexus', that is the capitalist employs the worker solely as a means to making profit and so will exploit or discard him as the need arises. The capitalist superstructure serves and legitimises this sub-structure with the family and education system producing healthy and disciplined workers, whilst the state, legal system and media ensure both physical and ideological control of the masses, ensuring that through materialism and exclusion of alternative ideas the working class is kept in a state of 'false consciousness'.

However, like all antagonistic modes of production, capitalism contains the 'seeds of its own destruction' due to its own inherent contradictions. The very heart of capitalism is competition in pursuit of profits, but ultimately such competition and cost cutting will lead to a collapse in the bourgeois class as more and more of its members 'go to the wall', and a growth in the size, unity and class consciousness of a workforce reduced to subsistence wages and threatened by mass unemployment. This, in turn, will create and exacerbate capitalism's periodic crises of boom and slump and increase class antagonisms and polarisation to the point where the workers will unite, throw off their chains, seize control of the state and means of production and so inaugurate the final MOP of Socialism-Communism. Here class conflict, inequality and false consciousness will no longer exist because the means of production will be communally owned by all the people. Man will at last be free from exploitation and alienation (see p 181), free 'to hunt in the morning, fish in the afternoon . . . and criticise after dinner' (*The German Ideology*).

Thus, whilst in Marx and Engels' view the capitalist mode of production is evil and exploitative and produces 'its own gravediggers', it also creates the economic forces of production necessary for material abundance, necessary for freedom from want and hardship, allowing man time to think, reflect and philosophise in a communist society based on the principle of 'from each according to his ability, to each according to his need'.

THE IDEA IN ACTION

Historical materialism was therefore designed not only as an academic theory but a programme of action, a 'guiding thread' for revolutionaries as well as for social theorists and historians. Engels converted it into a guiding light for socialists throughout the world declaring it to be not just an historical interpretation but a scientific law. As Engels proclaimed at Marx's graveside: 'Just as Darwin discovered the law of development of organic nature, so Marx discovered the law of development of human history.'

Its radical analysis of historical exploitation, oppression and inequality and its vision of a utopian future inspired communist revolutions throughout the world and a crude version of historical materialism became the 'Bible' of the Soviet Revolution in Russia and Eastern Europe. As Marx so boldly proclaimed: 'The philosophers have only interpreted the world – the point however is to change it.'

The theory of historical materialism, however, has also been the subject of intense criticism and debate both within Marxism and from without.

ECONOMIC DETERMINISM

The key controversy, one that still inspires heated debates, is the underlying element of economic determinism within historical materialism. According to cruder versions of this theory:

■ The economic substructure determines all else. Political social and ideological factors are all subordinate to economic ones and have no independent causal influence on history. All social conflicts, institutions and behaviour can be explained in terms of the economic stage of development.
■ Modes of production are clearly defined stages of economic development and all societies must follow the same pathway to socialism.

Many sociologists and historians would totally reject such a deterministic and simplistic analysis arguing that political and social forces have as much influence on social change as economic ones. Max Weber, in particular, led this critique using his concept of the *Protestant ethic* (see p 297) to highlight the importance of cultural factors in that most crucial of social changes, the Industrial Revolution. Detailed historical analyses of past and present societies have shown that a division of history into four or five modes of production is too simple, whilst present-day 'communist' societies such as Russia and China are clear evidence of the way industrial advance can be achieved without going through *laissez-faire* capitalism first. Within Marxism itself the dictates of orthodox Marxism and the inhumanities committed in the name of historical materialism led to a radical reassessment of economism. Some, like the Frankfurt School (see p 101), turned back to the early Marx for a more humanistic and flexible interpretation. Others like, Louis Althusser and structural Marxists (see p 1) sought to make it more scientific but both schools of Marxist thought gave far greater emphasis to political and especially ideological factors in late capitalism.

The source of this controversy is partly Marx, partly Engels and partly the fact that Marx's work was never completed and was being continually revised. Marx's own style, his dogmatism and claims to scientific certainty, all aided this impression of economic determinism. For example, whilst declaring that 'men make their own history' he went on to say that 'they do not make it under conditions chosen by themselves'.

However, both Marx and Engels publicly denied economic determinacy in their theory of historical materialism. Engels claimed that it was only a 'guide to study' and attacked crude interpretations that were evolving even in his own time.

According to the materialist conception of history, the ultimately determining element in history is the production and reproduction of real life. More than this neither Marx nor I have ever asserted.
. . . If someone twists this into saying that the economic element is the only determining one, he transforms that proposition into a meaningless senseless phrase. The economic situation is the basis, but the various elements of the superstructure . . . also exercise their influence upon the course of the historical struggles and in many cases preponderate in determining their form. There is an interaction of all these elements in which, amid all the endless host of accidents . . . the economic movement finally asserts itself as necessary . . . (Carver 1981)

In his later writings Engels gave even more support to the influence of ideas on history, whilst in his later years Marx accepted the possibility not only of a Soviet road to socialism but also of a peaceful, democratic one. This debate reflects an underlying conflict in the theory of historical materialism and Marxism generally in its attempt to be both a theory and a revolutionary guidebook. If historical materialism is correct, if socialism is inevitable, if political factors are subordinate to economic developments, why engage in revolutionary action?

Engels added to this impression of determinism by his increasing use of scientific terminology and concepts and by his claim that dialectical materialism was 'the Science of the general laws of motion and development of nature, human society and thought' (Carver 1981). Marx, at least in his less deterministic mood, would reply that whilst economic developments create the framework for change only men can actually make it happen. Therefore *not* to engage in the class struggle is to impede social progress.

THE ROLE OF THE STATE

The state in advanced capitalist and especially socialist countries has not 'withered away' but grown in size and intervention. Within capitalism the state, the key political force, has become the major institution managing the economy and ensuring not only physical control of the masses but ideological control. This political dominance of the economy is even more profound in centrally-planned economies and there, despite ideological claims to the contrary, the state is an oppressive totalitarian force suppressing rather than promoting human rights.

THE POLARISATION OF CLASSES

The prediction of the polarisation of advanced capitalist societies into two major classes has obviously not come about. Rather the reverse, with the middle class growing, the working class shrinking and the whole class system becoming fragmented and truncated by such non-economic forms of stratification as age, race and gender.

Moreover, far from the working class growing in unity and revolutionary consciousness, it has remained highly conservative. The 'communist' revolutions of the twentieth century have occurred not in the prosperous industrial West but the poor agrarian societies of the East and the Third World more often by political force than economic revolution.

MODES OF PRODUCTION

The concept of modes of production as an analysis of historical development has not proved as easy to apply to real societies as predicted. Few societies neatly fit this scheme. Few can neatly be labelled capitalist or feudal. Even Marx recognised this problem and allowed for mixed modes and even for the possibility of some societies 'skipping a stage in the great leap forward to Socialism'.

However, whatever its shortcomings in theory and practice, histori-cal materialism has proved central to Marxist theory and a major stimulus to social scientists (and revolutionaries) throughout the world. It continues even today, a hundred years later, to inspire debate, research and the hopes of millions of people for a freer, more rational and just society. Very few sociological ideas have had anything like as much influence and as Terrell Carver (1981), one of Engel's biogra-phers, concludes, 'The materialist interpretation of history is the main item in the intellectual legacy left us by Engels.'

Unfortunately today there is no unitary 'interpretation of this famous view of history on which all Marxists agree. Rather the mate-rialist interpretation of history represents a set of shared disagreements' (Carver 1981).

SEE ALSO

☐ **Structural Marxism** and
☐ **Critical theory** as modern versions of this thesis.
☐ **Social solidarity**
☐ **Social Darwinism** and
☐ **Structural functionalism** as very different theories of social change.

SUGGESTED READING

Any of the original works by Marx and Engels are worth trying (see Further Reading, below and on page 185). The following are readable summaries of their key ideas:
Callinicos A. *The Revolutionary Ideas of Karl Marx*, Pluto Press, 1983
Carew Hunt R.N. *The Theory and Practice of Communism*, Penguin, 1950
Hoffman, J. 'The Life and Ideas of Karl Marx' in *Social Studies Review*, Vol. 1 No. 2, Nov. 1985
Marx K. and Engels F. *Manifesto of the Communist Party*, ed. A.J.P. Taylor, Penguin, 1967
Ruis, *Marx for Beginners*, Unwin paperbacks, 1986
Simon R. *Introducing Marxism*, Fairleigh Press, 1986
The following are short outlines of Engels' life and times:
Carver T. *Engels*, OUP, 1981
McClellan D. *Engels*, Fontana, 1977

FURTHER READING

Engels F. *The Condition of the Working Class in England*, Blackwell, 1845
Engels F. *Anti Dühring* (1887–8), Foreign Languages Publishing House, 1959
Engels F. *The Origins of the Family, Private Property and the State* (1884),
   International Publishers, 1942

EXAMINATION QUESTIONS

1 'Marx's concept of class may have been adequate for understanding nineteenth-century industrial capitalism but is inadequate for comprehending
contemporary industrial society.' Discuss. (WJEC June 1986)
2 To what extent did Marx provide an adequate explanation of social change?
(WJEC June 1987)
3 'The Marxian assumption of two basic antagonistic classes is, in certain
important respects, sociologically unsatisfactory' (Anderson and Sharrock eds
Applied Sociological Perspectives). Critically examine this view. (AEB November 1985)
4 In the view of some conflict theorists, social stratification orginates in the
economic relations of a society and it results in *exploitation, domination* and
conflict. Thus it has been argued that society can be divided into two main
classes in antagonism to one another
   (a) Give brief definitions of the **three** terms shown in italics above
   (b) Choose **one** society and show how these terms can be applied
   (c) Name and illustrate **two** other concepts drawn from within the conflict
   approach which you would use to bring out the nature and consequences of
   social stratification
   (d) Does evidence suggest that industrial societies nowadays can be divided
   into two main classes?

                                          (JMB June 1986 Paper II)

12

FEMINISTS *and*

PATRIARCHY

THE AUTHORS

The term 'feminism' derives from the Latin *'femina'* meaning woman, and originally meant 'having the qualities of females'. It has been adopted as the general title for the Women's Movement, for the struggle by women for equal rights and as a theory of sexual equality in the twentieth century, replacing the term 'Womanism' in the 1890s.

A term which attempts to represent and unite the whole of the Women's Movement is bound to reflect a wide variety of definitions and emphases. *A Feminist Dictionary* (1985) cites just a few examples, extending from the advocacy of women's rights and the struggle against male domination to simply an awareness of and attempt to end women's subordination to men.

[Feminism] may be defined as a movement seeking the reorganization of the world upon a basis of sex-equality in all human relations; a movement which would reject every differentiation between individuals upon the ground of sex, would abolish all sex privileges and sex burdens, and would strive to set up the recognition of the common humanity of woman and man as the foundation of law and custom. (Teresa Billington-Grieg, 1911)

With a capital 'F' it is a theory, a position. With small 'f' it is an organic conviction based on experience. (Osha Davidson, 1984)
(Both from Kramarae C. & Treichler P.A., *A Feminist Dictionary*)

Feminism, therefore, is a social movement whose aim is to liberate women socially, politically and ideologically by abolishing patriarchy and showing that such social divisions as gender are culturally, not naturally, created by men to further their own power, privilege and dominance. It is a philosophy

based on the recognition that we live in a male-dominated culture in which women remain unacknowledged, and where women are forced into sex roles which demand that they be dependent, passive, nurturant, etc. Men too must assume sex roles [but these] are not nearly as crippling as women's. (*Banshee*, 1981) and it is a method of analysis, a new perspective on society:

It asks new questions as well as coming up with new answers. Its central concern is with the social distinction between men and women, with the fact of this distinction, with its meanings, and with its causes and consequences. (Juliet Mitchell and Ann Oakley, 1976)

The history of the Feminist Movement has yet to be written and certainly goes back beyond its presently recorded beginnings in the late eighteenth century when, inspired by the ideals of the French Revolution, Mary Wollstonecraft published A *Vindication of the Rights of Women* (1792). She and others in the first wave of feminism fought for equal rights for women in education, law, employment and marriage. This wave culminated at the beginning of the twentieth century in the Suffragette Movement and its successful campaign for political rights, in votes for women. In the inter-war and post-war years it allied with the Labour Movement and especially the Labour Party as part of a socialist programme of social reform.

The modern Women's Movement can be dated from publications like Betty Friedan's *Feminine Mystique* (1963) and Germaine Greer's *The Female Eunuch* (1970), the women's demonstrations in America and Western Europe against female inequality and the growth of the Women's Liberation Movement in the 1960s and 1970s. Academically, the growth of feminist publications and Women's Studies has forced all disciplines – sociology in particular – to recognise their underlying male bias and to re-evaluate many of their key concepts which previously rendered women invisible and powerless. Social class, *the* key concept in traditional sociology, for example, treated women, especially married women, merely as an appendage of their husbands and totally ignored gender as an influential factor or potential source of social stratification.

Politically, feminists appear to have had considerable success with a range of legal and social reforms on such key issues as equal pay, equal opportunities in employment and equal rights in divorce. More women now hold top positions in key institutions, especially in America, and Britain has her first female Prime Minister. However, real change, especially for the average woman, is very limited. What feminism has done is make women more conscious of their subordination, their rights and their need to fight every day at home, at work and in society at large for sexual equality.

Within the Feminist Movement a wide variety of theoretical views can be discerned, each identifying different causes, and so different solutions to inequality, patriarchy and gender divisions. Some of these are discussed below.

THE IDEA

The term patriarchy, literally, means 'rule of the father' (or patriarch) but has been adopted by feminists to refer to male domination over women in all its forms – physical, political and ideological. In particular it refers to the social and political structures, cultural institutions and forces which keep women oppressed and powerless in male-dominated societies.

Patriarchy can be traced back to the Bible, to the assumption that God is male and to the Book of Genesis where, after Eve ate the forbidden fruit in the Garden of Eden, God condemned her and all womankind to subordination to men, 'in sorrow thou shalt bring forth children, and thy desire shall be to thy husband and he shall rule over thee'. Every known society is ruled by men and, although examples of female equality can be cited (e.g. the Tchambuli tribe of New Guinea), there is no known example of female rule (matriarchy).

Feminist writers, however, totally reject the idea that patriarchy is either inevitable or natural. They have instead developed a variety of theories to show that patriarchy is man-made, a physical and ideological force used by men to keep women in their place.

TRADITIONAL FEMINISM

Traditional feminism pointed to the family as the key source of male domination and female oppression. In the past the right of the father to rule the family, and in particular his wife, was sacrosanct, enshrined in custom, tradition and often law. He could rightfully demand complete obedience and exercise his authority, and punishments, in any way he saw fit. In many primitive and traditional societies, women were a form of exchange, their marriages arranged and their rights to free speech and divorce non-existent. Even today in advanced democratic societies women as wives and daughters are ruled by men in the home as their husbands and fathers make all the key decisions and control all the finances. Feminists have highlighted the extent of domestic violence and even rape endured by women in the home and the way that, by bringing girls up to be passive and feminine, the traditional socialisation process idealises and reinforces male dominance. Hannah Gavron, for example, highlighted the prison-like nature of the home for many women by calling her 1966 study *The Captive Wife*. The patriarchal nature of society, therefore, merely reflects and reinforces male domination in the home. 'Patriarchy's chief institution is the family', argued Kate Millett (1971).

Traditional feminists have further highlighted numerous examples of male domination and female segregation outside of the home, for example:

■ That most working women do only 'women's work' (e.g. nursing, secretarial work, etc.) and are almost always in subordinate positions to men;
■ That in almost every field of work – even such apparently female areas as nursing and catering – men hold the top jobs. Fewer than five per cent of architects, engineers, scientists and solicitors in Britain are women and, in every field, the higher up the hierarchy you go the fewer women you find;
■ That, as at home, men dominate most key posts and key decisions, be it in the boardroom or Parliament. A mere 30 or so out of 650 MPs are women, and although Britain has her first female Prime Minister, Mrs Thatcher has usually been the only woman in her present Cabinet.

And so the list goes on. But patriarchy's real power is not physical force but institutional control. It is the power of an all-pervasive ideology which proclaims that male dominance and female subordination are both natural and normal; that for women to be dominant or aggressive is deviant and unfeminine. Such sex-stereotyping is promoted not only in the media (e.g. Page Three) but through the socialisation process, and is even reflected in our everyday language. Girls are brought up to be passive and feminine. Key terms such as *history* and *mankind* reflect male dominance. It is simply assumed that they include women as well. Those who deviate from such gender roles are often socially chastised, be it by gossip, by being ostracised or stigmatised as a tomboy, single parent or prostitute. So all-pervasive is this ideology of patriarchy that it is rarely criticised, and most women defer to it without question!

MARXIST FEMINISM

Marxist feminists, however, take a broader, more theoretical view. They see patriarchy as simply a further division and form of exploitation and oppression generated by the capitalist mode of production. Like social class, patriarchy is rooted in the ownership of private property and, according to Friedrich Engels (1884), Karl Marx's life-long collaborator, monogamous marriage developed not to unite men and women in marital bliss, but to protect private property.

Monogamy arose out of the concentration of considerable wealth in the hands of one person – that of a man – and out of the desire to bequeath that wealth to this man's children and to no-one else's.

Men, therefore, needed to use marriage to control women and to ensure 'undisputed paternity'. For Engels, male dominance was, therefore, based on economic dominance; remove that and patriarchy would collapse. Whilst arguing that true sexual equality could only come about in a socialist society where property was communally owned, Marx and Engels did see some elements of capitalism as progressive. The demand for female labour, they argued, would bring women out of the home, give them some economic independence and bring them together with male workers as socialists, conscious of and united against exploitation and inequality. Feminist Marxists have added to or re-analysed this view, highlighting the way women, especially as wives, help capitalism function more efficiently by acting as a form of social control and as a reserve army of labour.

THE DOMESTIC LABOUR DEBATE

■ As (unpaid) housewives, women ensure that the male labour force is kept both healthy and compliant. No husband takes strike action or any other form of rebellious act lightly, knowing the effect on their wives and children. Instead of taking out their frustration with capitalism on their bosses, men often take it out on their wives.
■ Women act as a reserve army of labour in the sense that they can be employed in times of boom and dismissed in times of slump far more easily than men. Moreover, they accept low wages, part-time and unskilled work, rarely join unions and are relatively compliant. They can be used, too, to break male unions and strikes. Their whole socialisation process has not only taught them to be obedient and passive, but to regard work as secondary to their primary role as housewife and mother.
■ Sexist ideology helps rather than threatens capitalism because it helps divide the working class into men versus women, and so makes them easier to control.

Moreover, evidence from socialist societies where the 'means of production' are communally owned and even where the traditional forms of family and marriage have been abolished does not show the automatic collapse of patriarchy. Though in communist countries, and particularly in Israeli kibbutzim, women are much freer, more equal and more likely to hold high office, the key positions, the key decisions, are still made by men. No women sit in the Politbureau, the main policy-making body in the USSR, and even in kibbutzim it is still women who are most likely to be doing the cooking and child-minding.

As David Lane (1970) has argued, collective ownership of the means of production is 'a necessary but not sufficient condition for female liberation'.

RADICAL AND REVOLUTIONARY FEMINISM

This developed out of dissatisfaction with this Marxist-feminist analysis, in particular its claim that patriarchy is like class, rooted in economic power and so, like class, can be abolished by socialism. In their view, patriarchy is a distinct form of oppression that pre-dates capitalism and all other forms of social stratification. Its roots are many and varied – economic, political, sexual, cultural, ideological, and even biological but they all add up to the same thing. Men as a class have power over women as a class. Men control society, hold all the key positions, make all the key decisions. Men control women at home and at work as subordinates; women still primarily do 'women's work' (e.g. nurse, secretary), still see the housewife role as their prime duty and are both kept subordinate and brought up to be passive by an all-pervasive patriarchal ideology that assumes male dominance, assumes that a woman's place is in the home, reinforces gender distinctions of masculinity and femininity, assumes heterosexuality is normal and severely punishes any woman who deviates from such 'natural' norms (e.g. single mothers, lesbians, career women). Some radical feminists go further and see the roots of patriarchy as biological. As Schulasmith Firestone (1972) argues, 'unlike economic class, sex class sprang directly from a biological reality'. Because women bear children they are dependent on men physically and economically. Men enjoy 'power over women' and so have reinforced their domination throughout the social structure. This sex class system, in her view, can only be eliminated ultimately by freeing women from their most basic biological role, having children, and whilst birth control techniques are a step in this direction, true liberation will only come with artificial reproduction, when babies can be born *outside* the womb.

Radical feminists, therefore, see patriarchy as a much deeper form of social stratification than Marxist feminists and so are far less optimistic about uprooting it. In their view, whatever the society, social group or even social situation, for example even simple conversations, men dominate women and only by raising women's consciousness (and men's) can women even begin to liberate themselves.

Analyses like these have increasingly uncovered the deep roots and multi-faceted layers of patriarchy, revealing not only the extent to which all social institutions are male dominated (even such areas as nursing and midwifery), but the extent to which male assumptions lie behind our very language and consciousness, rendering women invisible and powerless. Some extreme feminists have therefore gone as far as to argue that true liberation can only come about in a women-only society; that lesbianism is the only real path to sexual freedom.

THE IDEA IN ACTION

The concept of patriarchy has been central to feminist understanding and analyses. It clearly highlights male domination and power in the home as well as in society at large. It combines the force of male authority with the subtleties of paternal care, so highlighting the way women's subordination rests on both physical and emotional power, relationships as well as force.

However, as the previous review clearly showed, it is also a concept which has inspired a multitude of very different definitions and theories – so much so that some feminists have called for its elimination from the 'feminist dictionary', proposing such alternatives as 'sex-gender system', 'phallocracy' and simply 'sexism'. Its usage led to a fierce debate within feminism in the late seventies because it seemed to hide as much as it revealed. It implies that male domination is universal and mono-causal (i.e. that it is caused solely by biology or capitalism), so obscuring the multitude of forms in which female oppression has occurred in contemporary and past societies. Moreover, it takes the concept of gender for granted (see page 86), failing to recognise that this, too, is a social construct. Finally, it fails to portray gender relations as varying and as being a continuous struggle in which women do resist, occasionally successfully. 'Patriarchy . . . suggests a fatalistic submission which allows no space for the complexities of women's defiance' (Sheila Rowbotham, 1979).

The wide variety of solutions advocated for abolishing patriarchy have equally undermined the power and force of this concept, not least with some extreme feminists not only aiming to abolish biology, but to abolish men.

As this debate has abated, however, as feminist studies have turned from theoretical overviews into detailed empirical studies, so the concept of patriarchy has become less controversial and, once clearly defined, more useful. It is now, according to Sarah Fildes (Haralambos ed. 1985) more generally accepted because, at the very least, 'it highlights and names the areas around which we need to construct theoretical accounts'. Patriarchy is now a key concept in all feminist analyses.

SEE ALSO

☐ Gender

SUGGESTED READING

Barratt M. *Women's Oppression Today*, New Left Books, 1980
Charver J. *Feminism*, J.M. Dent & Sons, 1982
Goldberg S. *The Inevitability of Patriarchy*, Smith, 1977 – a very different and,
    from a feminist point of view, controversial account.
Maynard M. 'Current Trends in Feminist Theory' in *Social Studies Review*
    Vol 2 No 3, January 1987, p23
Oakley A. *Subject Women*, Penguin, 1981

FURTHER READING

Engels F. *The Origins of the Family, Private Property and the State* (1884),
    International Publishers, 1942
Fildes S. 'Women and Society' in Haralambos ed. *Development in Sociology*,
    Vol 1 pp 109–39, Causeway Press, 1985
Firestone S. *The Dialectic of Sex*, Paladin, 1972
Frieden B. *Feminine Mystique*, W.W. Norton, 1963
Gavron H. *The Captive Wife*, Penguin, 1966
Greer G. *The Female Eunuch*, Paladin, 1971
Kramarae C. and Treichler P. *A Feminist Dictionary*, Pandora, 1985
Lane D. *Politics and Society in the USSR*, Weidenfeld & Nicolson, 1970
Millet K. *Sexual Politics*, Abacus Books, 1971
Mitchell J. and Oakley A. eds, *The Rights and Wrongs of Women*, Penguin,
    1976
Rowbotham S. 'The Trouble with Patriarchy' in *New Statesman*, 28 December
    1979
Wollstonecroft M. *A Vindication of the Rights of Women* (1792), Penguin,
    1985

EXAMINATION QUESTIONS

1 Assess the view that authority patterns between the sexes have a biological
basis. (Cambridge Local Examinations Syndicate June 1986)
2 'Until the recent emergence of feminist perspecti/es, sociology had been
dominated by men and therefore by male concerns and prejudices. In short,
sociology was actually the sociology of men.' Explain and assess this state-

ment. To what extent does feminism constitute a distinct and valid perspective in sociology? (JMB June 1986)

3 Compare and contrast the respective social position of women in *two* different types of society. (London University January 1987 Paper 2)

4 Discuss the view that a major reason for the subordination of women in the labour market is the institutionalization of the mother-housewife role as the primary role for all women. (WJEC June 1987)

5 Describe and account for the differences and similarities in the ideologies used to support discrimination on the basis of *either* colour *or* sex in any *two* societies. (London University January 1987 Paper 1)

6 'Regardless of the type of society, as long as women are allocated domestic roles they will continue to have lower status than men.' To what extent do you agree with this statement? (London University January 1988 Paper 3)

13

THE IDEA

The term 'gender' is usually used simply to refer to the physical and social distinctions between men and women. Sociologists, however, and feminists in particular, are keen to define it more exactly and to try and determine the extent to which gender behaviour is natural and innate or social and 'man'-made.

Sociologists, therefore, use the terms:

■ Sex to refer to the physical and biological differences between men and women (e.g. physical features, sexual organs);
■ Gender to refer to 'social' differences in behaviour and roles, in the personal attributes we call masculinity and femininity.

The central issue in the gender debate is whether the behaviour of men and women in society is determined by biology or by culture. Are men and women naturally different or are they made to be so by the society they live in? Are men naturally the 'doers' – the workers, warriors, writers and decision-makers – and women the 'carers'? Are men naturally aggressive, rational and unemotional, and women naturally passive, intuitive and emotional? Is a man's place out in the world – working, fighting and organising – whilst a woman's place is in the home? And most especially, are men naturally the dominant sex, and so entitled to rule society – and women?

This naturist–nurturist debate, as it has been called, has raged throughout the social sciences for decades.

THE NATURIST ARGUMENT

The naturist argument rests on the assumption that the social differences in society between the two sexes are a direct reflection of biological differences. Men are physically stronger than women, so they organise society; women produce children so they have a natural maternal instinct to be passive, caring and dependent. Thus the present gender division of labour of men at work and women at home is both naturally and socially efficient as each specialises in the tasks they are best at. As Sigmund Freud proclaimed, 'Anatomy is destiny' (see 'Sex and Gender' in *Society Today*, 12 May 1983), and a vast array of biological, genetic, psychological and sociological evidence has been produced to support this thesis, such as Tiger and Fox's (1972) concept of the human biogrammer, a genetic predisposition for men to be 'masculine' and women 'feminine' in the way we understand these terms today. Similarly, in intelligence tests and exams, boys tend to outperform girls, especially in the hard and logical disciplines of maths and science, so 'apparently' proving their right to positions of authority and decision-making in society at large.

THE NURTURIST ARGUMENT

The nurturist argument sees human behaviour as largely a reflection of the social and cultural environment within which a child was brought up. Their evidence includes the following:

■ A critique of the naturist argument that the biological and psychological differences between the sexes are that great. Though, for example, men, on average, may be physically stronger than women, women survive better in tests of endurance and stamina. Wars like those in Vietnam and Israel have shown women to be just as aggressive, just as capable of killing as men when put in such situations. And as for intelligence, it is, in fact, girls who are the brighter sex – up until puberty when they tend to give way to boys for fear of appearing competitive and unfeminine. The two sexes do tend to think differently: boys are generally better on visual-spatial tests and girls have superior verbal skills, whilst personality tests often reveal that boys are just as emotional and sociable as girls, they just don't like to be seen as being so. As most reviews such as Maccoby and Jacklin (1974) or Lloyd and Archer (1982) clearly show, though, there are natural differences between the sexes, they are not that great, and certainly not great enough to explain existing social differences or justify sexual inequality.

■ Anthropological evidence shows that in other societies and cultures, even other times in a society's history, men and women behave differently and even swap roles. Thus, for example, in Margaret Mead's classic study of three tribes in New Guinea (1950) she found extensive differences in sex-roles and gender behaviour. Whilst the Arapesh (both men and women) were compassionate and caring, the Mundugumors were harsh, violent and aggressive. And amongst the Tchambuli tribe there was a virtual exchange of roles as the men did 'women's work' and painted and decorated themselves whilst the women went out hunting and fighting. In many primitive societies it is the women who do the heavy, physical work, even during pregnancy, and amongst the Triobander Islanders it was women who were sexually aggressive, who took the sexual initiative.

■ A detailed analysis of the socialisation process reveals the extent to which male–female differences are socially constructed (or at least socially exaggerated) and identifies the ways in which boys and girls are brought up to be distinctly different and socially divided. In the family, for example, from the moment of conception, the two sexes are treated differently: dressed in different clothing, even different colours, given different toys, punished differently and even touched and spoken to in a different manner. At school, work, in the media and even in the very words we use, boys and girls are treated differently and react accordingly. We don't (usually) have a 'Page 3' for women or a problem page for men; the terms 'tomboy' and 'cissy' are fearful sexual sanctions, and few Western men today would wear skirts, though some of the greatest fighters in history quite happily did so – the Romans, the Greeks and even the Vandals.

It is evidence and arguments like this that have reinforced and bolstered the feminist case that sexual differences do not explain gender differences. There is, in their view, no natural division of sexual labour and absolutely no natural justification for the sexual inequalities that exist in British society today.

■ At work, though over forty per cent of the British workforce is female, they are heavily concentrated in 'women's work' – the caring professions such as nursing and teaching, or in subordinate roles such as secretaries. Very few women get to the top of any profession; very few get in to such male preserves as engineering and science, very few get on to boards of directors. Women suffer low pay, poor promotion, worse conditions, and even trade unions often discriminate against them.

■ At school, sex stereotyping has been, until recently, fairly rampant, with girls usually 'opting' for such 'female' subjects as cookery and typing, often doing badly in mathematics and the 'hard' sciences and being advised by careers personnel to look for a job rather than a career on the assumption that their primary post would be as a mother and housewife.

■ In government: despite comprising over half the population, women are only represented by thirty or so MPs out of 650. Parliament, the Cabinet and Whitehall are all very much male preserves.

It is evidence like this that has led feminists to reject the idea that it is nature that is behind such extensive gender inequalities and to argue instead that it is power, male power to control society, to fashion it in a 'masculine' image, that is really at work. And for this analysis they have coined the term patriarchy (see page 77).

THE IDEA IN ACTION

The concept of gender has proved crucial in highlighting one of the key elements in human society and social stratification: the distinction between men and women, which predates and cross-divides all other forms of social difference, be it class, status or race.

This has revived the nature/nurture debate and helped highlight inadequacies in the naturist argument. It has also stimulated the feminist argument that we live in a 'man-made' society in which male dominance is not only institutionalised but taken for granted as 'normal', even by women!

If gender differences are socially constructed and not biologically determined, there is at least the hope of a 'sexual revolution' and the liberation of women from sex roles, sex stereotyping and patriarchy.

However, two main sets of criticisms of the use of this concept have emerged in recent years:

■ Writers like David Morgan (1986) and Linda Birke (1986) have expressed concern that the distinction between sex and gender, between biological and social influences on human behaviour, has been made too rigidly. Rather than either sex or gender being the only influence, they should be viewed as 'interacting' factors. No one can seriously argue that physical, genetic and especially hormonal factors have no influence on gender behaviour. The opposite view would equally be an exaggeration. Rather it is the balance between these two views, and more especially, how humans culturally interpret that balance, that is crucial. As Linda Birke argues, no woman can escape her own biology; what feminists should therefore be analysing is the way female biology is interpreted, the way gender identity is constructed and reconstructed in a constant and dynamic process of social interpretation. To see women simply as 'passive victims' of sex stereotyping and socialisation is as deterministic and simplistic a view as arguing that 'anatomy is destiny'. Rather, women must recognise their biological experiences and gain control of the way their resultant gender identity is interpreted.

This shift in emphasis from the *content* of sex stereotyping to the *processes* by which feminine images are constructed is reflected in a whole range of recent feminist work on the arts and mass media (e.g. Betterton, 1987; Beechey, 1985). Modern advertisements and television programmes, for example, are no longer quite so stereotyped. They now attempt to portray 'real' women in situations outside the home and kitchen, 'doing' things, working alongside and even organising men. Images of women are, therefore, changing, but who controls our pictures of women and femininity, and why and how do they do so? Modern gender analysis must adopt a more complex and dynamic approach to keep pace with such changes in interpretation.

The concept of gender has become extremely narrow. It has been used almost exclusively to analyse women – men have escaped its searchlight and only a limited amount of work has been done, in sociology at least, on homosexuality, transsexuals and all the other possible forms of gender.

Firstly, true sexual revolution will not merely involve liberating women, but men too. It is men's notions of gender and sexuality that imprison women in images of femininity. According to the patriarchy argument, so long as men continue to think of women as mothers, home-makers and sex objects, and so long as they control the 'means of cultural reproduction' (i.e. mass media), what hope do women have of a more positive and equal image?

Secondly, as Andrew Tolson (1977) has argued, men are as much a victim of sex stereotyping as women, possibly more so. They are brought up to live up to a 'macho' image of strength and power. They must not admit weakness or show their emotions or feelings. They thus lose a key element in their humanity. As Sheila Rowbotham (1979) has pointed out, 'Men are ashamed of their own sensitivity to suffering and love because they have been taught to regard these as feminine. They are afraid of becoming feminine because this means that other men will despise them and they will despise themselves.'

Men are as imprisoned in their work roles as women are in the home. They lose out a lot on family life and fatherhood and it is argued that it is the *absence* of the modern father as a person and role model which forces young males to turn to images of masculinity outside the home, especially on television, for example to follow shallow and stereotyped representations of how to be a 'man'.

Attempts have been made to set up 'men against sexism' groups such as 'Achilles Heel', but so far they have had very little success. Whilst women can feel the anger and passion of oppression, men can only feel guilt. As the French writer Emmanuel Reynaud (1981) argued,

When a man finds himself stifled by the meaninglessness of his life and makes an effort to put a final end to his patriarchal power, he will not have far to go to find the enemy. The struggle has to start, above all, in himself. To get rid of the 'man' embedded in himself is the first step for any man getting out on the path towards getting rid of power altogether.

Within sociology, too, there have been very few attempts to study masculinity, especially by men. One notable exception is an article by Carrigan, Connell and Lee (1985) that extensively criticises the male liberation approach, arguing instead for a more dynamic analysis of what they call 'hegemonic masculinity'. Hegemonic masculinity is a concept that not only involves analysing the dominant image of men over women but the way men who fail to live up to the male stereotype – the young, unemployed, and especially the homosexual – are marginalised and suppressed. There is now a wider recognition even in the media that 'masculinity is in crisis', that men are under threat, from women, modern life and especially unemployment, and that gender images are changing.

Over the last two decades . . . social attitudes and images of masculinity have loosened up in Britain. Men are expected to show more interest in fashion, in childbirth, in their children, are encouraged to express their emotions and to pay more attention to women's needs. The soft and gentle man is not such a rare creature. (Segel, 1981).

However, this has not brought about any significant changes in patriarchy, nor produced a coherent programme of academic study. This is a crucial gap in sociological research, reflecting perhaps male sociologists' own fears about self-examination.

Thirdly, as 'gay liberation' so clearly highlighted in the 1960s and 1970s, a gender revolution does not only involve men and women, but all other 'genders'. Again, this topic is a key element in the nature/nurture debate, in the argument whether homosexuals, transsexuals and the like are born or made. As Anthony Smith (1976) concludes, 'No-one knows whether [homosexuality] has a genetic cause or not . . . but most biologists would put heavy bets on the environment as the main contributor.' Hence the extensive delving by psychiatrists and others into the background of homosexuals in search of the event or incident that turned them from the 'normal' path of heterosexuality. Ken Plummer (1975) and others using a symbolic interactionist approach, however, point to the way society has created 'homosexuality' by the way, only very recently, it has labelled certain forms of sexual behaviour deviant. Homosexuality was accepted as 'normal' in Roman and Greek times. It is only in modern times (the late nineteenth century onwards) that homosexuals have had to 'hide in the closet' or come out fighting for gay liberation against the ideological and physical oppression of heterosexual society.

The study of transsexuals (people trapped in the body of the opposite sex) highlights these points even more. Jan (James) Morris's (1974) description of his own transition from a male to a female body is a fascinating account of sexual liberation, whilst anthropological studies of the Xaniths of Oman and the Mohave Indians of North America have postulated the possibility of a *third* gender, people who are biologically male but act and look like women. Ironically, such societies seem far more capable of coping with and tolerating such gender variations than our own.

The concept of gender in its broadest sense, therefore, has the potential for moving from the margins of sociology into the mainstream, from being a minor topic to ranking alongside 'class' as a key concept in analysing social stratification, ideology and knowledge. It highlights the fact that a truly liberated society will not only be free of class divisions but of gender roles and stereotypes. It would need to be an androgynous as well as a classless society. However, whilst feminists have grasped the analytical value of this concept with both hands, male sociologists still seem fearful of this nettle – fearful, possibly, that it will taint their own masculine identity and reputation?

SEE ALSO

☐ Patriarchy

SUGGESTED READING

Buswell C. 'Gender Relations and Sociological Problems' in *Social Studies Review*, Vol 4 No 5, May 1989, p200

Clarke E. and Lawson T. *Gender: An Introduction*, UTP, 1985

Delamont S. *Sociology of Women*, Heinemann, 1980

Garrett S. *Gender*, Tavistock, 1987 – a useful overview of the whole topic from a female perspective

Lloyd B. and Archer J. *Sex and Gender*, Penguin, 1982 – summarises and assesses much of the biological and sociological evidence

Mayes P. *Gender*, Longman, 1986 – an overview of the whole topic from a
   female perspective
Mead M. *Male and Female*, Penguin, 1950 – studies of tribes in New Guinea
   make stimulating and easy reading
Nicholson J. *A Question of Sex*, Fontana, 1979 – summarises and assesses
   biological and sociological evidence
Oakley A. *Sex, Gender and Society*, Sun Books, 1972 – one of the first
   important feminist studies to challenge traditional assumptions about
   gender
Seager J. and Olson A. *Women in the World*, Pan Books, 1986
Souhami D. *A Woman's Place*, Penguin, 1986
Stanworth M. *Gender and Schooling*, Hutchinson, 1983 – a thoughtful study
   of gender in the classroom
Tolson A. *The Limits of Masculinity*, Tavistock, 1977 – the topic seen from a
   male perspective
Weeks J. *Sexuality*, Tavistock, 1986 – covers the whole topic of sexuality

FURTHER READING

Beechey V. and Donald J. eds. *Subjectivity and Social Relations*, OUP, 1985
Betterton R. *Looking On*, Pandora, 1987
Birke L. *Women, Feminism and Biology*, Wheatsheaf, 1986
Carrigan T., Connell B. and Lee J. 'Towards a New Society of Masculinity' in
   Theory and Society No 14, 1985, pp 551–604
Fildes S. 'Gender' in Haralambos M. ed. *Developments in Sociology*, Vol 4
   pp 111–136, Causeway Press, 1988
Maccoby E.E. and Jacklin C.N. *The Psychology of Sex Differences*, Stanford
   University Press, 1974
Morgan D.H. 'Gender' in Burgess R. ed. *Key Variables in Social Investigation*,
   Routledge & Kegan Paul, 1986
Morris J. *Conundrum*, Faber, 1974
Plummer K. *Sexual Stigma*, Routledge & Kegan Paul, 1975
Reynaud E. *La Sainte Virilité*, quoted in *Achilles Heel*, nos 6 and 7, 1981, p 62
Rowbotham S. 'The Trouble with Patriarchy' in *New Statesman*, 28 Dec 1979
Segel L. *Is the Future Female?*, Virago, 1981
Smith A. *The Body*, Penguin, 1976
Tiger L. and Fox R. *The Imperial Kingdom*, Secker & Warburg, 1972

EXAMINATION QUESTION

Examine the view that gender, not class, is the most important social division
in industrial societies. (AEB June 1988 Paper 1)

14

THE AUTHOR

Andre Gunder Frank (1929–   ) was born in Berlin but was educated in America. He received a Ph.D. in Economics from the University of Chicago in 1957 and he has taught at Iowa State, Michigan State and Wayne State Universities in the USA, Sir George Williams University in Montreal, the Catholic University of Louvain in Belgium and the Freie Universität in Berlin, Germany.

In 1962 Frank went to Latin America and taught in universities in Brazil, Mexico and Chile. This experience, in particular the impact of the Cuban Revolution and emerging ideas of what was to be called the Dependency School of thought, fundamentally transformed his training and beliefs about the world economic system. Starting with *Capitalism and Underdevelopment in Latin America* (1969) Frank produced a stream of works that led him to being seen in the English-speaking world as the leading exponent of what has been called dependency, neo-Marxist or underdevelopment theory. In the late 1970s Frank returned to Europe as Visiting Research Fellow at the Max Planck Institute in Germany and is at present Professor of Development Studies at the University of East Anglia.

THE IDEA

Modernisation Theory (see page 269) argued that economic development takes place as a series of stages through which every country must progress if it is to build up enough 'steam' to 'take-off' as an industrial nation. From such a perspective the 'underdevelopment' of the Third World is due not only to a lack of skills and technology but to the failure of such peoples to develop a modern 'culture of enterprise', to sweep away traditional ignorance and superstition. What such 'backward' countries need is increased contact with the First World through trade and aid as a means to 'sparking off' their Industrial Revolution.

A.G. Frank rejected the very basis of this analysis, arguing instead that the key reason the Third World has not developed is not because of its own inadequacies but because the Western nations deliberately underdeveloped it. Such a relationship of exploitation and dependency can be traced back to the sixteenth century when the great European powers like Britain, France and Spain conquered and colonised the continents of Africa, Asia and Latin America and made them an integral part of their imperial systems. Such colonies supplied the mother country with cheap food and raw materials and in turn acted as new markets for the industrialised country's manufactured goods. There thus developed a world capitalist system based on an international division of labour by which the colonial powers made 'their' colonies specialise in one or two primary products on terms highly advantageous to the mother country and through such a system of unequal exchange the Western economies developed and the Third World ones underdeveloped. Where necessary the colonial powers even destroyed local industries that might compete against theirs, the classic example of this being the destruction of the thriving Indian textile industry by the British to ensure the success of the Lancashire cotton mills.

There thus developed, argues Frank, a world system of dependency and underdevelopment by which such *core* nations as Spain exploited such *peripheral* ones as Chile in a chain-like system of expropriation by which these satellite countries became totally dependent on the metropolis. The key link in this chain was (and still is) the city. The colonial powers used existing cities (or built their own) as the main means not only for governing such areas but for draining them of their surplus. The ruling elites of such colonies lived in the cities and generally collaborated with the colonial powers, using their control of local markets (and after independence their control of the government) to exploit the peasantry in the countryside, buy up their produce cheaply and export it to the West. Thus the cities were used to exploit the countryside and the ruling families of the Third World became more closely linked to the Western way of life than to their own people. So, to preserve their own privileged life-styles and maintain their elite rule, they often use the military to protect western interests and factories against their own people. In return the West supplies such dictatorships with aid and even weapons. There has thus developed a chain of dependency that through the world capital cities stretches across the globe and deep down into the villages of the Third World. Through such countries economic surplus is sucked upwards and outwards to the wealthy West:

a whole chain of metropolises and satellites, which runs from the world metropolis down to the hacienda or rural merchant who are satellites of the local commercial metropolitan centre but who in their turn have peasants as their satellites. (A.G. Frank, 1967)

Today with the decline of colonialism, it is the multinationals who govern this system. In their relentless pursuit of profit they search the world for cheap labour, raw materials and new markets – Volkswagen in Brazil for example – but the profits always go to the West. Dependency is also maintained by the Third World's reliance on the West for aid, but this does not come cheaply as interest charges or western factories have to be paid for. Soon these debts outstrip the poorer countries' ability to repay and so they default like Brazil and Mexico, creating a world financial crisis. They cannot repay their debts because their exports do not earn much. It is the First World that controls the world prices of food and raw materials and deliberately keeps them low to maintain their own high standards of living. The only way for the Third World to break this monopoly is to form their own power bloc as OPEC did in 1972/3, but this is very difficult.

Thus, according to Frank's model, 'satellite' countries can never develop so long as they remain part of the world capitalist system. One solution is 'isolation' as in the examples of Paraguay or China. Another is to 'break away' at a time when the metropolis country is weak, as in times of war or recession – as happened in the two World Wars and 1930s depression. This may require a socialist revolution to overcome the *comprador*, the ruling classes of the Third World, but to achieve this requires extensive organisation of the new urban proletariat or landless peasantry. Here Frank is rather pessimistic, believing that sooner or later the metropolis will reassert its control. For him the most 'ultra-developed' areas, the poorest countries of the Third World are precisely those that had the closest ties with the mother country in the past but have now been economically 'scrapped' as no longer useful (e.g. north-east Brazil).

Thus for A.G. Frank, development and underdevelopment are two sides of a world process by which the First World has developed at the expense of the Third World. Such poor countries are so locked into this system that it is almost impossible for them to escape.

THE IDEA IN ACTION

This fundamentally different explanation of development to the western-style modernisation theory inspired a whole generation of radical writers and Third World leaders. It offered a highly detailed analysis of the way they were being exploited and oppressed and, in depicting each link in the chain, offered the hope of breaking it. A host of subsequent studies found strong evidence in support of Frank's thesis. Barnet and Müller's study of the multinationals (1974), for example, identified the way that companies like ITT and General Motors, far from spreading jobs and technology in the Third World, in fact 'drained off' local investment capital. Teresa Hayter's study of aid (1971) revealed the very high cost to Third World countries of such loans and the way western technology (and arms) are used more to bolster oppressive dictatorships than to lay the basis of development. New hospitals, airports and hotels are not only of no use to the ordinary peasants of the Third World but actually distort their economies and turn them into debtor nations. According to the World Bank, the Third World today pays $21 billion more in servicing debt than it receives in aid.

Hayter further cites evidence of the way the economies of the Third World are distorted, of how the dependence of poor countries on a few cash crops serves the West's need for cheap food but leaves their own people starving. The key here is that the West keeps world food prices low, but the price of technology high. Eight hundred million people live in absolute poverty and near to starvation today whilst the West suffers from overeating. As Cardinal Arns pointed out at the 1985 International Development Conference in Rome, every time the US raises its interest rates, 'thousands die in the Third World because money that could be used for health care and food is sent outside'. When Third World governments attempt to break away from western control financial controls are tightened and ultimately the CIA or American army is sent in to restore 'order' (the Bay of Pigs, Chile, El Salvador, Nicaragua).

Many Latin American scholars have tried to formulate economic policies by which their governments can get better trade relations with the West or even, like OPEC, gain control of their own export prices.

However Frank's thesis has also been extensively criticised by both right- and left-wing writers. Frank's theoretical concepts like dependency metropolis and satellite are very vague and even circular because the present international system leaves the First World countries as dependent on the Third World as it is on them.

Modernisation theorists argue that both the multinationals and western aid do bring considerable benefits citing the examples of 'economic miracles' in both Brazil and Mexico in the 1970s (though both went bankrupt in the 1980s) and the growth of newly developing countries like Taiwan and South Korea.

Similarly, liberal writers like John Goldthorpe (1980) and the Brandt Commission (1980) believe Frank's ideas are too radical, too Marxist. Colonialisation did benefit many poor countries and the First World needs the Third World to grow and industrialise as a source of new investment and new markets. What is required, argues the Brandt Report, is a 'rebalancing' of the world economic and financial system in favour of the South, not its abolition.

Marxist writers have criticised both Frank's theory and his failure to provide a revolutionary programme for breaking the chains of the world capitalist system. Writers like Samir Amin (1976) have criticised Frank's historical analysis as too generalised. It fails to show the 'unevenness' of Third World development which ranges from the total backwardness of Ethiopia to the growing industries of South Korea and Taiwan. Similarly by concentrating only on North–South relations it ignores exploitation and dependency *within* the Third World (e.g. Asian multinationals dominating Eastern markets).

Ernesto Laclau (1977) has argued that dependency theory is not a true Marxist analysis. It only describes how the surpluses of satellite countries are extracted and distributed. It fails to provide the heart of a Marxist analysis, an explanation of the relations of production and of the modes of production, the economic stages from feudalism to capitalism that Third World countries have gone, or are going, through. Frank's theory only analyses the external feature of the world capitalist system, not the internal dynamics of the class struggle so vital to Marxist revolutionary practice.

Bill Warren (1980) goes even further, arguing that far from underdeveloping the Third world, capitalism and imperialism are 'progressive' forces, helping backward nations along the inevitable historical path from feudalism to capitalism and eventually socialism. Just as in the western nations, early capitalism produces extreme poverty and exploitation but these are short-term transitory problems. Through western expansion the Third World has not only acquired the skills, capital and technology for industrial progress but become conscious of and increasingly organised against western capitalism. The Third World is developing an industrial and urban proletariat, developing a 'typical' class struggle, seizing control of its own resources and as the newly industrialising countries have shown, stimulating the present crisis within western capitalism. The mass unemployment and deep economic recession of the First World is ironically partly a reflection of Eastern competition from Taiwan, South Korea and Singapore.

In such recent works as *Reflections on the World Economic Crisis* (1981) Frank acknowledges such criticisms and the possibility of industrial development in the Third World, if the multinationals can be brought under control. But, whatever its shortcomings, dependency theory has proved a major contribution to both the theory and practice of development and offered a radical alternative to modernisation theory.

SEE ALSO

☐ Modernisation theory

SUGGESTED READING

Bennett J. and George S. *The Hunger Machine*, Polity Press, 1987
Brandt W. *et al. North–South. A Programme for Survival*, Pan, 1980
Foster-Carter A. 'The Sociology of Development' in Haralambos ed. *Sociology New Directions*, Causeway Press, 1985
George S. *How the Other Half Dies*, Penguin, 1972
Harrison P. *Inside the Third World*, Penguin, 1981
Hayter T. *Aid: Rhetoric and Reality*, Pluto, 1985
Rodney W. *How Europe Underdeveloped Africa*, Bogle L'overture, 1972

FURTHER READING

Amin S. *Unequal Development*, Harvester, 1976
Barnet F.J. & Müller R.E. *Global Reach*, Jonathan Cape, 1975
Frank A.G. *Latin America: Underdevelopment or Revolution*, Monthly Review Press, 1969
Frank A.G. *Capitalism and Underdevelopment in Latin America*, Monthly Review Press, 1969
Frank A.G. *Sociology of Development and Underdevelopment*, Monthly Review Press, 1971
Frank A.G. *Crisis in the Third World*, Heinemann, 1981
Hayter T. *Aid as Imperialism*, Penguin, 1971
Hayter T. *The Creation of World Poverty*, Pluto, 1981
Laclau E. *Politics and Ideology in Marxist Theory*, New Left Books, 1977
Warren B. *Imperialism, Pioneer of Capitalism*, New Left Books, 1980

EXAMINATION QUESTIONS

1 Assess the relative merits of modernisation and dependency theories of development and underdevelopment. (AEB November 1985)

2 Examine sociological explanations of the persistence of marked inequalities between developed and underdeveloped societies. (AEB June 1985 Paper 2)

3 'The problems of the Third World cannot be explained or resolved by modernisation theory or dependency theory alone, but by some combination of the two.' Discuss. (AEB June 1988 Paper 1)

4 'The problems of the Third World are a direct result of past and present exploitation by the developed nations.' (AEB November 1988)

5 'Developed nations benefit directly from the underdevelopment of the Third World.' Examine this view. (AEB November 1989 Paper 2)

6 'Aid to underdeveloped countries does nothing to reduce their dependency on the developed nations.' Examine this view. (AEB June 1989 Paper 2)

15

THE FRANKFURT SCHOOL *and*
CRITICAL THEORY

THE AUTHORS

The Frankfurt School of social theory emerged from the Institute of Social Research established at Frankfurt University in 1923. It was sponsored by a wealthy businessman, Felix Weil, and it was the first Marxist-orientated research centre to be affiliated to a major university. In the wake of the First World War, the Russian Revolution of 1917 and the defeat of revolutions in Central Europe, it represented a major attempt by western Marxists to reappraise Marxist theory in the light of contemporary developments in advanced capitalist (and socialist) societies: the rise of fascism and Stalinism, the growth of monopoly capital, the power of the modern media. It was hostile to all forms of repressive idealogy and totalitarian control. It hoped to offer a more humanistic path to socialism and a 'free' society.

Tom Bottomore (1984) has divided the development of the Frankfurt School into four distinct periods.

1923–33

Under its first director, Carl Grunberg, the institute embarked on a series of empirical rather than theoretical research projects, though theoreticians like George Lukács and Karl Korsh did publish articles in the Institute's journal.

1933–50

Under its second director, Max Horkheimer, and his very talented associates, Erich Fromm, Herbert Marcuse and T.W. Adorno, the institute took a highly theoretical and philosophical direction in an attempt to develop an interdisciplinary social theory that could not only explain and criticise modern society but also transform it. However, with the rise of Nazism in Germany most of the leading members of the Institute, being both Jews and Marxists, had to flee abroad. The majority

emigrated to America and from 1934 to 1949 the Institute was affiliated to Columbia University. It was during this period that the
foundations of critical theory were laid, springing from Horkheimer's
inspirational essay *Traditional and Critical Theory* (1937) and developing through a series of theoretical analyses of monopoly capitalism,
the new industrial state, the role of technology, the culture industry and
the decline of individualism.

1950–70

Critical theory and the 'Frankfurt School' (now re-established in
Germany) came increasingly to dominate radical thinking in Western
Europe and even America (especially as Marcuse continued to live
there). It became a vanguard of the new left, neo-Marxism and a major
influence on the radical student movements of the 1960s.

1970 ONWARDS

This period saw the decline of the first Frankfurt School in terms of
both its theoretical influence and its membership. The theoretical
approaches of its leading members now became so diverse that they not
only broke away from a common association but even lost their involvement in Western Marxism. The Frankfurt theorists became increasingly pessimistic about the possibility of social revolution, about
the revolutionary potential of the working class, and came under
increasing criticism from new developments in Marxist thought.

With the death of Adorno in 1969 and of Horkheimer in 1973 the
original Frankfurt School died in all but name. However, it has enjoyed
a significant and substantial revival in the 1980s through the work and
ideas of Jürgen Habermas (see page 131).

In many ways the term Frankfurt School is a misleading title. It was
never a single school of thought, its membership was highly diverse,
wide-ranging and often changing, though its 'inner circle' of Horkheimer,
Marcuse and Adorno remained fairly stable throughout.

Their major works are too numerous to list, but include:

■ Max Horkheimer: *Critical Theory* (1972)
■ Theodor W. Adorno *et al.*: *The Authoritarian Personality* (1950)
■ Herbert Marcuse: *Reason and Revolution* (1954)
■ Herbert Marcuse: *One Dimensional Man* (1964)

THE IDEA

It is difficult to categorise *critical theory* as a single and unified set of sociological ideas in the traditional way. Rather it represented a theoretical framework, an interdisciplinary approach combining Marxism with Freudian concepts, philosophy with psychoanalysis, economic research with historical and cultural analyses across a wide variety of sociological fields from the family to the media, the economy to the state. Its underlying theme however was a 'critical' analysis of all forms of domination in modern society.

This overriding concern reflected the times the Frankfurt theorists lived in – the rise of totalitarian societies, the horrors of the Nazi concentration camps and Stalin's purges, the spread of authoritarianism and suppression of individual thought and freedom. Advanced capitalism and Soviet socialism emerged as the most powerful social systems ever developed by man, capable of fulfilling all the material needs of their mass populations, yet capable too of controlling and manipulating people on a mass scale that seemed to realise all the fears of George Orwell's *1984*.

Whilst the new communist states used Marxism as the basis of their ideological control of the masses (as well as physical force and terror) Western capitalism used the more subtle ideologies of consumerism and individualism to lull the working classes of America, Britain and Western Europe into a sense of 'false consciousness' and material satisfaction. The critical theorists sought to analyse such dominant ideologies and to try and explain why all the attempts to date to break the power of the ruling classes or the dominance of the state, be it by revolution or democracy, had failed.

Critical theory was, thus, in the same tradition as Marx's concept of 'alienation', Durkheim's 'anomie' and Weber's 'iron cage', a cry for the freedom of the individual amid the all-pervasive and stifling forces of bureaucracy, technology, the media and the state. The modern world is portrayed as a spiritual desert within which the individual is a lost soul searching for meaning and understanding amid material abundance, struggling for freedom and control against the faceless forces of technical progress, red tape and mass culture. The Frankfurt theorists sought to show that far from existing reality being real, it is an ideological distortion that conceals and legitimates the power of the ruling class; that far from existing society being rational, free and progressive, it is irrational and oppressive because it takes away or destroys the basic freedoms of human life – our ability to choose and make collective and rational decisions. Far from Western capitalist societies being the bastions of individual freedom as their propaganda proclaims, they are just as powerful an example of the 'totally administered society' creating a 'one dimensional man', as the communist societies they so revile and criticise.

The aim of critical theory was to liberate the individual in modern society by critically analysing such forces of domination, highlighting their weaknesses and so raising class consciousness about such ideological conditioning. By also outlining what a truly liberated and rational society would look like they equally hoped to inspire the masses to revolutionary thought and action.

The Frankfurt theorists used a Marxist framework as the basis of their criticism but they were as critical of traditional Marxism as of any other ideology. They criticised classical Marxism for being too deterministic, for overplaying the power of economic forces in historical development and underplaying the role of the individual, for becoming a repressive ideology used by tyrants like Stalin to suppress the masses, and the truth! However they did not intend to undermine Marxism, but to reinvigorate and revive it in the light of contemporary developments, to humanise and enliven it as the basis for predicting and promoting a more individualistic socialist society, 'a community of free human beings' (Horkheimer, 1937). Critical theory thus became a code word for neo-Marxism, a major attempt to liberalise official Marxism and create a more flexible, humanistic and radical interpretation of western society that combined the ideas of early Marx with such non-Marxist ideas as those of Freud and Weber.

Tom Bottomore (1984) has identified four key themes in critical theory:

CRITIQUE OF POSITIVISM AND EMPIRICISM

A fundamental critique of positivism and empiricism as the basis of modern scientific analysis, as a theory of knowledge and as the basis of modern sociology. In such key works as *Traditional and Critical Theory* (1937) and *Reason and Revolution* (1941), Horkheimer and Marcuse, respectively, rejected the idea of sociology as a science, arguing that positivism is too deterministic a basis for analysing human behaviour. Positivism treats people as things within a highly deterministic scheme of causes and effects, fails to distinguish between fact and value and, by presenting what is in society as what should be, legitimises the existing social order and obstructs change. In particular, the power of science has been subverted to support and promote a new form of 'technocratic' domination, by which technological, economic and political decisions are now sanctified by the stamp of 'scientific' approval, all criticism suppressed by a welter of unchallengeable scientific jargon and technical detail, all 'progress' justified in the name of science. The ruling elites now use science to obscure and legitimise their control, to make modern society seem impersonal and all-powerful whilst, in fact, they control and direct it. Instead of positivism being a means to discovering the truth, be it about nature or society, it has become a source of 'instrumental reason' used by the capitalist class (and the communist state) to increase exploitation of man and nature, profits and controls, to promote an image of reality supportive of the ruling elites. Science no longer involves itself in philosophical debates about the rights and wrongs of decisions about nuclear weapons, chemical pollutants, or space research. It merely serves the decisions of the powerful, irrespective of the effect on mankind – yet it gives the appearance of pursuing truth and knowledge.

In contrast to positivism, Horkheimer (1937) propounded 'dialectical theory', a critical approach to all knowledge as the basis for both promoting pure reason and for liberating human thought. By never accepting any argument, fact or theory as totally proven, dialectical theory hoped to provide a basis for both criticising and changing the world.

ANALYSIS OF NEW FORMS OF DOMINATION IN ADVANCED SOCIETIES

Like Weber, the Frankfurt theorists saw modern man as being over-awed by a new form of control – the forces of techno-rationality, an inner logic of all modern social systems, be they capitalist or communist, democratic or totalitarian, that has seen the rise of scientific techniques and technology as the overriding powers in society, sweeping aside individual opposition, rights and freedoms in the name of logical progress. They cited as examples of this trend the growth of monopoly capitalism, the growth of state control and planning of the economy, the spread of bureaucracy, of automation and mechanisation – all rational and apparently sensible developments, but all of which create an increasingly impersonal and alienating world in which the individual seems increasingly powerless, isolated and frustrated. Social control and centralised planning become all pervasive but no one seems to be in control, so opposition becomes pointless. Like Weber, Horkheimer and Marcuse became increasingly pessimistic about man's ability to resist such domination. In *One Dimensional Man* (1964), for example, Marcuse argued that the two main classes in capitalist societies have disappeared as effective historical agents. Domination is no longer by class but by the impersonal forces of scientific-technological rationality. There is no opposition as the working class has been assimilated by mass consumption and rational production processes.

ANALYSIS OF THE CULTURE INDUSTRY

The culture industry is seen as a key form of mass manipulation and deception whereby all forms of culture have been reduced to mass culture, fused into being merely a form of entertainment, devoid of any form of qualitative statement about the human condition, of any form of social criticism, and subverted by the advertising industry into a new form of consumer control. Adorno, in particular, sought to analyse all forms of culture, be they literature, art or music, to highlight the fact that in contrast to the great works of the past, modern culture no longer offers a critical analysis of the present or a vision of the future. It doesn't even reflect individual talent and creativity but is simply mass produced to sell on the mass market, to entertain the masses and keep them under control. Marcuse went on to highlight the way the culture industry produces and satisfies 'false needs' as a means to creating new markets for monopoly capital, to perpetuating consumerism and materialism and so averting criticism and dissatisfaction with capitalism. Modern man is encouraged to pursue pleasure and luxury, sex is no longer just a source of human reproduction and personal relationships but a major form of mass sales, for example of cars or magazines. At one point Marcuse himself put his faith into sexual freedom as the basis of a counter-culture and a more liberated society (1966) as he became something of a guru to the student revolutions of the 1960s.

FEAR OF THE DECLINE OF INDIVIDUALITY
IN MODERN SOCIETY

Horkheimer and his associates were committed to the value of individuality but became increasingly pessimistic about its survival amid the forces of mass society and 'the trend to a rationalized, automated, totally managed world' in an age 'which tends to eliminate every vestige of even a relative autonomy for the individual'. Using psychoanalytical concepts they even identified a trend to particular character types produced by society to promote conformity. Their classic study here was *The Authoritarian Personality* by Adorno *et al.* (1950), an analysis of the personality traits that helped give rise to fascism, aggressive nationalism and racial prejudice – a standardised individual whose thinking is rigid, stereotyped, superstitious and blindly submissive to authority. In contrast, individuals in the past were more autonomous and critical. This decline of individual and strong personalities is seen as a result of a change in the socialisation process. As capitalism develops, the role of the family and, in particular, the authority of the father, declines in the face of the growth of state power. With the father's power weakened, especially by the length of time he is away from home at work, the son turns to other role models and sources of identification such as heroes or stars promoted by the state or culture industry. Lacking a true father-figure the son is less able to stand up for himself, more self-conscious and anxious to prove his manhood, but by submitting to authority rather than by challenging it. Hence, argued Adorno, the mass support of Germany's youth in the 1930s for Hitler and the magnetic power of other fascist demagogues in this period and since!

Indeed the Frankfurt theorists themselves became increasingly despairing about this process. Horkheimer turned to religion whilst Marcuse put his faith for liberation in student and sexual revolution, and Adorno pinned his hopes on critical and authentic artists. They were equally fearful that despite all its rational and centralised planning, capitalism was driving western society to catastrophe through its underlying cycle of overproduction, anarchy, depressions, unemployment and war.

THE IDEA IN ACTION

Critical theory and the writings of the Frankfurt School became a major force in radical thought in post-war Europe and America, inspiring both neo-Marxism, the new left and student revolution. It reflected post-war fears about materialism, cultural decline, irrationality and imminent destruction through the nuclear arms race. Its key themes of the growth of mass society, increase in social controls and ideological conditioning and decrease in individuality; its critique of monopoly capitalism, the state and the role of science and technology, reflected currents of thought elsewhere in the western world, and its fears for the individual in the face of big business, big government and big brother inspired the young and other frustrated groups.

However critical theory's lack of theoretical unity and the diversity of its membership led to its eventual break-up and decline as its original members went off in different directions and lost faith in both Marxism

and the revolutionary potential of the modern working class. Their
ideas and theories increasingly came under criticism:

■ Their theoretical work lacked coherence and structure, was based
more on generalisations than detailed analyses.
■ Despite their claim to its being an interdisciplinary approach, critical theory was in fact quite a narrow analysis limited to contemporary
society and primarily philosophical in nature. It lacked historical depth,
and breadth, and was weak on economic analyses of advanced capitalism despite the contributions of Friedrich Pollock and Franz Neuman.
They often looked back to a golden era of early capitalism as a period
of true individualism, but never analysed such a speculative claim.
■ Whilst claiming to make a major reassessment of Marxism the
Frankfurt theorists left out its core component – an analysis of class in
capitalist societies and, in particular, the role of the working class as a
revolutionary force. Critical theory has been described as 'Marxism
without the proletariat'. The Frankfurt School lost faith in such revolution and tended to assume that class (and so class conflict) would
disappear in the face of the totally administered society.

    Even in its chosen sphere of social control and conformity:

■ it failed to analyse historically or empirically whether the condition
of the individual in modern society was actually worse than in the past,
or worse under capitalism than communism. Critical theorists tended
to use a middle-class bourgeois model of modern man rather than the
'man in the street', tended to ignore the very real growth in individual
freedom in post-war western society. The decline they talked of was
more that of the intellectual and the educated middle class than that of
the mass of the population.
■ It overemphasised the power of the culture industry and dominant
ideology, ignoring its weaknesses and the way people have resisted and
obstructed such conditioning.
■ It ignored the wide variety of attempts by the working class and
subject groups in post-war society to resist capitalism and domination:
the growth and power of socialist and communist parties in western
Europe, the power of modern trade unions, the rise of women's liberation and other radical movements, such as students, ethnic groups or
environmentalists, against the power of the state, big business,
bureaucracy or technology. In trying to explain why a Marxist-type
revolution had not occurred in the West, they tended to overemphasise

the power of the 'system' to crush or absorb opposition, to control people's thoughts and behaviour.

■ Finally, whilst studies like *The Authoritarian Personality* (1950) and *One Dimensional Man* (1964) were significant contributions to analyses of the relationship between modern man and mass society, of social control and conformity, fascism and prejudice, they lacked the detail and depth of theoretical analyses to have a lasting influence.

Essentially critical theory was a defence of individuality, a plea for consideration of the individual person in both mass society and modern social theory. It defended subjectivity and attacked the power of positivism in both sociology and Marxism. It proclaimed the individual amid the crushing forces of conformity and rationality inherent in the modern social system. However, it was only one amongst several postwar social analyses, one amongst a variety of Marxist reappraisals and though initially very influential, its growing pessimism and its theoretical weaknesses saw its decline in the face of more radical theories and successful social movements such as the revolutions in the Third World, the student revolution of May 1968 and other attempts to defeat or overthrow the 'system'. Its preoccupation with culture and philosophy has now been bypassed by more recent developments in Marxist thought more in tune with such central concerns as economic, historical and class analysis. Though the original Frankfurt School is now dead, its spirit lives on in the neo-critical writings of Jürgen Habermas, Clause Olte, Klaus Eder, Albrecht Wellmer and others.

At heart the Frankfurt philosophers believed that man is essentially a rational being who could only live and breathe, be truly human, in a rational and free society. They lost faith in the possibility of such a society ever emerging.

SEE ALSO

☐ **Historical materialism** as the parent theory of this revision of traditional Marxism.

☐ **Structural Marxism** as a radical alternative interpretation of the master.

☐ **Alienation** as a reflection of Marx's early views provides the basis for the humanist themes of critical theory.

☐ **Legitimation crisis** shows how Jürgen Habermas has extended and revised the ideas of the Frankfurt School of the 1930s.

SUGGESTED READING

Bottomore T.B. *The Frankfurt School*, Tavistock, 1984 – a concise and read-
    able overview
Marcuse H. *One Dimensional Man*, Routledge & Kegan Paul, 1964 – a
    popular version of 'critical' ideas

FURTHER READING

Adorno T.W. *et al. The Authoritarian Personality*, Harper, 1950
Habermas J. *Legitimation Crisis*, Heinemann, 1973
Horkheimer M. *Traditional and Critical Theory*, Fischer, Frankfurt, 1937
Horkheimer M. *Critical Theory*, Herder & Herder, 1972
Marcuse H. *Reason and Revolution*, Humanities Press, 1954
Marcuse H. *Eros and Civilisation*, Beacon Press, 1955

EXAMINATION QUESTION

'Marx's concept of class may have been adequate for understanding nineteenth-century industrial capitalism but it is inadequate for comprehending
contemporary industrial society.' Discuss. (WJEC June 1986)

16

HAROLD GARFINKEL *and*
ETHNOMETHODOLOGY

THE AUTHOR

Harold Garfinkel (1917–   ) was born in Newark, New Jersey. He
studied under Talcott Parsons but was heavily influenced by phenomenological ideas, especially those of Alfred Schutz. In both his doctoral thesis, *The Perception of the Other* (1952), and in his work at the
University of California Los Angeles, he made the analysis of the
structure of everyday life the focus of his research, attracting to him
such students as Aaron Cicourel, Harvey Sacks and David Sudnow.
With the publication of *Studies in Ethnomethodology* in 1967 he is
credited with founding ethnomethodology as a distinct sociological
approach.

THE IDEA

Most sociologists as well as most ordinary people tend to take social
order for granted, tend to assume that society really exists 'out-there'
and has reality of its own. Whilst sociologists seek to analyse the social,
economic and political forces underlying everyday reality or concentrate on its more extraordinary features (the deviant or powerful),
ordinary people are simply too busy getting on with their daily lives to
give it much thought – until, that is, it is disrupted by a power cut, a
strike or a domestic crisis and they have to 'pick up the pieces' out of
the resultant chaos and confusion. Ethnomethodology rejects such a
view of social order, arguing instead that what keeps society in order
is everyday reality – the common agreements, mutual expectations and,
especially, shared meanings behind the routines and commonsense of
daily life. Thus, as the word itself implies, ethnomethodology is the
study of 'the methods people use to make sense of the world about
them'. Its aim is to highlight the rules and background knowledge
behind our everyday routines and social encounters by producing
detailed 'ethnographies' of descriptions of quite ordinary events and
situations.

Harold Garfinkel was inspired to investigate this much neglected, even 'extraordinary' area of social life by his study of a group of jurors and the 'common sense' methods they used to make sense of the evidence before them. A key feature of his research was his use of 'natural experiments' to bring to light the highly precarious nature of social order. So, for example, to highlight the importance of routines in daily life he would get his students to deliberately disrupt them – by singing on a crowded bus or asking old ladies and pregnant women to give up their seats for them. To illustrate the extent to which we all use a vast store of background knowledge and essentially depend on the context of a conversation or action in order to interpret it, Garfinkel set up an experiment in which ten students were sent to see a counsellor, ostensibly about their personal problems. The counsellor sat behind a screen, gave only yes and no answers and these at random. Yet the students made sense of this 'nonsense' by using their own background knowledge of the problem and what they thought a counsellor would say. Had they known the counsellor was a fake, their 'interpretations' of his answers might have been very different.

From such experiments Garfinkel developed three key concepts to explain how ordinary 'members' of society not only have the capacity to interpret reality but to create (and recreate) it daily: *documentary method, reflexivity* and *indexicality*. By documentary method Garfinkel referred to the way we identify certain underlying patterns out of the enormous variety of phenomena we see and experience everyday. We then use such general patterns to make sense of the individual phenomena we experience in the future. Social life is therefore reflexive – each individual item is seen as a reflection or evidence of a more general theme and vice-versa. Thus, not only is 'each used to elaborate the other' but a self-fulfilling prophecy develops. Our general idea of reality directs us to select and interpret individual items of evidence in a predetermined way that tends to confirm our original picture of life. Finally, argued Garfinkel, no words or actions make sense outside the context of the conversation or situation involved. Such indexicality occasionally has to be 'repaired' as, for example, when a gesture or phrase has been misunderstood.

Thus, for Garfinkel and most ethnomethodologists, language and the 'activity' of talk is a central means by which we not only make sense of the world but actually 'create' it. Words are not just symbols of what is going on but are the very means by which things get done, by which society functions. So central is this notion to ethnomethodologists that writers like Harvey Sacks have tried to establish 'conversational analysis' as a distinct sub-discipline.

Garfinkel was especially at pains to refute the traditional socio-logical assumptions that social order has a reality of its own above and beyond the views and accounts of it by ordinary people and that sociologists' interpretations of life are any more accurate and scientific than those of ordinary members of society. Far from ordinary people being 'cultural dopes' simply acting out the directives of society, they, by their interpretations, actions and accounts, are actually 'creating' it. Thus, in Garfinkel's view, the sociologists' methods of making sense of society are essentially no different (and certainly not superior) to ordi-nary people's. The man-in-the-street is therefore in a sense his own so-ciologist. The role of the sociologists is therefore simply to describe and explain how people daily create and recreate the 'worlds' they live in.

THE IDEA IN ACTION

Ethnomethodology is generally seen as part of the interpretative tradi-tion in sociology. It starts from the phenomenological assumption that society only exists in so far as its members perceive its existence and that therefore the best way to understand how it works is to study it from within, subjectively, from its participants' point of view. Garfinkel's prime aim was to put the ideas of Alfred Schutz into practice.

Initially ethnomethodology stimulated enormous interest as it severely challenged the very foundations of traditional sociology. It argued that nothing in social life should be taken for granted; that even the 'hardest' of data on social reality should be scrutinised in terms of the social processes by which it was collected. Aaron Cicourel (1976) showed, for example, that far from the official statistics on crime being an accurate reflection of the amount of criminal behaviour, they were more a reflection of the activities and interpretations of the officials collecting and interpreting such facts and figures, in particular the police. Thus, in a sense, the police (and behind them the politicians and courts who make and administer the laws) create our image of the reality of crime. Maxwell Atkinson (1978) reinterpreted suicide statis-tics in a similar manner.

Inevitably, such a challenge to the basis and superiority of tradi-tional sociology incurred the wrath, criticism, even derision of 'estab-lished' approaches. Ethnomethodology was criticised as:

■ Tedious, boring and leading nowhere. It offered only descriptions, no grand theories.
■ Portraying people as creative but failing to give them any sense of

purpose or motive as to why they acted or interpreted in a particular way.

■ Failing to give any real consideration to the influences of power and social differences on people's behaviour or the structure of society.

■ Portraying life as no more than a multitude of individual everyday existences, untouched by such external forces as war or unemployment.

■ Ethnomethodology's own approach can be turned back on itself. If ethnomethodologists' descriptions of 'life' are no better than ordinary people's and only further add to reality, rather than explaining it, what is the point of doing such study?

Nevertheless Garfinkel and his students have highlighted a vital but neglected area of study – everyday life – and shed new light on accepted assumptions. Thus, while some see it as a 'flash in the sociological pan' with little more to offer, its supporters like Benson and Hughes (1983) see it as a 'fundamental break with a whole tradition of social scientific thought' and one that is here to stay.

SEE ALSO

☐ **Phenomenology** as the parent theory that gave birth to this strand of interpretative sociology.

SUGGESTED READING

Atkinson M. 'Societal Reactions to Suicide. The Role of Coroners' in Cohen S. ed. *Images of Deviance*, Penguin, 1971 – sums up Atkinson's ideas.
Atkinson M. *Discovering Suicide*, Macmillan 1978 – an excellent example of an ethnomethodologist at work.
Benson D. and Hughes J. *The Perspective of Ethnomethodology*, Longman, 1983
Cicourel A. *The Social Organisation of Juvenile Justice*, Heinemann, 1976
Sharrock W.W. and Anderson R. *The Ethnomethodologists*, Tavistock, 1986

FURTHER READING

Garfinkel H. *Studies in Ethnomethodology*, Prentice Hall, 1967

EXAMINATION QUESTIONS

1 'Social life is very much dependent upon people's definitions and interpretations of the social order.' Using a variety of examples, explain and illustrate this assertion. Assess the adequacy of this explanation of social order. (JMB June 1987)

2 'All knowledge is relative because it is socially constructed.' Assess this view. (AEB November 1988)

3 'What is defined as a suicide is more a matter of what the coroner thinks, than what the dead person intended.' Discuss with reference to recent studies of suicide. (AEB June 1989 Paper 1)

17

ERVING GOFFMAN *and*
STIGMA

THE AUTHOR

Erving Goffman (1922–82) was born in Manville, Canada. He took
degrees at the Universities of Toronto and Chicago and then joined the
Department of Social Anthropology at the University of Edinburgh.
From fieldwork in the Shetland Islands (1949–51) emerged his first
major publication *The Presentation of Self in Everyday Life* (1956).
From research for the National Institute of Mental Health emerged his
famous study *Asylums* (1961). In 1962 he became Professor of Sociology at the University of California, Berkeley; in 1968 he was made the
Benjamin Franklin Professor of Anthropology and Sociology at the
University of Pennsylvania and in 1981 he received the ultimate acco-
lade when made President of the American Sociological Association.

Goffman's style of sociology was highly individualistic and difficult
to categorise. He is generally associated, though, with the ideas and
concepts of symbolic interactionism and was strongly influenced by
George Herbert Mead (see page 191).

Goffman's key works include:

  The Presentation of Self in Everyday Life (1956)
  Asylums (1961)
  Encounters (1961)
  Behaviour in Public Places (1963)
  Strategic Interaction (1970)
  Gender Advertisements (1979)

Goffman's central interest was in analysing human interaction and
the presentation of people's 'selves' in everyday situations, particularly
in public places. He is therefore often seen as the founding father of
dramaturgy, the analysis of human behaviour which sees life as a play
and people as actors performing roles in front of ever-changing audi-
ences. Though the script for such roles is often written out beforehand,
most of it is improvised. Thus, like Mead, Goffman does not see human

behaviour as predetermined but as an expression of individuality, creativity and freedom within the limits of a particular social context. As he outlined in *Asylums*, even in the most controlled of situations, people can establish some sense of freedom, space and most especially identity. The central aim of all his work was to dramatise the way all of us try to establish and defend our self-image, both publicly and privately, and to illustrate the wide variety of 'fronts', 'props' and strategies we employ to preserve our individuality and humanness. In his analyses, the human self emerges through a process of continual conflict between society's definitions and those the individual has of himself.

In later works, *Frame Analysis* (1974) and *Forms of Talks* (1981), Goffman delved deeper into all forms of human communication. He died in 1982.

THE IDEA

Despite our individual eccentricities and imperfections we all like to think of ourselves as normal. We tend to avoid, segregate and stereo-type those who are in any way different for fear of being contaminated. In a collection of essays entitled *Stigma* (1961) Goffman turned his eye for the dramatic from the 'presentation of self' by ordinary people to the strategies employed by those with 'spoiled identities' in our society – the Jew, the mentally ill, the divorcee, the blind, the stutterer. How do such social 'outcasts' maintain any semblance of dignity and self-esteem in the face of such massive rejection and humiliation?

Goffman identified three main types of stigma:

■ Physical defects such as being a cripple, a dwarf or deaf.
■ Personal weaknesses or blemishes on a person's character or back-ground such as a prison record or being unemployed.
■ Social stigmas of the company a person keeps or the racial or religious group he belongs to, for example ethnic minorities.

Stigmas may therefore be ascribed or achieved, something you are born with or something you 'earn'. It may be highly visible like having no nose or being known as a prostitute, or an invisible but 'dark' secret like homosexuality. It may be a source of public sympathy like polio or one of public shame, like being an ex-convict.

The essays in *Stigma* (1961) are an extensive discussion of the wide variety of strategies people use in the face of being stigmatised or to prevent such a label being applied in the first place. Much obviously depends on the defect involved and how visible it is. Some try to 'repair' it by, for example, plastic surgery or going 'straight'. Some try to hide it by special clothing, dark glasses or aliases. Some learn how to pass it off in public or how to prevent the sneers and looks of others by joining in 'normal' society. Others withdraw – the handicapped into homes, junkies into a drug culture – into the security of 'worlds' where their defects are considered normal. Some even fight back by forming pressure groups like Gay Lib or Black Power to force society to change its view of them and grant them equal rights with other humans. The stigmatised have to go through a special *moral career*, a particularly painful socialisation process, as they learn to live in a society where they are not considered complete, are looked down on and often segregated. Their self-image is often shattered, especially if stigmatisation occurs late in life, as the result say of a crippling car accident or an addiction to drink. Such individuals feel strangers in their own society and face enormous strain between their public images and their private lives. Their egos are rarely intact.

However, as Goffman emphasises, the stigmatised are only one of the two 'faces' of stigma. The other is society at large and its definitions of normality. We are the audience whose reactions force the abnormal and the deviant to act in an unusual manner. It is we 'normals' who discriminate, segregate and construct an ideology about the 'handicapped' as inferior or a threat, in order to justify our rejection, fear and prejudice about them. Yet we are all well aware of our own imperfections as we 'face up' to everyday situations. So, argues Goffman, the normal and the stigmatised are not two separate classes of people but two ends of a continuum which varies according to the people, time, place and situation involved. What may be abnormal in one situation may not be in another. Thus we are all 'normal deviants', we all play 'two-headed roles' as we joke about or sympathise with the stigmatised.

Stigmas are not, therefore, a reflection of inherent weaknesses in a person's body or character. They are a social label created by the 'reaction' of others in society. The individual involved fails to live up to people's expectations and stereotypes about normal looks or behaviour and so is 'disqualified from full social acceptance'. The study of stigma therefore is not only an analysis of a special form of 'image management' but of a particular form of social control. The abnormal are labelled deviant and sub-human as a way of controlling or excluding them. Ironically, in Goffman's view labelling people in this way creates the very behaviour it was designed to suppress. Faced by the 'abnormal' reactions of ordinary people, the stigmatised inevitably act strangely!

THE IDEA IN ACTION

Such a powerful and intricate description of how even the outcasts of society seek to maintain their self-esteem and personal identity, of how society at large creates abnormality and deviance by its own reaction, obviously had a profound effect on many social sciences and forced many a psychiatrist or social worker to reanalyse 'abnormal' behaviour as possible highly rational, given the totally unusual situations the handicapped in society often find themselves in. However, like other forms of interactionism it was criticised for failing to explain where such social labels as stigma come from, who has the power to stigmatise and why some groups suffer such discrimination and not others. It was more a study of social psychology than of social structure. For all that, works like *Stigma* and *Asylums* continue to stimulate and entrance, continue to give depth and colour to our understanding of the various social 'worlds' that make up society. Few have given sociology such style, individuality and insight as Erving Goffman.

SEE ALSO

☐ **Labelling theory** and
☐ **Symbolic interactionism** as the parent theories of this idea.
☐ **Self-fulfilling prophecy** as another example of this type of social interaction.

SUGGESTED READING

Burns T. *Erving Goffman*, Tavistock, 1986 – a short and readable overview of Goffman's life and work
Goffman E. *Asylums*, Penguin, 1961
Goffman E. *Stigma*, Prentice Hall, 1964
Smith G. 'The Sociology of Erving Goffman' in *Social Studies Review*, Jan. 1988 – a very useful short summary and assessment

FURTHER READING

Goffman E. *The Presentation of Self in Everyday Life*, Penguin, 1956
Goffman E. *Encounters*, Penguin, 1961
Goffman E. *Behaviour in Public Places*, 1963
Goffman E. *Strategic Interaction*, Blackwell, 1970
Goffman E. *Frame Analysis*, Harper, 1974
Goffman E. *Gender Advertisements*, Macmillan, 1979
Goffman E. *Forms of Talk*, University of Pennsylvania Press, 1981

18

JOHN GOLDTHORPE, DAVID LOCKWOOD ET AL *and*

EMBOURGEOISEMENT

THE AUTHORS

The embourgeoisement thesis cannot be traced back to any one author. Rather it arose in the late 1950s and early 1960s from a variety of writers – sociologists like Clark Kerr, Jessie Bernard and F. Zweig, political scientists like Richard Rose and David Butler, and politicians like Tony Crosland. It can even be traced back to Werner Sombart and Robert Michels' idea early in the twentieth century, that instead of the middle and working classes in advanced industrial societies conflicting, as Karl Marx had predicted, they were converging.

Amid the growing prosperity of the late 1950s ('You've never had it so good', proclaimed the Prime Minister, Harold Macmillan) the spread of mass-produced consumer goods, the apparent elimination of poverty, the expansion of tertiary industries and the decline of primary ones, it appeared that Britain was becoming a middle-class society and we were all adopting a bourgeois lifestyle. In particular this thesis was used to explain the continued dominance of the Conservative Party over British politics and the failure, yet again, of the Labour Party to regain power in the 1959 Election. The post-war 'liberal' dream of a classless society in which 'ideology was dead' and consensus 'ruled OK' seemed about to come true. The proletarian revolution seemed no more than a figment of Karl Marx's imagination, the working class was 'withering away' and, instead of revolting against capitalism, the masses seemed to be embracing it.

This thesis was tested, and largely refuted, in a famous series of studies of 'affluent workers' by John Goldthorpe, David Lockwood, Jennifer Platt and Frank Bechhofer, published in 1968. Goldthorpe and Lockwood are leading figures in the field of social stratification; Goldthorpe through the Oxford Mobility Studies of the 1970s, Lockwood through such publications as *The Blackcoated Worker* (1958) and *Sources of Variation in Working Class Images of Society* (1975).

Platt and Bechhofer are now lecturers at Sussex and Edinburgh Universities respectively.

THE IDEA

Goldthorpe and Lockwood summed up the embourgeoisement thesis as the belief that:

as manual workers and their families achieve relatively high incomes and living standards, they assume a way of life which is more characteristically 'middle class' and become in fact progressively assimilated into middle-class society. (Goldthorpe & Lockwood, 1968)

The thesis of the 1950s and '60s tended to focus specifically on the upper working class: skilled manual workers earning high wages in the newer industries. Such 'affluent' workers appeared to be assimilating with the lower middle classes in four main ways:

■ Economically. The income and consumption patterns of the middle and working classes seemed to be increasingly similar. Such skilled workers could now afford to buy the luxury goods, cars and even the homes previously seen as the preserve of the middle class.
■ Culturally. Affluent workers appeared to be adopting middle class attitudes and lifestyles in terms of their leisure activities, voting habits and even the way they brought up their children.
■ Technologically. In the new automated factories the traditional divisions and distinctions between men and management seemed to be disappearing. Skilled workers were accorded the status of white collar technicians and worked alongside management as part of a 'team'. As machines took over the more physical and mundane tasks so men were freed for the more interesting and demanding ones. Harmony and job satisfaction seemed to replace conflict and alienation.
■ Ecologically. As such workers moved from the declining industries of the North to the newer, expanding ones of the South so the traditional working-class communities were broken up and their sense of class solidarity replaced by the self-reliance and individualism normally associated with the middle class.

To test this thesis in the most favourable of conditions, Goldthorpe and Lockwood examined a sample of 229 manual workers at Vauxhall Motors, Skefco Ball Bearings Company and Laporte Chemicals in the prosperous and growing area of Luton. These workers were highly paid, all married and 57 per cent of them owned their own homes. This study looked for evidence of 'embourgeoisement' in four main areas: attitudes to work, interaction patterns in the community, aspirations and social perspectives and political views. It used three main headings:

ECONOMIC FACTORS

Despite their high wages such affluent workers did not earn as much as their non-manual counterparts. They did not enjoy such perks as expense accounts, pension schemes or company cars. They did not have the same job security and so 'continuity' of earnings. They did not have the same opportunities for promotion and much of their high earnings was based on overtime.

NORMATIVE FACTORS (ATTITUDES AND VALUES)

The Luton workers did not enjoy their work. They generally found it extremely boring, even alienating. They only accepted it because of the high wages. They had little commitment to the company in the way a white-collar careerist has and rarely joined even its social clubs. They had a very instrumental attitude to work; they did it for what they could get out of it.

Similarly they held typically working class attitudes rather than middle class ones. Sixty-seven per cent saw themselves as working class, only 14 per cent as middle class; 80 per cent voted Labour at the 1959 Election and saw it as the party of the working class; the vast majority were strong union men. Finally, they did not see society as the middle class do, as a ladder of opportunity open to individual talent (prestige model) but rather in collectivist terms of solidly supporting the trade union as the means to higher earnings (power model).

RELATIONAL FACTORS

Nor did these workers aspire to middle class lifestyles or status by either living on private estates or joining institutions like the local golf club. By and large the Luton workers kept to themselves, mixed primarily with their own kin and friends and showed no desire to move up into more exclusive social circles.

Thus the Luton study did not find this sample of affluent workers to be typically middle class. Neither, however, were they typically working class. They could afford 'luxurious' lifestyles; they had adopted a privatised and home-centred way of life with a particular concern for their children's education and futures. Their support for both the union and the Labour Party was primarily instrumental rather than emotional, a means to higher wages and welfare benefits rather than to socialism. They were very materialistic and saw society not in the traditional working class way of 'us and them' (power model) but according to the distribution of money with a large central class made up of the majority of 'working people' and two extremes of very rich and very poor. The traditional manual–non-manual division was not seen as significant. Goldthorpe and Lockwood therefore concluded that this new 'breed' of affluent worker was neither middle nor working class (despite a number of points of 'convergence' with both) but a new privatised working class: workers from traditional working class backgrounds whose behaviour was an adaptation to the more middle class environments they had moved into; but such environments (not such incomes) did not 'determine' how they behaved as the embourgeoisement thesis seemed to claim.

THE IDEA IN ACTION

Generally, Goldthorpe and Lockwood's study is seen as the authoritative refutation of the embourgeoisement thesis, and a variety of studies since have supported its idea that the modern working class is more privatised and instrumental and that the class structure today is 'fragmenting' as industry and lifestyles change.

The 'Affluent Worker' study was also acclaimed for its style of research. Its neo-Weberian 'action' approach clearly showed up the weaknesses of mass surveys and showed the advantages of interpreting attitudes as well as facts and figures.

Ironically, amid growing unemployment and union militancy, the 1970s saw the emergence of an alternative and Marxist thesis of manual–non-manual 'convergence', but this time of the lower middle classes adopting 'proletarian' attitudes and behaviour – the proletarianisation thesis of Braverman (see p. 31). It too was finally rejected.

However, with the election and re-election of Mrs Thatcher in 1979, 1983 and 1987 the embourgeoisement thesis has enjoyed something of a revival. It has been used to explain the considerable support she seems to inspire from skilled workers living in the South East. In contrast the Labour Party seems to be continuing to try to appeal to a working class that is shrinking and exists only in the traditional heartlands of the North, Scotland and Wales.

SEE ALSO

☐ **Convergence thesis** and
☐ **Post-industrial society** as more general theories of a progressive trend towards a classless society.
☐ **Deskilling** as part of the alternative thesis of proletarianisation.

SUGGESTED READING

Goldthorpe J.H. and Lockwood D. *et al. The Affluent Worker*, CUP, 1968
Marshall G. *et al. Social Class in Modern Britain*, Hutchinson, 1988 – an updated analysis of this issue.

FURTHER READING

Goldthorpe J.H. and Lockwood D. *et al. Social Mobility and Class Structure in Modern Britain*, Clarendon Press, 1968, 1980
Lockwood D. *The Blackcoated Worker*, Allen & Unwin, 1958
Lockwood D. 'Sources of Variation in Working Class Images of Society', in Bulmer M. (ed), *Working Class Images of Society*, Routledge & Kegan Paul, 1975

EXAMINATION QUESTIONS

1 What do you consider to have been the most significant changes in the British class structure since the nineteenth century? (Cambridge Local Examinations Syndicate June 1986)
2 Examine sociological explanations of changes in the support for different political parties in Britain over the past twenty-five years. (AEB June 1988)
3 The 'fact' and the 'consciousness' of class do not always coincide. What problems does this produce for sociologists? (AEB June 1984)
4 'The majority of white collar workers are now in the same class position as manual workers.' (AEB June 1988)
5 Outline the major studies of social mobility in Britain and examine the criticisms of them. (AEB June 1989 paper 2)

19

ANTONIO GRAMSCI *and*

HEGEMONY

THE AUTHOR

Antonio Gramsci (1891–1937) was born in Sardinia, Italy, the son of poor, lower middle-class parents. He won a scholarship to Turin University in 1911 and joined the Italian Socialist Party in 1913. He helped found and edit the radical newspaper *L'Ordine Nuovo* and became a key figure in the syndicalist, or factory council movement of the 1920s. However, in 1921, he and other activists broke away to form the Italian Communist Party and he became its General Secretary in 1924. In the same year he was elected to the Italian Parliament but was imprisoned by Mussolini in 1926. Mussolini described him as the 'Sardinian hunchback' with a 'brain of undeniable power'. At his trial the prosecutor declared 'we must prevent this brain from functioning for twenty years'. He was not released until 1937, dying shortly afterwards from a cerebral haemorrhage and the acute deprivations of prison life.

Gramsci is generally considered one of the outstanding Marxist theorists of the twentieth century and his *Prison Notebooks* (1971) are regarded as a Marxist classic – thirty-three notebooks comprising 2848 closely-packed pages and written in the worst possible conditions. He was profoundly influenced by the great Italian philosopher Benedetto Croce and by Machiavelli, Marx and Lenin. Gramsci's aim was to unify social theory and practice, to criticise orthodox Marxism and its claims to scientific certainty, in particular its economic determinism, its insistence on the inextricable link between base and superstructure, on the inevitability of the underlying laws of historical materialism, that capitalism is bound to collapse, irrespective of any help from radical individuals or revolutionary groups. In contrast he argued for a more

humanist, active approach, emphasising human subjectivity and involvement. For him, politics, ideology and culture are independent of
the economic system, not controlled by it. A true socialist revolution
not only involves proletarian control of the state and the means of
production, but also ideological and moral leadership. Moreover, his
own experiences of backward peasant life in Southern Italy and the
industrial North convinced him that any socialist revolution would
require alliances with other social groups in society, particularly the
peasantry. It had to be a mass, even popular movement. A minority
revolution of the working class alone on the Bolshevik model would
not be enough to secure power.

THE IDEA

Gramsci's emphasis on culture and ideology, on mass revolution, is
best expressed in his concept of hegemony, a term that originated in
Greek times to refer to the dominance of one state or ruler over
another, Gramsci extended it to refer to the predominance of one social
class over another, to the ability of those controlling society to impose
their world view, their ideology, on the masses, partially by force but
mainly by consent, or at least acquiescence.

Gramsci defined hegemony as 'moral and philosophical leadership,
leadership which manages to win the active consent of those over
whom it rules' – leadership designed to create a national-popular
collective will.

Gramsci argued that no ruling class could dominate by economic
control, or even by political force alone. Such naked oppression would
only inspire revolution. What is also needed is ideological control, the
consent of the governed, and this is achieved through such important
socialising agencies as the family, church, law, media, schools, and
even trade unions. They all promote and legitimise the ideas of the
ruling class to the point where such values are accepted uncritically and
unconsciously as normal. They form the basis of everyday life, even
underlie our notions of 'common sense'. Thus whilst the ruling class
can ultimately enforce its rule through the state (the law, police, army,
etc.), its real control lies through its intellectual dominance over civil
society.

Complete ideological dominance, however, is rare and never complete. It always faces new challenges from alternative groups, new
ideas, new crises. It rests on gaining the support of the mass of the
population through establishing an 'historic bloc' of shifting alliances

between the dominant class and other sectors of society; alliances which are always open to dispute and collapse. This opens the way for subordinate classes like the working class to seize the moral, intellectual and political leadership, win widespread support and overthrow the ruling class. In capitalist societies the working class is in a particularly strong position to resist and expose bourgeois indoctrination. Their everyday experiences of working life under capitalism has revealed its essentially exploitative and oppressive nature. However, to turn such knowledge into revolutionary action will require sustained education of the masses by radical intellectuals to raise such proletarian understanding into revolutionary class consciousness and, ultimately, action. A true working-class revolution will, therefore, first require an intellectual struggle to expose bourgeois ideology; a cultural revolution in which the working class seizes philosophical and moral leadership before gaining political and economic control of the state and society. The role of the Communist Party is therefore, in Gramsci's view, to help promote working-class consciousness and help win the support of other groups in forming a revolutionary alliance. Such intellectual liberation and alliances, however, could equally come about through the workers themselves through such movements as syndicalism and factory councils.

THE IDEA IN ACTION

Gramsci's concept of hegemony has had a major influence on post-war western Marxism, offering a major alternative to the rigid orthodoxy of Soviet communism. It offered new insights into the complexities of advanced capitalism, and in particular into the lack of revolutionary consciousness amongst the working class of western Europe even under the fascist regimes of the 1930s. It equally offered an alternative, non-violent socialist strategy, more in keeping with the liberal freedoms and individual rights of western society than the Bolshevik model of a political revolution based on the use of violent force to seize and sustain power.

Gramsci's use of the term hegemony differed from that of more orthodox Marxists such as Lenin and Mao Zedong, who used it to refer to political leadership or state domination. His interpretation and strategy differed in the following respects:

■ Its emphasis on ideological, moral and cultural factors as opposed to simply political and economic ones, on the importance of an intellectual revolution, of promoting mass class consciousness within civil society as well as seizing control of the state;

■ Its emphasis on the masses, on groups other than the working class being involved in the revolution, so allowing for the inclusion of such non-proletarian but radical groups as students, women, Blacks, etc. Such a broad analysis beyond the working class alone has greatly helped western Marxists explain the student revolution and the Women's Liberation movement of the 1960s and 1970s.

■ Its emphasis on creating a National-Popular movement dependent on conditions in each country helped stimulate the growth of independent Communist parties and socialist groups with national strategies which did not require to wait for a world revolution or directives from Moscow.

■ Its emphasis on the unity of theory and practice encouraged radical intellectuals to get involved with the working class and promoted the idea, as Marx said, that men make their own history rather than wait for underlying, impersonal historical forces to do it for them.

Gramsci's analysis tried to show not only how ruling classes seized power, but how they sustained it, not only by force and economic control, but by ideological leadership which, if successfully broken, usually preceded its political downfall. In the *Prison Notebooks*, for example, Gramsci contrasted the success of the Jacobins in the French Revolution who, by including in their own propaganda the aspirations of the masses, were able to gain the support of the peasantry, with the failure of the Italian Risorgimento which failed to broaden its support, and so collapsed. He pointed out how the bourgeoisie, the ruling class under capitalism, has been able to retain power, despite the instability of the capitalist economy, primarily by maintaining its intellectual ascendancy even against socialist challenges; how conservative governments have achieved passive revolutions without the use of force, but by convincing the masses, even large sectors of the proletariat, that its ideas are their ideas. Mrs Thatcher's Conservative government of Britain in the 1980s not only used the state and the law to roll back the Welfare State and crush militant trade unions and local authorities, but established an ideological climate in which the values of liberal capitalism were dominant, in which market forces, privatisation and inequality were not only accepted, but promoted, under which socialism was in danger of being driven out of modern Britain as even the working classes deserted the Labour Party. Thus, to gain power, the working class must transcend its own immediate interests, combine with other sectors of society and win over the majority of the population to the moral correctness of its cause. A modern socialist revolution, in Gramsci's view, is as much one of ideas as of political force, as much one requiring mass support as minority leadership. For him, the ideal society is one in which the laws of the state coincide with the dictates of individual conscience.

Inevitably Gramsci's more humane, open and gradualistic analysis of socialist strategy has been subjected to severe criticism by more orthodox Marxists for being too liberal, for denying the historical importance of the laws of historical materialism, and by the Communist Party for compromising the revolutionary purity of the proletariat. Structuralists like Louis Althusser (see page 1) and Nicos Poulantzas (see page 252) have been especially scathing. Nevertheless, this concept has provided western Marxists with a major means of analysing the complexities of advanced capitalism, of explaining the lack of revolutionary fervour amongst the European working class and the success in gaining and holding power of such New Right governments as Margaret Thatcher's in Britain and Ronald Reagan's and George Bush's in America. Gramsci's ideas have inspired the New Left in western Europe and the growth of Eurocommunism, providing a strategy for promoting peaceful revolution by exposing the exploitation, oppression and inequality of western capitalism, and so winning over radical groups to the socialist cause. Probably his major legacy has been the emergence, ten years after his death, of the Italian Communist Party as a major force in post-war Italian politics; a true reflection of Gramsci's desire to combine theory and practice.

SEE ALSO

☐ **Alienation** and
☐ **Ideology** as background ideas to Gramsci's theories.
☐ **Structural Marxism**
☐ **Critical theory** and
☐ **Legitimation crisis** as three very different versions of this key Marxist idea.

SUGGESTED READING

Bocock R. *Hegemony*, Tavistock, 1986 – a broad analysis of the whole idea of hegemony

Hoffman J. 'The Life and Ideas of Antonio Gramsci' in *Social Studies Review*, January 1988

Joll J. *Antonio Gramsci*, Fontana, 1977 – short, readable study of his life and work

McNeil P. 'Battle for Common Sense' in *New Statesman/Society*, 21 November 1988 – a discussion of Thatcherism as a modern day hegemonic ideology.

FURTHER READING

Gramsci A. *Selections from the Prison Notebooks*, New Left Books, 1971

EXAMINATION QUESTIONS

1 'All societies have ideologies that justify inequality.' Discuss and illustrate this statement. (London University June 1986)
2 Examine Marx's view that the ideas of the ruling class are, in every age, the ruling ideas. (AEB June 1987)

20

JÜRGEN HABERMAS *and*
LEGITIMATION CRISIS

THE AUTHOR

Jürgen Habermas (1929–) was born in Düsseldorf, Germany. His father was the head of the Bureau of Trade and Industry, his grandfather a Protestant minister. He studied at the Universities of Göttingen, Bonn and Marburg plus a period in the 1950s at the Institute for Social Research, home of the world famous Frankfurt School and critical theory. From 1962 to 1964 he lectured in philosophy at Heidelberg University and was then appointed Professor of Philosophy and Sociology at Frankfurt University. In 1971 he became director of the Max-Planck Institute in Starnberg, but in 1982 returned to Frankfurt where he still works as a Professor of Philosophy and Sociology. He has received numerous academic prizes, including the Hege (1974) and Sigmund Freud (1976).

As a youth in Germany during the 1940s, Habermas was horrified by the Nuremberg Trials and accounts of Nazi atrocities. However, his conversion to neo-Marxism, critical theory and radical politics really came when he worked as a research assistant for Theodor Adorno and other leading members of the Frankfurt School. At one point he was a strong supporter of the student radicals of the 1960s and he still retains strong links with a variety of left-wing social and intellectual movements in America and Europe. Though essentially an academic, intellectual life for Habermas is not just a vocation but a means to promoting a better, more rational and just society, 'one geared to collective needs rather than arbitrary power' (Pusey, 1987).

Habermas is generally seen as the leading proponent of neo-critical theory, but his work is not simply an extension of the key themes of the Frankfurt School of Adorno *et al.* (see page 101), but also a departure from them. Like them, Habermas aims to develop a 'critical' theory capable of both challenging and reconstructing existing social theory and offering a new and, in his case, very positive vision of future society. Like them, he is strongly motivated by contemporary historical events, the degeneration of the Russian Revolution into Stalinism, the failure to date of mass revolution in the West, the decline of proletarian class consciousness, the growth of issued-based protest movements at a time when late capitalism and its powers of mass control have grown and been strengthened by the spread of bureaucracy, state power, monopoly capital and the mass media. Social criticism and opposition has been stifled, individual rights and freedoms restricted, at a time when the capitalist system is facing new types of crisis, particularly those of economic disorder and political legitimacy.

The key themes of Habermas's work to date can be summarised as:

A critique of positivism and the instrumental uses of science and technology.

A reconstruction and update of critical theory.

A reconstruction of Marxism, in particular reassessing historical materialism to take account of state control of the economy and the contemporary importance of ideological power.

A new theory of knowledge and communication.

His overall aim is to produce an analysis of the march of 'reason' through human history, its use in the past as a weapon against error, superstition, myth and tyranny, its subversion today in serving the ideological controls of advanced capitalism, its use in late capitalism as an instrument of oppression, stifling all criticism through the spread of bureaucracy, techno-rationality and scientism. By developing a new theory of knowledge capable of undermining positivism and such instrumental rationalism, capable of liberating human communication, he hopes that, once again, rational thought can rule and so produce a more just and free society. This analysis of social theory and rationalism has culminated in his most recent work, a massive two-volume debate with the key thinkers of both social science and philosophy called *The Theory of Communicative Action* (1981).

His other major works have been:

Towards a Rational Society (1970)
Knowledge and Human Interest (1968)
Legitimation Crisis (1973)
Communication and the Evolution of Society (1979)

THE IDEA

The term 'legitimation' refers to the way a government or social system attempts to justify its existence and power. All governments need to legitimise their rule, to justify their right to power, to promote their authority as a means to gaining popular support, or at least, acquiescence, without which they are likely to collapse. Traditional societies used myth, magic or the authority of God to legitimise their rule; modern governments claim to represent the will of the people as reflected in the results of elections and written constitutions. The term 'crisis' refers to the situation whereby the strains within society have reached such a point that the whole social system cannot cope and is in imminent danger of collapse.

The aim of Habermas's *Legitimation Crisis* (1973) was to try and identify the crisis points within advanced capitalist societies and how the modern state continues both to manage such crises and maintain the legitimacy of the capitalist system. He sought to take account of contemporary developments, not least the growth in state power and the decline of class conflict and class consciousness, especially amongst the working class. He sought to explain that although advanced capitalism seems stronger than ever, it is in fact undergoing constant crises that ultimately will threaten the legitimacy of the system, and so cause its collapse. Classical Marxism, with its overriding emphasis on economic factors, can only offer a limited explanation of contemporary developments. Habermas, by emphasising cultural and ideological factors as well, sought to update and reconstruct modern Marxism and critical theory.

In *Legitimation Crisis* (1973) Habermas analyses late capitalist societies in terms of three key sub-systems – the economic, political and socio-cultural. For society to be stable all three sub-systems must be in balance and closely interrelated. Advanced capitalism, for example, requires the state to manage the economy as a way of overcoming the instabilities and conflicts of market forces and to alleviate the inequalities created by exploitation and the pursuit of profit. Hence the growth of state planning and regulation of the economy and the expansion of the welfare state to combat poverty, ill-health and industrial pollution. However, the state in turn must maintain popular support and mass loyalty. Therefore it must tax private enterprise to pay for educational and welfare services, never appear to be biased solely towards big business, and develop techniques, both ideological and physical, for securing mass conformity and control. The socio-cultural system must create the correct ideological climate and social consensus to support capitalism and motivate its members into the 'enterprise culture'. If any one of these sub-systems fails to function effectively in balancing the social system then a crisis will occur.

Habermas identified four possible crisis tendencies within the modern capitalist system, each of which might trigger off a chain of crises elsewhere – economic crises and crises of rationality, legitimation and motivation. The whole capitalist system is riddled with inherent contradictions created by the very nature of it being an irrational system designed to promote inequality and exploitation rather than a just distribution of wealth and power. It is in a permanent state of crisis management and is only kept in balance by one sub-system compensating for the deficiencies of another. For example, an economic crisis caused by a decline in profits may be offset by state hand-outs to 'lame duck' industries. However, this may in turn generate a rationality crisis, may bring to the surface what Marxists call the irrationality or anarchy of a market economy in which there is no rational planning according to human need, but only the unstable forces of supply and demand, underpinned by the motivation of private profit and personal gain. Thus, government hand-outs to ailing private enterprises may in turn produce inflation and a financial crisis as the government has to borrow such sums. This, in turn, generates a legitimation crisis as the state is seen to be favouring business against labour, or industry against finance, especially if it attempts to manage this financial crisis by cutting welfare spending. It will be seen as politically biased, lose popular support and have its legitimacy as representative of the people questioned. This may lead to a motivation crisis, to people questioning why they should work for the 'system' or vote for it. With the spread of monopoly capital, the welfare state and affluence, there is a general decline in people's motivation to work. The work ethic and spur of competition are no longer so strong, whilst the growth of bureaucracy increases people's sense of alienation. Increasingly unable to participate in formal politics, disillusioned with decision-making by faceless bureaucrats and planners, more and more people turn to extra-parliamentary movements such as Women's Liberation or environmental groups as a way of challenging the 'system'.

A full-blown legitimation crisis would threaten the whole state apparatus with disintegration and produce either a radical change in the social structure or a spate of authoritarian repression as the state sought to reassert its authority and control by force. Consider as an example of such a cycle of crises the state of British capitalism in the 1970s and 1980s as it went through a downswing in the business cycle. The economic crisis of low productivity and rising inflation led to the attempts in the 1970s by both Conservative and Labour governments to manage the crisis by state subsidies and wage restraint. These 'irrational' policies led to crises of legitimation and motivation as even Labour's own supporters, the trade unions and working class, went on strike against the 'system' and helped bring down their 'own' government in 1979. The election of Mrs Thatcher has seen an attempt to reassert the power of the state, re-establish the legitimacy of pure capitalism and remotivate the British people by liberating market forces and reviving the nineteenth-century ideologies of self-help and individual enterprise.

Legitimation in late capitalist societies is thus primarily based on ideological control, on the ability of the state and cultural apparatus (media, etc.) to convince the mass of the people that the existing system is just, fair, rational, and so, legitimate. Like Weber, Habermas sees the essence of modern legitimacy – whether in organised capitalist societies or bureaucratic socialist ones – as rationality, the logic of reason and debate. This principle underlies the social, political and ideological structures of modern societies. It is reflected in the spread of bureaucracy, technology and economic planning. Today we judge the rationale of all proposals, decisions and plans in terms of their merits by reasoned discussion and debate. Such logical thought is most clearly reflected in modern science and its techniques of experimentation and constant testing. It is through reason that modern civilisation with all its benefits of mass education, mass democracy and mass prosperity has emerged.

However, like his mentors of the Frankfurt School, Habermas sees rationality today as a distortion of pure reason, as a form of 'instrumental' reason used to promote the capitalist system rather than the needs of mankind at large. Whilst in the past reason has been a progressive force liberating human thought from the tyrannies of myth, superstition and arbitrary power, helping man escape the oppressions of poverty and ill-health, today it is being used to make an inherently irrational system – late capitalism – appear rational, just and legitimate. Science and technology are now being used as instruments for increasing exploitation of both man and nature as a means to promoting the profits of monopoly capital and increasing social control. Through new technologies, workers have been deskilled or eliminated, consumers and voters mass-manipulated and the planet raped and polluted. Modern bureaucracy and technical experts have taken over all forms of planning and decision-making, leaving the individual today feeling trapped, isolated and frustrated in an 'iron cage', powerless against an impersonal system that, whilst apparently rational, is equally faceless and oppressive. Yet the power of science and technology, this new ideology Habermas calls 'technocratic consciousness', seems irresistible and all-pervasive. Who can challenge such apparently progressive forces as automation, nuclear power or the space race? Certainly scientists and technologists rarely do question the ethics or use of biotechnology or new chemicals, rarely consider their value to mankind at large rather than to corporation profits. Rationality today serves the 'system' rather than, as in the past, challenging it; it legitimises and reinforces capitalist domination and so helps perpetuate and reproduce capitalism.

This is how, argues Habermas, modern capitalism has advanced, has overcome its inherent crises, retained its legitimacy and ideological control and subdued both the class struggle and class consciousness. As Michael Pusey (1988) argues, 'Revolution conceived in the classical way after the French and the Russian experience as the forcible seizure of power no longer makes sense in the context of late capitalist society.'

Habermas, however, is far more optimistic than his forefathers in the Frankfurt School. He still believes that pure reason can be liberated to provide the basis for both collapsing capitalism and to create a truly free and rational society. This is because legitimation, when based on irrationality, is ultimately limited. It is limited by:

■ The ability of the state to continue managing crisis situations and the ability of the sub-systems to compensate for each other.
■ The general consensus that holds society together, the normative value systems underlying our legal, political and other social systems that set limits on oppressive behaviour by the state or its agents.
■ The inherent logic of rationality by which, even in the most oppressive social systems, rational debate must occur, and ultimately this will lead to critical reflection and questioning of irrationality. This is especially so in western democracies where public debate, limited though it may be, has to take place as part of our political system. Ultimately Habermas therefore hopes that the 'inherent' irrationality of the capitalist system and 'technocratic consciousness' will come to light, so creating a legitimation crisis which, in turn, will set off crises elsewhere in the system. Further, the spread of post-industrial society will break down traditional social institutions and sources of legitimation (the break-up of local communities and family life) and increase the extent of bureaucratic administration and planning, leaving the masses alienated, rootless and increasingly dependent on a state which can no longer balance their increasing demands for welfare with capital's demand for reduced taxation and state spending. The very forces of instrumental rationality which are at present upholding late capitalism

ultimately contain the seeds of its own destruction and the collapse of its legitimacy. The whole system would collapse in a chain-like reaction, set off by popular discontent and the inner logic of rationality, that would ultimately unmask the underlying irrationality of advanced capitalism and reveal its true nature. According to Habermas, the alternative to this liberation of reason from service to the 'totally administered society' is that we continue on our present course and ultimately destroy ourselves in one of a number of ways, be they nuclear war or global pollution.

THE IDEA IN ACTION

Habermas's concept of legitimation crisis forms part of his most general political sociology and theory of historical materialism. His overall aim has been to try to combine philosophy and sociology as the basis of a revived critical theory based on analysing the process and progress of rationalisation within modern societies. He has sought to revive and reconstruct both critical theory and modern Marxism. In contrast to classical Marxism which emphasised the primacy of the economic substructure in historical materialism (see page 67), Habermas has argued that political and cultural factors do have an independent force, even an inner logic of their own – as highlighted in his thesis of legitimation crisis. Whilst economic factors may have been the determining influence in early capitalism, they alone cannot explain developments in late capitalism where ideological forces are also obviously of considerable importance. Whilst Marx's economism is still preeminent in Habermas's theory of historical materialism, he has also added the ideas of Hegel, Parsons, Freud and, in particular, Weber's analysis of rationality and the development of reason in human history. His ideas have stimulated other colleagues at both the Frankfurt Institute and the Max Planck Institute. Claus Offe, for example, has undertaken research into the corporate power of the state in late capitalism and into the 'achievement principle as a major legitimating principle in advanced capitalist societies'.

Criticisms of Habermas's work, including his concept of legitimation crisis, however, have been as extensive as its praise. They have even been encouraged by Habermas as part of his 'critical' debate.

MARXIST CRITICISMS

Marxist writers criticise his work, like that of the original Frankfurt School, for over-concentrating on modern society, for overemphasising ideological forces and for failing to provide a detailed analysis of historical change and, in particular, of the economic organisation of advanced capitalism. In their view he overemphasises the cultural forces in late capitalism and underestimates the power of an economic crisis alone to bring down capitalism. In particular, they claim he underplays, though does not ignore, the power of class conflict as the key dynamic in social change, emphasising instead the power of reason and the inherent contradictions of the capitalist system. However, though Habermas's concept of legitimation sees class as a latent rather than an active force in modern politics, his thesis does take much better account than traditional Marxism of such new sources of extra-parliamentary political action such as the Peace Movement and Women's Liberation as both protests against the 'system' and calls for a more rational society: 'the new conflicts are not sparked by problems of distribution but concern the grammar of forms of life'.

LACK OF DETAIL

His theory of legitimation crisis fails to outline in detail the mechanisms by which the different sub-systems are interrelated or the means by which, for example, an economic crisis becomes a rationality or legitimation crisis. The very generalised nature of Habermas's analysis, which is deliberate, as a rejection of determinist-type claims to cause and effect, also leaves many readers feeling frustrated because he refuses to predict in detail the 'chain of crisis reaction' by which capitalism will collapse. He hopes for radical change, hopes that critical reflection will release 'repressed traces of reason' but, equally, accepts the ability of the system to continue managing crises and regress deeper into irrationality. He is opposed to social engineering of the type seen in eastern Europe as merely creating a new form of domination and irrationality imposed from above. His ultimate faith is in pure democracy, free communication, critical reflection and rational discourse.

Habermas's political sociology, his thesis of legitimation crisis, his analysis of historical materialism and his theory of communicative action have stimulated extensive debates throughout the social sciences, inspiring major debates on the modern state, the nature of modern communication, modernity and even art. His prime aim is to inspire critical reflection as the mechanism to releasing popular understanding about the true nature of modern society and its underlying irrationality, and so stimulating a rational debate about a more just and free society. As Michael Pusey (1987) points out, 'Scarcely anyone would now challenge [the view that Habermas] is one of the most important figures in German intellectual life today and perhaps the important sociologist since Max Weber.'

SEE ALSO

☐ Alienation
☐ Historical materialism and
☐ Hegemony and
☐ Critical theory as background ideas.

SUGGESTED READING

Pusey M. *Jürgen Habermas*, Tavistock, 1987 – the best short introduction to Habermas's ideas.
Wilby P. 'Habermas and the Language of the Modern State', *New Society*, 22 March 1979

FURTHER READING

Habermas J. *Theory and Practice*, Heinemann, 1963
Habermas J. *Knowledge and Human Interest*, Heinemann, 1968
Habermas J. *Towards a Rational Society*, Heinemann, 1970
Habermas J. *Legitimation Crisis*, Heinemann, 1973
Habermas J. *Communication and the Evolution of Society*, Heinemann, 1979
Habermas J. *The Theory of Communicative Action*, Suhrkamp, Frankfurt, 1982

EXAMINATION QUESTIONS

1 'In politics, the key word is "legitimacy".' Describe what you consider to be the most powerful processes of legitimisation in advanced industrial society and evaluate their effectiveness. (London University June 1987)
2 Using examples, compare and contrast the different ways in which authority is legitimated. (London University January 1987 Paper 1)

21

EDMUND HUSSERL, ALFRED SCHUTZ *and*
PHENOMENOLOGY

THE AUTHORS

Phenomenology is a philosophical theory developed by Edmund Husserl and converted into a sociological perspective by Alfred Schutz.

Edmund Husserl (1959–38) was a German philosopher, born in Prossnitz, Moravia (now part of Czechoslovakia), the son of a prosperous Jewish merchant. He studied at the Universities of Leipzig and Berlin and graduated in mathematics. He was converted to philosophy by the philosopher-psychologist-priest Franz Bretano and the logician Bernard Bolzano. After lecturing at the University of Halle (1887–1901) he was appointed Professor of Philosophy at Göttingen and later at Freiberg University.

The early twentieth century was a critical period in human history, not least with the First World War and the rise of fascism. Such crises of western civilization profoundly affected Husserl and greatly stimulated his philosophical desire to go 'back to basics'. Although baptised a Christian, as a Jew Husserl suffered at the hands of the Nazis, was deprived of honours and recognition in his final years and only the heroic efforts of a Franciscan monk saved his later manuscripts.

Edmund Husserl is undoubtedly one of the most important philosophers of the twentieth century. He not only founded phenomenology but profoundly influenced such key thinkers of this century as Jean-Paul Sartre, Max Scheler and Martin Heidegger, stimulated such schools of thought as existentialism and influenced not only the social sciences but history, the arts and literary criticism.

His key works are:

■ *Logical Investigations* (1901)

Ideas for a Pure Phenomenology and Phenomenological Philosophy (1913)
The Crisis of the European Sciences and Transcendental Phenomenology (1936)

Alfred Schutz (1889–1959) was an Austro-American businessman and social philosopher. He was born in Vienna, studied law and social science at the University of Vienna, developed a close interest in phenomenology and began an intellectual collaboration with Husserl until the threat of the German invasion of Austria forced him to emigrate to America in 1939. Though he became a banker by profession, he continued his studies in social philosophy and took up the post of Professor at the New York School of Social Research in 1952. He introduced Husserl's philosophy of phenomenology to sociology and, by combining it with other interpretative schools of thought, such as G. H. Mead's, developed phenomenological sociology as the leading version of 'interpretative' sociology in the western world in the late 1960s and 1970s. Phenomenological sociology became a major challenge to positivism, to the idea of sociology as a science, and stimulated further interpretative perspectives such as ethnomethodology and Habermas's version of critical theory.

Schutz's key works included:

Collected Papers (1971)
The Phenomenology of the Social World (1972)
The Structures of the Life-World, co-authored with T. Luckman (1974)

THE IDEA

The word phenomenon has two basic meanings:

It is a thing or occurrence (or person) that is slightly unusual, possible extraordinary, the explanation of which is still in doubt.
It is an object of perception, perceived by any of the senses.

The first definition is the scientific, everyday one based on the assumption that the external world actually exists and has a reality of its own from which our senses, especially our eyes, merely pick out facts or objects of particular or extraordinary note, such as the phenomenon of rust eating metal or the phenomenal power of the sun.

The second definition refers to the way that our brain, through our senses, both perceives and makes sense of an external world that may or may not have a reality of its own. This is the basis of phenomenology, the philosophical view that the physical world does not exist as a distinct and objective reality that never changes and is the same to all people, but is a relative world, dependent, as far as human beings are concerned at least, for its existence on interpretation – on the meanings that we humans assign to it. There is, for example, no such thing, according to phenomenology, as a chair or table; these are merely shapes of wood which we have endowed with certain functions and meanings. To grasp this idea more clearly, imagine visiting another society (or even another planet) of which you have no knowledge, and trying to make sense of their way of life.

Whilst objects in the physical world do physically exist, irrespective of human 'labelling' (e.g. trees, mountains), facts in the social world do not. Concepts like crime and love are entirely human creations, entirely dependent on human perception, interpretation and meaning for their existence. There is, for example, no such thing as a crime; it all depends on human interpretation of a particular act in a particular situation (e.g. killing someone may be self-defence, an accident or heroism as well as murder). All human knowledge is, therefore, relative. Equally, society is not a thing out there with an existence of its own as portrayed in positivist analyses (see page 44) but is something we create and recreate in our everyday lives through our routines, interaction and the common assumptions we share with others. The key to such interpretation and communication is language and we learn our particular societies' common assumptions about life through socialisation. The social world is a world known in common with others through lived experience.

Phenomenology, therefore, is the study of human consciousness and of the way people interpret the world they live in. Husserl's aim was to establish a philosophy free of all preconceptions, a philosophy that 'went back to basics', that sought to discover the essence of essences, the very heart of man's 'Life World'. The essence of his own philosophy was the view that to be human at all is essentially to be a genuine human being in a social world guided by reason. His essential aim was to attain ultimate knowledge of everything, reducing everything to primary presuppositions. Phenomenology is not based on one single principle or assertion but seeks to analyse all original experience, to uncover the basic structures of human intentionality, consciousness and life world. The 'rational' methods of deduction and induction, the traditional philosophical tools of analysis alone are not enough. Intuition, too, must be used to analyse and understand all forms of human perception.

Alfred Schutz sought to apply such philosophical ideas to study of the social world. He began by arguing that Max Weber's notion of subjectivity and interpretation was too shallow: it only referred to individual interpretation and meaning, so failing to bring out the inter-subjective nature of the social world, the way that it is a shared and common world, not a series of private and solely personal ones, the heart of which is language, socialisation and, in particular, common sense. Thus, though we all have constantly to interpret and make sense of the world around us, we actually experience it as a given, orderly world which exists out there, independent of any one individual. The basics of such social order are :

■ Common sense – a common stock of knowledge about how to inter-pret and act in our own particular society or social group.
■ Typifications – common ways of classifying objects (house, man) and experiences (hate, nightmare) which build up into 'stocks of know-ledge'.
■ Reciprocity – common assumptions that others see the world in the same way that we do.

All three elements of this intersubjectivity create the apparent order of everyday life. We learn such common sense through socialisation and language, and we adapt, alter our perception of it, as and when necessary. Social order for phenomenologists is thus a 'negotiated' order, a practical framework forming the basis of most people's 'life world' as they seek to go about their daily lives and work. We all have our own individual backgrounds, interests and motivations, our own view of ourselves and the world, but we can only execute them, only live as human beings, by working together, using common meanings and assumptions. When such common assumptions break down, when this underlying consensus collapses, then social confusion and disorder arise, either on a very limited scale as, for example, when you mis-interpret what someone said or did, or on a massive scale when, say, the value of money is no longer commonly agreed (e.g. hyperinflation in Germany in the 1930s).

Schutz's view of the social world was, therefore, a highly inter-pretative one in which social order was a negotiated reality based on common assumptions and interpretations.

The role of the social scientist is that of understanding it in its essence. To do this he must suspend or 'bracket off' his own attitudes, taking nothing for granted but trying to see the world, or a particular social situation, as those involved in it do, because it is they (and their assumptions/interpretations) who are creating it. The researcher must on one hand withdraw from the social world in order to study it objectively and without preconceptions, and yet use his own human consciousness, understanding, and even intuition to make sense of the world as other humans see it. He must, in a sense, act like a stranger, someone coming from outside, anxious to understand how people in society act, feel and see, so that he too can participate fully within their world. The phenomenological researcher is as concerned with people's motives, feelings and imagination, with all forms of sense perception, as he is with actual behaviour and action, if he is to understand not only how people behave, but why. The subjective elements of human behaviour and social life are as important if not more important than the 'objective facts'. Open-mindedness, seeing before thinking, are crucial to phenomenological research if all phenomena, all assumptions in and about the social world are to be revealed and understood in their essence.

Phenomenological analysis, like scientific research, may start with empirical observations, but then seeks to go deeper into the meaning of action, into abstract typifications, into what Husserl called 'eidetic analysis' – seeing through the particular to discover what is essential to a particular phenomenon, be it a social organisation or relationship, developing second-order typifications and ideal types of the sort proposed by Max Weber.

THE IDEA IN ACTION

Phenomenological sociology has had a major influence on mainstream sociology since the 1960s, offering a major challenge to scientific sociology. Rather than developing a sociological school of its own, it has spawned a variety of 'interpretative' approaches such as ethnomethodology, and stimulated interpretative and subjective elements within such existing 'sociologies' as Marxism (e.g. Habermas's interpretation of critical theory).

It challenged 'scientific' sociology on two key fronts :

■ Its view of man and society.
■ Its method of research.

Positivist or scientific sociology tends to portray society as similar to the natural world, as something above and beyond the individual, something with a reality of its own, a world in which the individual is something of a puppet, his behaviour determined largely by external forces. Positivism, therefore, argues that the scientific methods of the natural sciences are as appropriate to understanding the social world as the physical one, since both are essentially of the same nature and governed by similar forces of cause and effect, from which can be discovered laws of nature capable of sustaining predictions about future behaviour. Phenomenologists utterly reject such an analysis. In their view, man is a conscious being, free, independent and rational, capable of constructing and controlling his social world. Man's actions are not externally determined or programmed, but purposeful and motivated. Man is not a puppet.

Human beings are not merely acted upon by social fact or social forces . . . they are constantly shaping and creating their own social worlds in interaction with others [so] special methods are required for the study and understanding of these uniquely human processes. (Morris, 1978)

Thus phenomenologists equally reject scientific method, whatever its claims to objectivity, as totally inappropriate to understanding society or a social situation from within, in terms of the meanings and interpretations of the social actors involved. The sociologist should ideally involve, not detach, himself in order to perceive the social world, its underlying assumptions, culture and typifications as others do. Hence phenomenologists' preference for techniques like participant observation. They equally reject the positivist claim to objectivity as a philosophical impossibility (no human being can totally suspend his own cultural assumptions and frameworks of thought) and a distortion of true reality whereby the social scientist merely imposes his interpretation on a situation, ignoring the views and motives of those involved. Similarly, social facts such as crime or marriage cannot exist, or be studied, as independent things with a reality of their own, but only as social constructs created by human beings to make sense of the world. Phenomenology has put the subjective elements to the forefront of social analysis in the same way that positivism highlighted objectivity.

Inevitably, phenomenology itself has been attacked and criticised, not least by scientific sociology.

■ Its concepts and language such as 'essences' and 'being in itself', are somewhat exotic for Anglo-Saxon tastes, hence the slow acceptance of its ideas in Britain and America.
■ It can be both exciting and tedious – exciting to move from abstract theories to real life, from grand concepts to common sense, but then such analysis can become quite technical, even boring. Conversations,

as we all know, can be extremely stimulating, until someone starts analysing your every word and what you 'really' meant.
■ Its research projects have tended to be small-scale, concerned primarily with small group activity and interaction, and so lack the
sweeping power of grand theory and its attempt to analyse the whole
of society.
■ It has been criticised as highly unscientific, as being little more than
the subjective interpretation of individual sociologists studying a particular social situation. The results of such studies have no basis for
generalising beyond that particular study, offer no basis for constructing laws about society and human behaviour.
■ There is an inherent contradiction in the phenomenological mode of
study, that not only must the observer highlight and explain the
feelings and assumptions of his subjects, but his own, as the study progresses, so that the reader can fully understand the layers of interpretation involved in a particular situation. Not only may this process
become an *ad infinitum* one which can become quite futile, but it
means that ultimately no one can offer an objective and superior
analysis, free of assumptions. If all analysis is no more than interpretation and no interpretation is superior to any other, then why do
sociology?
   Phenomenologists have replied to such criticisms by claiming that
what their research projects might lack in objectivity, they make up for
in terms of validity and quality by being highly accurate and detailed
accounts of what really happens in given social situations. It is this
emphasis on qualitative research, on insight and subjective factors,
which has distinguished phenomenological theory and method from
more scientific sociologies.

SEE ALSO

☐ **Ethnomethodology** and
☐ **Symbolic interactionism** as offshoots of phenomenology.
☐ **Positivism** and
☐ **Structural functionalism** as alternative approaches to sociological analysis
and practice.

SUGGESTED READING

Pivcevic E. *Husserl and Phenomenology*, Hutchinson, 1970

FURTHER READING

Husserl E. *Logical Investigations*, Routledge & Kegan Paul, 1901
Husserl E. *Ideas for a Pure Phenomenology and Phenomenological Philosophy*, Macmillan, 1913
Husserl E. *The Crisis of European Sciences and Transcendental Phenomenology*, North West University Press, 1936
Morris M. B. *An Excursion into Creative Sociology*, Columbia University Press, 1977
Schutz A. *The Phenomenology of the Social World*, Heinemann, 1972
Schutz A. and Luckman T. *The Structures of the Life World*, Heinemann, 1974

EXAMINATION QUESTIONS

1 Interpretivism as a methodology in sociology is based on the assumption that the social world can only be understood as subjective reality. The most common research techniques used by interpretivist sociologists are participant observation and unstructured interviews. Such methods produce qualitative data which enables the researcher to gain insights into how social actors construct their own reality. Criticisms of this methodological approach range from the technical and moral problems of setting up and carrying out the investigation to more fundamental doubts about the validity of the data obtained in this way.
   (a) Briefly define the following terms.
      (i)   subjective
      (ii) qualitative data
      (iii) constructing reality
   (b) Using at least **one** empirical study with which you are familiar, demonstrate how participant observation and/or unstructured interviews can be used in the way indicated in the passage.
   (c) Outline **one** problem involved in setting up or carrying out **either** participant observation **or** unstructured interviews and **one** criticism of the validity of data obtained from this research technique.
   (d) Explain and illustrate how the choice of methodological approach influences the type of results and explanations which sociologists arrive at. (JMB June 1987 Paper 1)
2 We are human and experience human society 'from the inside'. Does this make sociology more convincing than the natural sciences, where an insider view is not possible? (Cambridge Local Examinations Syndicate June 1986)
3 'Sociologists who adopt an interpretative approach emphasise the creativity of human beings; sociologists who adopt a positivist approach stress the passivity of human beings.' Discuss, illustrating your answer by reference to sociological works with which you are familiar. (Oxford Delegacy May 1986)

4 Drawing upon research studies from any area of social life with which you are familiar, compare and contrast the positivist and interpretative approaches to research in sociology. How far do you think it is possible that clear distinctions can be made between positivist and interpretative research methods? (JMB June 1986)

5 Sociologists have often distinguished between theories of social structure and theories of social action. Outline and assess these two approaches to sociological theory. (AEB June 1989 Paper 2)

22

IVAN ILLICH *and*
DESCHOOLING

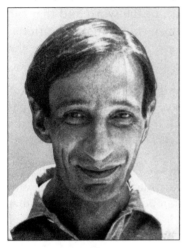

THE AUTHOR

Ivan Illich (1926–   ) was born in Vienna. He studied theology and philosophy at the Gregorian University in Rome and took his doctorate in history at the University of Salzburg. In 1951 he went to the United States where he served as assistant pastor in an Irish-Puerto Rican parish in New York. From 1956 to 1960 he served as Vice-Rector of the Catholic University of Puerto Rica. He co-founded the widely-known and controversial Centre for Intercultural Documentation (CIDOC) in Guernavaca, Mexico. Between 1964 and 1976 he directed research seminars on 'Institutional Alternatives in a Technological Society' with a special focus on Latin America.

The concept of deschooling is part of Illich's broader critique of the power of professionals in advanced industrial societies, of the way the modern citizen is seduced into conformity and an uncritical acceptance of the authority of those in power. His hope is that his radical attacks on the monopoly power of professionals will inspire ordinary people to demand greater freedom of choice, more control over their own lives, health and education and ultimately lead to a 'de-institutionalisation' of modern society.

Illich has written extensively for such journals as the *New York Times, Le Monde, The Guardian, Espirit* and the *New York Review of Books.*

His own publications include:

- *Celebration of Awareness* (1970)
- *Tools for Conviviality* (1973)

Energy and Equity (1974)
Medical Nemesis (1975)
Shadowing Work (1981)
Gender (1983)
and the key work for our present discussion
Deschooling Society (1973)

THE IDEA

Illich's thesis is that schools in advanced industrial societies have failed
to teach people to learn in the broadest sense of the word and that the
only solution to liberating learning is to abolish traditional educational
institutions – to deschool society. Schools are in crisis and so are the
people who attend them:

Schools have lost their unquestioned claim to educational legitimacy. Most
of their critics still demand a painful and radical reform of the school, but
a quickly expanding minority will not stand for anything short of the
prohibition of compulsory attendance and the disqualification of academic
certificates . . .

As attention focuses on the school, however, we can be easily distracted
from a much deeper concern: the manner in which learning is to be viewed.
Will people continue to treat learning as a commodity – a commodity that
could be more efficiently produced and consumed by greater numbers of
people if new institutional arrangements were established? Or shall we set up
only those institutional arrangements that protect the autonomy of the learner
– his private initiative to decide what he will learn and his inalienable right to
learn what he likes rather than what is useful to somebody else? We must
choose between more efficient education of people fit for an increasingly efficient society and a new society in which education ceases to be the task of some
special agency.

For Illich real education involves:

   The acquisition and learning of such specific skills as woodcraft,
typing and foreign languages.
   A broad 'liberating' experience in which the individual explores,
creates and uses his powers of imagination, initiative and judgement to
the full. The individual should learn to think for himself and develop
his talents to the full.

In Illich's view, far from fulfilling such ideas, modern schools are
repressive institutions which indoctrinate pupils, smother their creativity and imagination, induce conformity and passivity. Though schools

claim to be providing a rich educational experience for each and every child, 'a voyage of discovery', their real aim, claims Illich, is to produce mass conformity to the established order. They do this through a 'hidden curriculum' in which the pupil has little or no control over what or how he learns. He is simply told what to learn by an authoritarian teaching regime under which success involves obedience and passive repetition. Pupils are not encouraged to think for themselves, are not allowed to criticise or question what they are being taught or the authority of the teacher, are not encouraged to create or initiate their own ideas but must 'swallow whole' those propounded by the teacher or textbook. Pupils learn to depend on the teacher for knowledge, learn not to question authority and that success depends upon conformity, particularly in the all-important end-of-course examinations that are the passport to the next stage in the education system or rewarding careers. Thus learning is transformed by our school system from being a process of continual and critical evaluation into a packaged commodity; from an end in itself by which the individual learns to think for himself, to a means of acquiring wealth, power and privilege.

The hidden curriculum teaches all children that economically valuable knowledge is the result of professional teaching and that social entitlements depend on the rank achieved in a bureaucratic process. The hidden curriculum transforms the explicit curriculum into a commodity and makes its acquisition the securest form of wealth. Knowledge certificates – unlike property rights, corporate stock, or family inheritance – are free from challenge. They withstand sudden changes of fortune. They convert into guaranteed privilege. That high accumulation of knowledge should convert to high personal consumption might be challenged in North Vietnam or Cuba, but school is universally accepted as the avenue to greater power, to increased legitimacy as a producer, to further learning resources.

But schools do not act in isolation. They are part of the overall social system and in Illich's view far from schools liberating the individual's mind and imagination they are part of the system of social control: 'All over the world schools are organised enterprises designed to reproduce the established order.' They do this by

■ Selecting for each successive level those who have, at earlier stages of the game, proved themselves good risks for the established order.
■ Socialising tomorrow's citizens into mindless mass conformity, deference and an uncritical acceptance of established authority.
■ Teaching pupils to see education as a commodity to be consumed in ever-increasing quantities so preparing them for the mindless consump-

tion of the goods and services propagated by mass advertising and modern industry.

In particular, the child learns that the professional is an expert whose authority must not be questioned. He alone has the knowledge and the power to teach, cure or tell us how to live our life. He alone knows what is best for us and so we unquestioningly place our children's education in the hands of the teachers, our health in the hands of the doctors and futures in the hands of politicians and civil servants. We come to depend on such experts and are indoctrinated into the belief that the only path to human happiness and fulfilment is to consume the ever-increasing quantities of goods pouring from our factories and employ ever-growing armies of professionals and bureaucrats.

Schools are the first and the key stage in this mass conformity. They are equally a key source of alienation in modern society, destroying man's creativity and initiative, skills and independence. Our education system creates a sense of powerlessness, meaninglessness and isolation amongst our young, especially if they fail.

Schools have alienated man from his learning. He does not enjoy going to school. If he is poor, he does not get the reputed benefits; if he does all that is asked of him, he finds his security constantly threatened by more recent graduates; if he is sensitive, he feels deep conflicts between what is and what is supposed to be. He does not trust his own judgement, and even if he resents the judgement of the educators, he is condemned to accept it and to believe that he cannot change reality.

Illich's aim is to smash this myth of the power and authority of the professional, to break this spell of conformity particularly at the key stage of school life. His solution is both simple and radical. It is nothing less than the abolition of our present education system, the 'deschooling of society' as the means to liberating society at large. In place of traditional schools Illich advocates the establishment of 'skill exchanges' and 'learning webs', centres where individuals can learn the skills they wish to acquire from expert instructors and/or come together with others of similar interests to exchange ideas, think out a particular problem and create new initiatives. The key difference here is that learning is active not passive, the result of conscious individual choice and initiative, not the unquestioning acceptance of predetermined and prepackaged knowledge. In this way Illich hopes to liberate human minds, to break the spell of mass consumerism and create a thinking society in which the individual is truly liberated and free to choose his own destiny and form of fulfilment.

THE IDEA IN ACTION

Ivan Illich's concept of deschooling has proved to be one of the most powerful critiques of modern mass education. It challenged the traditional assumptions:

■ That education is always a good thing.
■ That progress depends on getting more and more people into the education system for longer periods of time.
■ That increased spending by governments on education will necessarily produce significant improvements in the economy.
■ That the educational experts – the professional teachers, lecturers, academics, necessarily know what real knowledge is, what is best for children to learn.

Illich's idea stimulated a radical rethinking of schooling in the West and, particularly, in Third World countries. It developed into a 'deschooling movement' in the 1970s in a number of countries and had a major impact on Chinese and Indian education. 'Free schools' sprang up in Britain, America and western Europe as radical alternatives to traditional schools. Pupils choose whether to attend, choose what to learn, and the teachers see their role not as instructors or authoritarian figures but as counsellors encouraging and guiding pupils' understanding and development, not dictating it. UNESCO set up international conferences on the topic of deschooling, accountability in education and alternatives to the traditional systems of mass education. What Illich particularly exposed was the power of the education profession over people's lives and ways of thinking, a power based on their monopoly control of educational knowledge, a power that is part and parcel of the overall structure of power and authority in advanced industrial societies.

His idea, however, also provoked a range of criticisms, not least from the educational profession itself, that his attack was unjustified and his alternatives unworkable. Harry Judge and Chanan and Gilchrist argued that most primary education in England and Wales is educationally sound. It is in the secondary level that the crisis exists and the aim should be to reform and improve secondary schools, not abolish them. Secondly, how exactly were Illich's skill centres and 'learning webs' to work; who was to run and fund them and would not they too need organisation and so face the very dangers of bureaucracy, authority and control from the top which Illich was trying to avoid. Thirdly, are teachers really that powerful? Do they really have such an influence over children's learning and futures and such an impact on society at large? Are they just middlemen in the overall structure of power and authority, themselves subject to instructions and control from above?

It is the broader structure of power, of which schools are only a part, that lay behind critiques of Illich by Bowles and Gintis (1976) and Christopher Jencks (1973). Whilst sympathetic to much of Illich's argument, Bowles and Gintis, using a Marxist analysis, believe that he made a fundamental error in blaming schools for all modern society's ills. Rather, in their view, the root cause is the economy. The education system only reflects the inequalities, oppression and alienation created by advanced capitalism and its class system. Only a class revolution can truly liberate the mass of people, not the abolition of our schools and colleges. Jencks was equally pessimistic about reforms of the school system, however radical, having any significant impact on society at large: 'None of the evidence we have reviewed suggests that school reform can be expected to bring about significant social changes outside the schools.'

By the 1980s most of the 'free schools' had died out. They tended to take in only the 'dropouts' from mainstream schools and suffered from parental indifference and severe financial problems. As Professor Ian Lister explained in an introduction to Illich's recent version of *Deschooling Society*:

Today educational reformers of all varieties have gone quiet. The spate of radical literature which was produced by Penguin Education has come to an end. The curriculum projects are over. Even traditional reform programmes are held up for lack of funds. The educational boom, of which they were all part, is over.

Nevertheless, Ivan Illich's concept of deschooling has had, and continues to have, a profound influence and world-wide impact on educational thinking about the structure and functioning of schools and on the sociology of education's ideas about the power of knowledge and the power of the professions. Could it be that his ideas even influenced the present Conservative Government's policies of increasing parental power in schools and making teachers more accountable?

SUGGESTED READING

Illich I. *Deschooling Society*, Penguin, 1973
Illich I. *Limits to Medicine*, Penguin, 1977 – densely packed with facts and figures but worth the effort.
Lund P. *Ivan Illich and His Antics*, SLO, 1978

FURTHER READING

Bowles S. and Gintis H. *Schooling in Capitalist America*, Routledge & Kegan Paul, 1976
Illich I. *Celebration of Awareness*, Calder & Boyars, 1970
Illich I. *Tools for Conviviality*, Calder & Boyars, 1973
Illich I. *Medical Nemisis*, Calder & Boyan, 1975
Illich I. *Disabling Professions*, M. Boyars, 1977
Illich I. *Shadowing Work*, M. Boyars, 1981
Illich I. *Gender*, M. Boyars, 1983
Jencks C. *Inequality*, Penguin, 1973

23

CLARK KERR ET AL *and*
CONVERGENCE THESIS

THE AUTHORS

Though the convergence thesis was a collaborative effort Clark Kerr is generally considered the main author. Clark Kerr (1911–   ) was born in Stoney Creek, Pennsylvania. He was educated at Swarthmore College, Stanford University and the University of California, collecting during his academic career an additional thirty-two honorary degrees. He taught and undertook research at Antioch College and the Universities of California and Stanford. Between 1940 and 1945 he was Associate Professor at the University of Washington and over the next thirty years rose from Director of Industrial Relations to University Chancellor, President and Professor of Industrial Relations at the University of California. Between 1974 and 1979 Kerr served as Chairman of the Carnegie Council of Policy Studies in Higher Education. In addition he has been involved in a wide variety of advisory posts in industrial relations including the National War Labor Board, the Waterfronts Employers, the International Longshoremen's and Warehousemen's Union, the Presidential Commissions on Intergovernment Relations and on National Goals and a wide variety of educational commissions. He has acted as an arbitrator in such fields as the newspaper, aircraft, canning and oil industries and lectured as far afield as Britain, Ghana and Kenya.

Clark Kerr's major publications include:

- *Unions, Management and the Public* (with E. Wright) (1962)
- *Labour and Management in Industrial Society* (1964)
- *Marshall, Marx and Modern Times* (1969)
- *Labour Markets and Wage Determination* (1977)
- *Education and Industrial Development* (1979)
- *The Future of Industrial Society* (1983)
- *Industrialism and Industrial Man* (with Dunlop, Harbison and Myers) (1962)

Clark Kerr and his colleagues J. T. Dunlop, F. H. Harbison and C. A. Myers were not the only proponents of the convergence thesis – Daniel Bell, Ralf Dahrendorf and variety of other writers have proposed similar theses, but, in their book *Industrialism and Industrial Man* (1962) they outlined one of the major and most detailed versions of this key idea.

THE IDEA

As industrialisation has spread and become the dominant feature of societies throughout the world so a number of writers have argued that though there are still very great differences economically, politically and socially between the First and the Third Worlds, between East and West, ultimately all societies will become the same. They will all converge into one single, uniform type of mass industrial society with similar economic, political and social systems. In this way, prophesy such writers, international differences and inequalities will be eliminated and a more peaceful and stable world of plenty, of unity and brotherhood will evolve. Whilst writers like Herbert Spencer pointed to the underlying laws of social evolution and Marx and Rostow to stages of economic progress, what Clark Kerr and his colleagues identified as the driving force of industrial development was the 'internal logic of industrialism'. And the prime dynamism behind such industrial convergence was, in their view, technology. As advanced industrial societies were inevitably forced to compete for and use the latest technology so, inevitably, they had to adapt their economic, social and political structures into increasingly similar patterns. 'The same technology calls for the same occupational structure around the world – in steel, in textiles, in air transport' (C. Kerr *et al.*, 1962). Equally, modern industry, whether in the capitalist West or communist East, will require similar types of worker with similar skills, qualifications and reward structures. Thus, as the range of occupations and pay systems become increasingly similar, so too the stratification systems of capitalist and communist societies will converge.

To illustrate their thesis Kerr *et al.* chose, as the basis of their comparison, two of today's apparently most 'divergent' societies, America and Russia. They sought to show that though the British Industrial Revolution generated a wide variety of industrial societies from the 'free market' model of the USA and the mixed economies of Britain and western Europe to the centrally planned systems of the USSR and China, all industrial societies have certain key features in common.

■ They all need an ever increasingly skilled labour force to cope with the demands of complex machinery and automation. Such a labour force will inevitably become increasingly differentiated by occupation and levels of skill and by the resultant differences in pay, hours, conditions and status.

■ To produce such variation in occupation, industrial societies will have to be both highly mobile and meritocratic. To recruit personnel with the necessary skills, class and social differences will have to be eliminated, appointments will have to be on merit and ability, not as in the past by ascription, and workers will have to move between jobs and from one area to another. Industrial societies will thus become more open and more equal.

■ The education system will have a central role in producing such a workforce, in transmitting the necessary skills, knowledge and attitudes required for advanced industrial work, in raising the general level of numeracy and literacy in the population at large whilst producing specialist skills in the fields of management, technology and the professions.

■ With the growth in industry, society will become more complex, cities will grow, mass communication and transport will become more important. Governments will have to take more responsibility for planning and controlling large scale industrialisation.

■ As industrialism progresses so cultural differences between countries will decline. A consensus or agreement on social values and norms will evolve as all industrial societies increasingly succumb to the common values of science and technology, of change and progress, of mass media and education, of competition, materialism and the work ethic.

As industrialism spreads world-wide and advanced industrial societies become increasingly alike so, claimed the convergence thesis, world conflict would decrease. The lifestyle and culture at present evident in the West would soon become typical all over the industrial world, be it in Japan, Russia or Latin America.

THE IDEA IN ACTION

The convergence thesis is a very optimistic vision of the future of the industrial world. It is very American in its aspirations and a typical product of the hope and idealism of the early 1960s. It is a functionalist idea of a gradual evolution towards one common, stable and peaceful world society and there is much evidence in support of its claims. Modern America, Russia and western Europe do have much in common. They are increasingly using (and exchanging) similar technology, and parts of their social and political systems also seem to be converging as seen in the western shift to greater economic planning and the development within communist countries of market forces and consumerism. And the newly industrialising countries of South Korea, Hong Kong and Singapore seem to be shedding their old cultural traditions as they industrialise and westernise.

However, such similarities and elements of convergence are more superficial than real, and detailed examinations of this thesis have revealed significant weaknesses in both its theory and in its claim that convergence is inevitable and controlled by some 'internal' technological logic:

■ It is too vague and imprecise in its concepts and definitions. Whilst it is relatively easy to find general similarities in all industrial societies – they all use large-scale factory systems, an extensive division of labour and are increasingly urbanised and consumer-orientated – it is equally easy to find significant differences. Simply compare the way 'democracy' works in Britain and Poland, France and South Korea.

■ Many of Kerr *et al.*'s claims about the key features of industrial societies are not necessarily true. Though advanced societies are more open and meritocratic than traditional ones, ascription and kin networks are still strong influences in ensuring that sons follow their fathers into occupations of a similar social status and power. Similarly, whilst advanced industrial societies may appear to be increasingly egalitarian, the reality is more that social divisions still exist, but are hidden by a general rise in the standards of living of all. The depression of the 1970s and 1980s has clearly revealed that social inequalities are as great as ever, with recent government figures showing that in 1986 16 million people in Britain lived in poverty, nearly 4 million were unemployed and that the North and South of England were almost worlds apart in terms of living standards, health and housing. Similarly, far from inequalities being eliminated in communist countries, social differences are alive and well and, according to Mervyn Matthews (1978), 'actively promoted' by political and bureaucratic élites anxious to preserve their power and privilege. Finally, as John Goldthorpe's study of modern Britain (1968) showed, social mobility, especially long-range, is not as great and unimpeded as convergence theorists would lead us to expect.

■ The major criticism, though, is of the thesis's determinism, especially its claim that industrialism and technology are the overwhelming forces determining the shape and direction of all industrial societies, making them all converge whatever their present political, social and economic make-up. Rather, as Goldthorpe (1984) and Parkin (1972), argue a variety of factors influence social development. In the West market forces largely determine the occupational structure, whereas in the USSR the Communist Party controls the distribution of wealth and power. Though very similar in economic structure (and technology) to the rest of western Europe, the Swedish government and people have decided to adopt a welfare state and tax system that redistributes wealth and opportunity more equally than such other capitalist societies as Britain and America. In the Third World developing nations are deliberately choosing a variety of alternative paths to industrialisation. Some, like South Korea, have chosen the free-market model of the West; others, like Cuba and Nicaragua, the centrally-planned models of communist Russia and China. Such decisions are not inevitable nor determined by technology but are essentially political choices influenced by historical links with the West or East, the possibilities of foreign aid and technology, and the present state of play between the superpowers. The balance of power between capitalism and communism is as great an influence on industrial development as any logic of industrialism, be it technology or any other single force. Rather, most writers conclude that the differences between industrial societies are as great as the similarities, that a multitude of interacting factors shape a society's direction. Though their own analysis makes them sympathetic to aspects of the convergence thesis, especially that all societies will eventually evolve into one prime type (communist), Marxists writers too generally reject this idea because in their view the fundamental difference between capitalist and communist societies lies in the ownership of the means of production and this will only be eliminated when private ownership is abolished in the West.

Thus by the 1970s and 1980s the convergence thesis seemed to be academically dead and buried. Certainly its claims that all societies industrialise in the same way, or at least emerge in a similar shape, and that technology is the driving force or logic behind modern industrialisation are no longer widely accepted. However, as Raymond Aron (1967) has argued, if used with care this search for industrial and social similarities or differences can be a valuable tool in comparative research, highlighting points of both convergence and divergence, and in showing that, far from living in isolated individual societies we are all increasingly part of a world economic system. As to the idea or hope that convergence will bring world peace, Aron argues that the two issues are separate and distinct:

In the end, the only true wars are between brothers. If the Soviet and American societies do resemble each other tomorrow, it would be wrong to imagine that they will love each other.

SEE ALSO

☐ Post-industrial society

SUGGESTED READING

Kerr C. *et al. Industrialism and Industrial Man*, Heinemann, 1962
Scase R. 'How Do Societies Compare?', *Social Studies Review*, Vol 4 No 4, March 1989

FURTHER READING

Aron R. *Eighteen Lectures on Industrial Society*, Weidenfeld & Nicolson, 1967
Goldthorpe J.H. *Social Mobility and Class Structure in Modern Britain*, Clarendon Press, 1980
Kerr C. *et al. Unions, Management and the Public*, Heinemann, 1962
Kerr C. *et al. Labour and Management in Industrial Society*, Anchor Books, 1964
Kerr C. *et al. Marshall, Marx and Modern Times*, Harvard University Press, 1969
Kerr C. *et al. The Future of Industrial Society: Convergence and Continued Diversity*, Harvard University Press, 1983
Matthews M. *Privilege in the Soviet Union*, Allen & Unwin, 1978

EXAMINATION QUESTIONS

1 Is there evidence to suggest that capitalist and communist societies display similar patterns of inequality? (Cambridge Local Examinations Syndicate June 1987)
2 Do capitalist and communist societies share a common stratification system? (Cambridge Local Examinations Syndicate June 1986)

24

THOMAS S. KUHN *and*

PARADIGMS

THE AUTHOR

Thomas Kuhn (1922–   ) was born in Cincinatti, Ohio, and, although he originally graduated as a physicist at Harvard University, under the influence of James Conant he became increasingly interested in the history of science. Thus he moved from research work in radio waves to a professorship in general education and the history of science at University of California at Berkeley in 1961. From there he went on to Princeton and he is now Professor of Philosophy and the History of Science at Massachusetts Institute of Technology. He has received a number of academic awards, has sat on such prestigious bodies as the American Social Science Research Council.

His publications include:

- ■ *The Copernican Revolution* (1957)
- ■ *The Essential Tension* (1977)
- ■ *Black Body Theory and the Quantum Discontinuity* (1978)

His key work though, the one that made his name and established the concept of paradigms, is *The Structure of Scientific Revolutions* (1962) and its second edition (1970). His main aim has been to explore the divergence between the idealised accounts of science produced by philosophers and the reality of actual scientific research.

THE IDEA

The popular image of science rests on three key features:

■ That the natural scientist is the 'explorer of nature' committed solely to the pursuit of truth and the discovery of facts.
■ That the essence of scientific method is objectivity, open-mindedness and the critical analysis of all facts and theories.
■ That the growth of scientific knowledge is a slow, gradual process by which facts are piled upon facts so increasing our understanding of nature and the forces governing it.

It is these features that have distinguished science from other academic disciplines, this image that has inspired public admiration and awe, this approach that has uncovered so many secrets of the universe, sent men to the moon, created test-tube babies and split the atom. It was this image that Kuhn's concept of paradigms fundamentally challenged and so inevitably caused a storm of controversy.

Kuhn argued that, far from scientific advances being gradual and cumulative, the history of science is in fact one of 'revolutions' in thought in which traditional theories and practices are suddenly overturned and discarded as a new paradigm or supertheory emerges which takes over control of a particular scientific community and leads its research in a totally new direction with a totally new view of what the natural world looks like. Moreover, far from being open-minded and objective, scientists are in Kuhn's view heavily committed to the particular paradigm that underlies their field of science, be it physics, chemistry, biology or whatever.

Kuhn defined paradigms as 'universally recognised scientific achievements that for a time provide model problems and solutions to a community of practitioners'. A paradigm is a unified and coherent framework, a way of thinking that a particular field of science has about the universe and the way it works. It guides scientists towards certain problems and provides many solutions, it governs their research programmes and is increasingly reinforced by the theories that develop from it. It is like a puzzle. It sets out the rules of the game, poses the challenges for each new generation of scientists and the aim is to solve the problems it poses and to discover the missing pieces required to complete its picture of nature. It sets the standards against which new discoveries will be acclaimed or rejected. It is the accepted view of what constitutes science in a particular discipline and the members of each scientific community are so committed to it, so take it for granted, that it is rarely questioned or criticised. Modern examples of paradigms would be the dominance of Einstein's theory of relativity in physics or Darwin's theory of evolution in biology. New generations of young scientists are socialised into the paradigm's underlying theory and research methods by their teachers and their textbooks. They are taught only the paradigm's principles and theories and rarely exposed to alternative ones. They gain entry to the 'scientific community' by producing the expected solutions in their experiments, passing examinations set by professors steeped in the paradigm's principles and setting up research projects directed at the paradigm's problems. The picture Kuhn therefore presents of modern science is of a series of tight-knit academic communities each based on a rather closed, even dogmatic, view of reality from which alternative visions are rigorously excluded and in which the standard of judgement is not objective reality but the subjective evaluation of one's peers.

Kuhn divided the development of science into three main stages:

■ Pre-paradigm – a state in which there is no general consensus or agreed theoretical framework within a particular discipline but a wide variety of competing theories as to the nature of their subject matter, appropriate research methodology and the types of problems that require solutions.

■ Normal science – the mature stage at which a particular scientific community agrees to unite behind a particular paradigm, its achievements and its guidelines as to research. The general aim is to fill in the puzzle and 'mop up', rather than to innovate. Though anomalies in the paradigm do arise they are either forced into the existing framework or the scientist involved is blamed as incompetent.

■ Paradigm revolution – however, in time, as the anomalies grow, as more and more questions arise that the dominant paradigm cannot answer and new phenomena are discovered that it cannot explain, so a crisis develops in the discipline to the point where even its 'leading lights' feel uneasy. There follows a period of hectic debate about fundamentals and a sudden willingness to try anything which is solved either by a new development in the existing paradigm or the emergence of a new paradigm with a new view of nature and a new puzzle to solve. During this revolutionary stage the discipline tends to divide into traditionalists and radicals and a battle for power and allegiance develops. This takes place at two levels: the theoretical and the political. Gradually, more and more of the scientific community are won over to the new paradigm, not by reason – because initially it lacks substantial proof and cannot by definition be tested by the old methods – but by 'conversion', a leap of faith, what Kuhn calls a '*Gestalt* shift', a sudden vision of the new wonders offered by the new paradigm – 'Lavoisier . . . saw oxygen where Priestly had seen dephlogistated air and where others had seen nothing at all' – and, once converted, not only is it impossible to revert back to the old view of nature, but it is impossible to hold, simultaneously, two paradigm visions because people holding different theories 'see different things and they see them in different relations to one another'. After a paradigm revolution scientists simply see and so respond to a different world. Such incompatibility of paradigms Kuhn called 'incommensurability'.

As conversions to the new truth spread, as evidence and research experiments in its favour grow, so too, in time, the older traditional professors of the discipline will have to give way to the new young converts eager for power and ambitious for authority. Once in power they will now preach the new orthodoxy, select the research projects and teams, rewrite the textbooks and set the exams. As the dust settles and the new paradigm gains general acceptance so a further phase of normal science is set in motion as a new generation of scientists explores the fresh challenges and novel problems posed by the new framework, until that too reaches its limits. As Max Planck remarked:

a new scientific truth does not triumph by convincing its opponents and making them see the light, but rather because its opponents eventually die, and a new generation grows up that is familiar with it. (Quoted in Kuhn, 1970)

As major examples of scientific revolutions, Kuhn cites the developments associated with the names of Copernicus, Newton, Lavoisier and Einstein, each of which involved the overthrow and rejection by the scientific community of one time-honoured theory for another, each of which produced a shift in the problems available for scrutiny and the standards by which their solutions were to be judged, each of which transformed the scientific imagination in such a way as to transform the world within which scientific work was done.

THE IDEA IN ACTION

Kuhn's idea of paradigms revolutionised our understanding of science and scientific knowledge. It inspired a wealth of detailed studies of major scientific advances and has been a major contribution to both the sociology of science and the sociology of knowledge. It also generated a storm of controversy and a major debate between Kuhn and Sir

Karl Popper, because it appeared to challenge the very foundation of modern science. In the second edition of his book (1970) Kuhn sought to reply to his critics but, in doing so, he so modified much of his original thesis that many writers now distinguish between the early and the later Kuhn.

The main criticisms of Kuhn's idea (and his responses) can be listed as follows:

■ That his key concepts were too vague to be workable. One writer counted twenty-two versions of the term paradigm in Kuhn's original work and though Kuhn (1970) tried to define this term more precisely, he also argued that it be dropped in favour of the term 'disciplinary matrix'. The concept of scientific community proved equally elusive with Kuhn referring both to the whole scientific community and to particular sub-disciplines, some with as few as twenty-five members. Similarly it proved difficult to distinguish a full-blown scientific revolution from a simple theoretical advance. Kuhn's answer was that this could only be done by more detailed studies of key advances and that ultimately it was for the scientific community involved to assess how 'revolutionary' an impact a new theory had on their discipline. He even conceded the possibility of micro-revolutions.

It was problems of definition like these that have made it so difficult to apply his concept to other academic fields. Whilst, for example, in his early work, Kuhn seems to describe the social sciences as being at a pre-paradigm stage, his later definition of scientific community makes sociology sound like a mature science.

■ That Kuhn's concept of 'incommensurability' made independent evaluations of alternative theories impossible and so left as the only standard of judgement the subjective evaluations of the scientific community. For critics such as Sir Karl Popper such a standard reduced scientific evaluation to 'mob psychology' and replaced the power of logic with the rule of power, so fundamentally challenging the authority of modern science. Though Kuhn later accepted the idea of 'partial communication' between paradigms and that standards do exist in science, he continued to argue that ultimately a scientific community is won over to a new paradigm not by proof but by persuasion, by experiencing and using its theoretical framework and vision of reality.
■ That Kuhn's concept of paradigms denied the possibility of objective knowledge because, according to his thesis, all knowledge, all understanding of nature depends on the paradigm through which it

is viewed. No fact speaks for itself. It depends for its discovery and existence on the meaning given to it by the paradigm involved. All knowledge, therefore, must be partial knowledge and absolute, total knowledge is impossible. Far from compromising on this relativist view of knowledge the later Kuhn developed it by arguing that knowledge depends not only on the paradigm used but the language involved – and we have no culture-free language to communicate in.

Despite such criticisms Kuhn's idea of scientific paradigms has proved a major contribution to our understanding of science and the sociology of knowledge. Moreover, far from trying to undermine the achievements of modern science he was simply trying to describe how they actually occur rather than how scientists claimed they appeared. As he argued, it is this very unity of approach, this paradigm consensus, that has enabled science to advance so rapidly whilst other disciplines have stagnated. Moreover, behind this scientific commitment to one paradigm also lies the scientists' desire to be original, to discover that earth-shattering new theory, and it is this tension between preservation and innovation that lies at the heart of science's monumental progress today.

SEE ALSO

☐ **Sociology of science** as an earlier functionalist analysis of the world of science.
☐ **Falsification** as the basis of an ongoing debate between these two philosophers of science and knowledge, Popper and Kuhn.

SUGGESTED READING

Barnes B. *T.S. Kuhn and the Social Sciences*, Macmillan, 1982 – an overview of Kuhn's work and contribution to social science

FURTHER READING

Kuhn T.S. *The Copernican Revolution*, Harvard University Press, 1957
Kuhn T.S. *The Structure of Scientific Revolutions*, Chicago University Press, 1962; 2nd ed. 1970
Kuhn T.S. *The Essential Tension*, Chicago University Press, 1977
Kuhn T.S. *Black Body Theory and the Quantum Discontinuity*, OUP, 1978

EXAMINATION QUESTIONS

1 'Knowledge is socially constructed and therefore varies from place to place and time to time.' Explain and discuss. (AEB June 1988 Paper 2)
2 With reference to sociology and at least one other social science examine the extent to which social science disciplines have their own bodies of theory, techniques of enquiry and specialised subject matter. (JMB June 1987)
3 'Once knowledge is seen as a social product, it is difficult to avoid a position of total relativism.' Explain and discuss this statement. (AEB Nov 1984)

25

OSCAR LEWIS *and*
THE CULTURE OF POVERTY

THE AUTHOR

Oscar Lewis (1914–70) was born in New York City and was educated at City College, New York, and Columbia University. He was Professor of Anthropology at the University of Illinois from 1948 onwards. He was field representative in Latin America for the US National Indian Institute (1943–4), consultant anthropologist for the Ford Foundation in India (1952–4) and from his research into the lives of peasants in Asia, Mexico and Cuba, he produced studies on village life in Northern India, *Five Families* (1959), *Children of Sanchez* (1964), *La Vida* (1968) and the series of oral histories of Cuban peasants he and his wife were working on when he died in December 1970 – *Four Men, Four Women and Neighbours* (1977).

THE IDEA

From his studies of both the urban and the rural poor in Puerto Rico and Mexico in the 1950s, Oscar Lewis developed the thesis that the poor live amid a (sub)-culture of poverty, one that not only keeps them apart from the rest of society but one which in many ways keeps them 'trapped' in poverty. Segregated into rural villages, shanty towns or inner cities, the poor adapt to their problems and frustrations and isolation by developing their own distinct set of attitudes, values and behaviour, their own 'design for living' in an unequal society. This sub-culture is characterised by a general sense of social disorganisation:

■ At the individual level there is a

strong feeling of marginality, of helplessness, of dependence and inferiority, a strong present time orientation with relatively little ability to defer gratification, a sense of resignation and fatalism. (Lewis, 1959)

■ At an economic level there is unemployment, underemployment and low wages,

a miscellany of unskilled occupations, child labour, the absence of savings, a chronic shortage of cash, the absence of food reserves in the home, the pattern of frequent buying of small quantities of food many times a day as the need arises, the pawning of personal goods, borrowing from local money lenders at usurious rates of interest, spontaneous informal credit devices organised by neighbours, and the use of second-hand clothing and furniture. (Lewis, 1959)

■ At the family level amid crowded quarters and a lack of privacy there is:

gregariousness, a high incidence of alcoholism, frequent resort to violence in the settlement of quarrels, frequent use of physical violence in the training of children, wife beating, early initiation into sex, free unions or consensual marriages, a relatively high incidence of the abandonment of mothers and children . . ., a belief in male superiority and a corresponding martyr complex among women. (Lewis, 1959)

■ At the community level there is a 'lack of effective participation and integration in the major institutions of the large society'. Hence the poor's lack of organisation and political 'clout'.

Such a sub-culture is not only a reaction of the poor to their marginal position in society but it is internalised and passed on to the next generation.

By the time slum children are aged 6 or 7 they have usually absorbed the basic valves and attitudes of their sub-culture and are not psychologically geared to take full 'advantage of changing conditions' or increased 'opportunities which may occur in their life time'. (Lewis, 1968)

Thus the culture of poverty helps perpetuate poverty, the poor help keep themselves poor; their fatalism creates a self-fulfilling prophecy which prevents them breaking out of poverty even with 'outside' help. The sub-culture cannot be eliminated simply by changes in 'the structure of the larger class society' (Lewis, 1969).

THE IDEA IN ACTION

The concept of the culture of poverty had a major impact both on the theories of poverty and on the policies of governments devised to tackle poverty in the 1960s, especially when blended with the idea of a cycle of poverty, because it provided a crucial explanation of how the 'cycle' was perpetuated. In his key analysis of the American poor, *The Other America* (1963), for example, Michael Harrington talks of 'a language' and a 'psychology of the poor'. This thesis underlay both the American 'War on Poverty' in the 1960s and the variety of British poverty programmes during this era of affluence. Billions of dollars were poured into the American ghettoes through programmes such as the Job Corps, Neighbourhood Youth Corps and especially Headstart, with the overall aim of breaking the cycle of poverty by breaking this sub-culture of fatalism and disorganisation. Teams of youth workers and teachers were sent in to revive 'community' spirits and activity, to teach the poor how to help themselves and, in particular, to resocialise the young back into mainstream values, encouraging them to compete for the American Dream and through education find a pathway out of the ghetto. Such a 'cultural' approach of identifying poor areas and sending 'missionaries' in to convert the poor back to the ideals of community action and individual self-help also lay behind such British programmes as the Educational Priority Areas and in particular the Community Development Project, albeit with less political backing and a lot less money involved!

However by the 1970s both the thesis of a culture of poverty and the poverty programmes based on it were coming under increasing attack:

■ Lewis's studies of the poor had concentrated almost wholly on individuals and their families so ignoring the wider structure of society at large.

■ Researchers amongst the poor in both Third World and advanced societies began to question the idea that the poor everywhere displayed such fatalism and disorganisation and/or that the attitudes of the poor were distinctly different from the rest of society. Ken Little in West Africa and William Margin in South America, for example, found thriving and highly organised 'community' life in the slums and shanty towns of the Third World. They found that though the poor were physically cut off from society at large and did not have the money to participate in its lifestyle, nevertheless they generally hoped to eventually. Much of the apparent 'disorganisation' in these slum areas was more a reflection of the middle-class bias of western researchers who failed to see the sense of community that lay beneath the surface.

■ Generally the poverty programmes of the 1960s failed. Much of the money and effort failed to get through to the poor, the extent of poverty in the 1970s generally increased as the depression grew and, far from breaking the culture of poverty, such failure only reinforced it. Both the community workers and researchers involved were left disillusioned with this thesis and many turned to more radical analyses, in particular those of Marxist writers.

Radical and Marxist writers criticised the culture of poverty thesis on two key levels:

■ That it was a false analysis of the causes of poverty. It tends to explain the reaction of the poor to living in poverty – it does not explain what caused poverty in the first place. Further it tends to 'blame the victim', to blame the poor for keeping themselves in poverty by their attitudes and apathy. Thus it diverted attention from the 'real' causes: the structure of society and the distribution of wealth. In both the early and advanced stages of capitalism there is a need for the poor – to provide a pool of cheap and unskilled labour to do society's 'dirty work', to motivate and discipline the better-off, to maintain high profits – and by definition there is a grossly unequal distribution of wealth. A real attack on poverty they argue, would require a 'war on wealth' – a massive redistribution of wealth and power and a fundamental shift in the ownership of the means of production from private hands to public ownership. The poor are therefore kept poor by the power of the rich and stay poor, not through their own way of life, but by the culture of capitalism which perpetuates such inequality. Such an analysis switches attention from the poor, from the attitudes of individuals, to the structure of power and attitudes of the well-off.

■ That it was used by western governments as a convenient ideological device for disguising poverty rather than tackling it. Whilst appearing to do something about poverty, the programmes of the 1960s in fact were designed not only to divert attention from inequality and make it appear that 'capitalism cared' (but at a very low cost), but primarily to keep the poor under control.

After the Race Riots in America in the 1960s, officials really were scared that the cities would explode and a 'class war' break out. The culture of poverty thesis, therefore, was used as an excuse for official intervention in poor areas under the guise of trying to help. The real aim of the war of poverty therefore was a 'war on the poor', invading their communities with social workers rather than the police, drawing the 'sting' out of their grievances by appearing to do something and yet drawing off the ablest and most articulate leaders of the poor by offers of jobs and better education. Ironically, it was these community workers, especially on the British Community Development Project, who became the most radical critics of the inadequacy of those official programmes.

Such sweeping criticisms of Lewis's thesis, especially as 'a tool of the capitalist class' are, however, somewhat unfair and more a reflection of the way his ideas were distorted than of what he originally said (Lewis, 1968).

Secondly, his own analysis was, in fact, quite radical and dealt with poverty in 'developing' not developed countries. He pointed not only to the attitudes of the poor but the structure of society, arguing that the culture of poverty is itself 'both an adaptation and reaction of the poor to their marginal position in a class-stratified, highly individuated capitalistic society'. He drew attention not only to the apathy of the poor but also their revolutionary potential:

The poor have a critical attitude towards the basic institutions of the dominant classes, hatred of the police, mistrust of government and those in high position, and a cynicism which extends even to the church. This gives the culture of poverty a high potential for protest and for being used, in political movements aimed against the existing social order. (Lewis, 1968)

My rough guess would be that only about 20% of the population below the poverty line . . . in the United States have characteristics which would justify classifying their way of life as that of a culture of poverty. (Lewis, 1968)

Finally, far from supporting the American 'War on Poverty', Lewis commented:

I can testify that most of them [officials and politicians] had only the vaguest conception of the difference between poverty and the sub-culture of poverty. (Lewis, 1969)

As Charles Valentine has argued:

the idea of a poverty culture appealed to many powerful people who appropriated and developed it for their own purposes, using it to justify a series of pernicious policies . . . for purposes which have nothing in common with his [Lewis's] aims. (Valentine, 1969)

Whatever the truth of such claims and counter-claims, the culture of poverty has proved a very powerful and influential thesis and one that, like all 'key ideas', has stimulated new insights and fresh approaches to one of the world's most pressing and enduring of problems.

SEE ALSO

☐ Labelling
☐ Self-fulfilling prophecy

SUGGESTED READING

Lewis O. *La Vida*, Secker & Warburg, 1968
Lewis O. *Children of Sanchez*, Penguin, 1964
Community Development Project, *Building the Ghetto*, CDP Interproject Editorial Team, 1977 – an excellent example of what happened in Britain when politicians and social workers tried to apply this concept to the inner cities of the 1970s through the Community Development Projects.

FURTHER READING

Harrington M. *The Other America: Poverty in the USA*, Penguin, 1963
Lewis O. *Life in a Mexican Village: Tepotzlan Restudied*, University of Illinois Press, 1951
Lewis O. *Five Families: Mexican Case Studies in the Culture of Poverty*, Basic Books, 1959
Lewis O. *Four Men, Four Women and Neighbours*, University of Illinois Press, 1977
Lewis O. 'C.A. Book Review The Children of Sanchez,Pedro Martinez and La Vida'. *Current Anthropology* Vol 8 No 5 Dec, 1967
Lewis O. 'C.A. Book Review Culture and Poverty: Critique and Counter Proposals', *Current Anthropology* Vol 10 No 2–3 April–June 1969
Valentine C. 'C.A. Book Review Culture and Poverty: Critique and Counter Proposals' *Current Anthropology* Vol 10 No 2–3 April–June 1969

EXAMINATION QUESTIONS

1 'Despite attempts to eliminate poverty in industrial societies, it persists and has recently increased.' Examine this view. (AEB June 1988)

2 'Sociological explanations of poverty have increasingly focused on structured social inequality rather than on the cultural characteristics of the poor.' Explain and discuss with reference to any one society. (AEB June 1985)

3 Outline the 'culture of poverty' thesis and examine the major criticisms of it. (AEB November 1988)

4 To what extent have sociological explanations of poverty helped us to understand poverty in Britain in the 1980s? (AEB November 1989 Paper 1)

26

KARL MANNHEIM *and*

IDEOLOGY

THE AUTHOR

Karl Mannheim (1893–1947) was born in Budapest, Hungary, and grew up amidst the upheavals in Central Europe of the First World War and the conflicts of communist and fascist revolutionaries. He served in the radical Hungarian government of 1918–19, but was forced to flee to Germany after a right-wing coup. He studied at the Universities of Berlin, Budapest, Paris, Freiberg, and Heidelberg which was still a major intellectual centre strongly influenced by the ideas of Max Weber. Mannheim became Professor of Sociology at Frankfurt University in 1926 but fled from the Nazis to England in 1933. From 1933 to 1945 he was a lecturer at the London School of Economics and then became Professor of Sociology and the Philosophy of Education at the London Institute of Education.

Mannheim's career after leaving Hungary is often divided into two main phases:

■ A German phase (1920–33) when heavily influenced by Georg Lukács he sought to establish the basis of a Sociology of Knowledge as a rational means to evaluating the rival claims of the revolutionary ideologies so rampant in his day. His key-work here was *Ideology and Utopia* (1929, 1960)

■ A British phase (1933–47) in which he sought to analyse the structure of modern 'mass' society, its fragmentation and atomisation, its willingness to adopt extremist ideas and totalitarian governments. In such works as *Man and Society in an Age of Reconstructions* (1940) and *Freedom, Power and Democratic Planning* (1950) he argued for greater social planning to re-establish social order and consensus, with education playing a central role.

THE IDEA

The term 'ideology' is usually used to refer to a predetermined, even biased view of the nature of man, of society and of what life ought to be like. Such a set of ideas and beliefs may be clearly thought out and expressed, as for example in a political manifesto or religious creed, or it may be implicit, an unconscious preference for a liberal or conservative point of view. In either case a degree of bias and partiality is evident. Facts and figures are being used to bolster a particular viewpoint rather than as a means to discovering the truth. From such a perspective knowledge is seen as something that actually exists, as a store of hard data about what life is really like, dug up and critically analysed by men like academics and judges, men of such independence and wisdom that they are untainted by everyday reality and self-interest. We talk, for example, of a world of ideas separated from everyday reality inhabited by men living in ivory towers.

Karl Mannheim however argued that all knowledge – with the notable exceptions of maths and physics – is ideological, simply a reflection of the values, aspirations and interests of the wide variety of social groups that go to make up modern society: sects, generations, parties and especially social classes. Far from 'facts and figures speaking for themselves', they are used to speak for class or group interests. Such bias may not necessarily be deliberate or conscious self-interest but it will always occur because without a predetermined mental framework it would not be possible for men to make sense of the social world. There is therefore, in Mannheim's view, no such thing as objective knowledge or absolute truth, only at best an approximate truth, a synthesis of the enormous variety of beliefs about what life is really like and what ought to be done. Mannheim therefore saw intellectuals as no more than the most articulate spokesmen of class or group interest; though he later accepted that they may be sufficiently independent as to be able to synthesise rival views and establish some sort of intellectual harmony. The role of the sociology of knowledge therefore was to try and identify which ideas derived from which social groups and from such evidence piece together their overall ideology and show how such a world view helped promote the group's own interests.

This 'sociological' view of knowledge was most clearly outlined in his book *Ideology and Utopia* (1929). By 'ideology' Mannheim referred to the beliefs and values of the ruling class of a particular society: 'In certain situations the collective unconscious of certain groups obscures the real condition of society both to itself and to others and thereby stabilizes it.' By 'Utopia' he meant the beliefs and values of those groups, usually the oppressed who were aiming for a radical reconstruction of society according to their particular vision of an idea future – a view of reality that is equally biased and distorted: 'certain oppressed groups are intellectually so strongly interested in the destruction and transformation of a given condition of society that they unwillingly see only those elements in the situation which tend to negate it'.

Moreover, he argued the relationship between such competing ideologies in dialectic. By the weaknesses and injustices of the existing social order, ruling ideologies ironically give 'birth' to utopias which eventually rise up, overthrow the existing ruling class and themselves become ruling ideas as has happened with, for example, capitalism in nineteenth-century Britain, or communism in twentieth-century Russia and China. Thus in Mannheim's view, life is a process of continual struggle for power between rival social groups backed by competing ideologies, and he sought to trace the social origins of the history of political ideas from chiliasm through to liberalism, conservatism and finally communism.

THE IDEA IN ACTION

Mannheim's view of knowledge has proved immensely influential, and he and Karl Marx are generally seen as the founding fathers of the sociology of knowledge. Together they broke the traditional assumption that knowledge and ideas have an independent life of their own. Rather, they highlighted the social roots of knowledge and ideas, and the power of ideas to influence and control people's behaviour. Though heavily influenced by Marx, Mannheim rejected the idea that class alone was the basis of ideology, nor did he see the possibility of a 'scientific' analysis that would unveil the distortion of class ideology and reveal the truth.

He was not as systematic a thinker as Marx and he lacked a theory to explain why certain groups adopted one ideology rather than another or why human societies are perpetually involved in a struggle for power. Yet his insights and analyses of individual ideologies were often quite brilliant. His essay on 'Conservative Thought', for example, is considered a classic.

Partly because of his refugee existence, partly because European thought, especially in Germany, was shattered by Nazism and the Second World War, he never created a new generation of sociologists in the way that Max Weber did. He had no immediate successors to continue and extend his analysis, though his influence on the sociology of knowledge today is considerable and is reflected in such phenomenological studies as those by Berger and Luckman.

SEE ALSO

- ☐ Hegemony
- ☐ Structural Marxism
- ☐ Critical theory
- ☐ Legitimation crisis as modern versions of ideological power.

SUGGESTED READING

Kettler D. *Karl Mannheim*, Tavistock, 1986 – a short overview of Mannheim's life and work in the Tavistock series of key sociologists

FURTHER READING

Berger P and Luckman T. *The Social Construction of Reality*, Penguin, 1967
Berger P. and Luckman T. 'The Sociology of Religion and Sociology of Knowledge' in Robertson R. ed. *The Sociology of Religion*, Penguin, 1969
Mannheim K. *Ideology and Utopia*, Routledge & Kegan Paul, 1929, 1960
Mannheim K. *Man and Society in an Age of Reconstruction*, Routledge & Kegan Paul, 1940
Mannheim K. *Freedom, Power and Democratic Planning*, Routledge & Kegan Paul, 1950
Mannheim K. *Essays on the Sociology of Knowledge*, OUP, 1952

EXAMINATION QUESTIONS

1 Show how **two** of the following concepts can contribute to an understanding of the sociology of knowledge:
    (a) ideology;
    (b) commonsense knowledge;
    (c) conscience collective.
2 Through a consideration of **two** different areas of social activity, assess the sociological **usefulness** of the concept of dominant ideology. (London University June 1986)
3 'No knowledge is absolutely true because all knowledge is socially constructed.' Examine this view. (AEB June 1989 Paper 2)

27

KARL MARX *and*
ALIENATION

THE AUTHOR

Karl Heinrich Marx (1818–93) has undoubtedly been one of the key influences
on modern sociology. He was born in
Trier, an ancient city in the Rhineland,
the son of a prominent local lawyer and
a Dutch mother. They were both des-
cended from distinguished families of
Jewish rabbis but had to convert to Chris-
tianity so that Marx's father could hold
public office. Possibly Marx's Jewish
background increased his own sense of
marginality and his ambivilance between
being a radical thinker and a revolutionary activist.

The eighteenth and nineteenth centuries were the 'Age of
Revolution:

■ The political revolutions in America, France and Europe.
■ The Industrial Revolution that swept Britain and western Europe.
■ The intellectual upheavals of the scientific revolution, of the age of
enlightenment and of Darwinism.
■ The nationalist movement that included the unification of Marx's
own homeland, Germany, in 1870.

Such immense social upheavals provided both the background and
the inspiration for Marx's ideas, ambitions and self-sacrifice – 'sacrific-
ing oneself for humanity'.

He studied law and philosophy at the Universities of Bonn and
Berlin, gaining his doctorate in 1841. However his involvement with a
radical group called the Young Hegelians prevented him from pursuing
an academic career so he turned to journalism as editor of such liberal
newspapers as the *Rhineland Times* – publications quickly suppressed

by the authorities for their radicalism. In 1843 he married Jenny von
Westphalen, the daughter of an aristocratic friend of his father. Soon
after, he met his life-long collaborator Friedrich Engels, a Manchester
businessman appalled by the conditions of the working class in England. Together they outlined their initial analysis of class conflict in
such works as *The Holy Family* and *German Ideology*, and in 1848
produced *The Communist Manifesto* for the newly formed Communist
League, but too late for the European revolutions of that year. As the
authorities in Germany clamped down on revolutionaries, Marx was
forced to flee to Paris and then London. For the next twenty-five years
Marx and his family lived in abject poverty, relieved only by some
financial help from Engels, occasional journalism and later some small
inheritances. The British government refused to grant the 'Red Doctor'
citizenship, three of his children died in infancy and, though Marx
himself suffered from a long list of ailments that included carbuncles,
insomnia and ophthalmia, he (and Engels) produced a flood of work:
over fifty volumes in all, much of which was written in the British
Museum, much too on the family's only table whilst his children played
'horsey' on his back. Through such works as *Gründrisse, A Contribution to a Critique of Political Economy* and most especially *Das
Kapital*, Marx attempted a 'scientific' analysis of world history and of
capitalism in particular. But he was also active in radical politics as a
leading figure in the International Workingmen's Association (the First
International) and a keen observer of the 1871 French Commune. He
died in 1883 aged 65 and is buried in Highgate Cemetery.

His ideas live on, not as with most thinkers solely in the world of
intellectuals but in the daily life of workers and peasants throughout
the world. Born into an age of revolution, he helped give birth to
revolutions of the twentieth century in the Second World of Russia and
Eastern Europe, and in the Third World of China, Asia, Africa and
Latin America; inspiring an international search for liberty and justice
through equality. As Friedrich Engels predicted at his graveside: 'His
name will endure through the ages and so will his work.'

THE IDEA

Peter Hamilton (Worsley, 1982) has divided up Marx's ideas into three
interlocking models of how capitalism works:

■ An economic model whereby capital is created and circulated.
■ A social model whereby one class, the bourgeoisie, exploits the
other, the proletariat.

■ An ideological model whereby ideas and the apparatus of the state are used to maintain and justify such exploitation (see **Historical materialism**).

The concept of alienation underlines all three models and is in essence a scathing moral indictment of a socio-economic system that denies man his true nature, separates him from the products of his own labour and sets man against man in an economic 'jungle'. For Marx the essence of human nature, what distinguishes man from the animals, is his consciousness, his imagination, his ability to control his own environment. This power is most clearly expressed in the productive process where, by working together, men transform nature – felling trees to make houses, clearing forests to make roads. However, whenever this form of self-expression and social co-operation is in any way limited or thwarted, the alienation will occur. In the *Paris Manuscripts* of 1844 (quoted in Bottomore and Rubel, 1961) Marx outlined four key forms of alienation:

■ When the worker has lost control of the end product. What he has produced, be it a table or chair, is no longer his but owned by his employer.
■ When, through the extensive division of labour in modern factories, the worker no longer feels involved in the production process. He is merely 'a cog in the wheel', motivated not by the intrinsic satisfaction of work but only by the extrinsic one of the wage at the end of the week.
■ When relationships between workers are not those of colleagues but of rivals, competitors for jobs, bonuses and promotion; and those between employer and worker are not the relationships of equals but of master and slave as employers seek to maximise the profits from their workforce.
■ Whenever the individual is denied the true essence of his human nature – self expression through work. His work no longer feels part of him, nor represents his true talents. It is no longer a source of pride and achievement.
    In Marx's own words:

In what does this alienation of labour consist? First, that the work is external to the worker, that it is not a part of his nature, that consequently he does not fulfil himself in his work but denies himself, has a feeling of misery, not of well-being, does not develop freely a physical and mental energy, but is physically exhausted and mentally debased. The worker therefore feels himself at home only during his leisure, whereas at work he feels himself homeless. His work is not voluntary but imposed, forced labour. It is not the satisfaction of a need, but only a means for satisfying other needs. Its alien character is clearly shown by the fact that as soon as there is no physical or other compulsion it is avoided like the plague. Finally, the alienated character of work for the worker appears in the fact that it is not his work but for someone else, that in work he does not belong to himself but to another person. (Bottomore and Rubel, 1961)

Though all previous economic systems that involved a class structure and exploitative relationships generated a sense of alienation, capitalism does so more markedly – not only because exploitation is at its highest but because its 'market forces' lead to men being treated not as individuals but merely as another commodity of production to be used or discarded as the need arises. Only in a classless society, where the means of production are communally owned, will alienation be eliminated forever. Amid the abundance of modern mass production, 'communist' man would no longer work to survive, no longer specialise but be free to express all his talents – to fish in the morning, hunt in the afternoon and criticise in the evening. All social divisions of gender, race, town and country, brain and brawn, will disappear amid a society of equal individuals.

THE IDEA IN ACTION

For Marx the concept of alienation has two distinct but interrelated meanings:

■ It is a subjective feeling, a sense of powerlessness and uninvolvement.
■ It is a structural analysis of economic systems that deprive men of both the fruits of their labour and control over their work.

Much written since, however, has separated these two interlinked ideas.

■ In the 1950s and 1960s American social scientist, M. Seeman (1959) broke down the concept of alienation into five psychological components (isolation, meaninglessness, powerlessness, normlessness and self-estrangement) and Robert Blauner (1964) linked four of these to different types of work structure, arguing that assembly-line work is especially alienating and craft work the most creative. Blauner believed that automation would remove alienation from modern work because it would put the worker in control of the machinery – a thesis totally rejected by Marxists such as Harry Braverman (1974) who argues that not only does automation not alter the relations of production (the bosses are still in control) but it is a means to increased exploitation since workers are 'deskilled' and eventually replaced by such machinery (see **Deskilling**).

■ Other writers have applied the term alienation to a whole range of modern malaises – the feeling of discontent, isolation, powerlessness and impersonality felt by many groups in today's mass society (the young, minority groups, women) and used it to explain the high rates of strikes and absenteeism in today's giant factories.

■ The concept of alienation has also been a major source of dispute between rival schools of Marxists, with humanists seeing it as a central theme in Marx's work (particularly with the recent publication of *Gründrisse*) and structuralists like Louis Althusser, arguing that Marx rejected this term altogether in his more mature works, in favour of exploitation. Herbert Marcuse (1964) blended it with the psychology of Sigmund Freud and inspired a generation of American hippies and radicals in the 1960s.

■ It is difficult to judge whether the sense of alienation is less in 'socialist' than capitalist societies since such a subjective feeling is almost impossible to measure. Certainly the workers in the Eastern Bloc countries do not seem to feel in control, if the rise of Solidarity, the destruction of the Berlin Wall and the revolutions of 1989–90 in Eastern Europe are anything to go by. Possibly the Chinese communes, Yugoslav factories and some small-scale experiments such as Kibbutzim have had greater success.

Thus, whilst the concept of alienation has been used in a wide variety of social sciences, many sociologists feel that it has lost all real meaning and is of little analytical value. Nevertheless, when used as Marx originally intended – as an analysis of work, of human nature and of the subjective effect of class exploitation – it still wields considerable moral, if not sociological force.

SEE ALSO

☐ **Anomie** as Durkheim's explanation of this industrial malaise.
☐ **Critical theory** as an attempt to expand this idea of early Marx into a humanist school of modern Marxism.
☐ **Historical materialism** as an overview of Marx and Engels' general theory of historical and economic development.

SUGGESTED READING

Bottomore T.B. and Rubel M. eds *Karl Marx. Selected Writings*, Penguin, 1961
Burns E. *Introduction to Marxism*, Tavistock, 1966
Callinicos A. *The Revolutionary Ideas of Karl Marx*, Pluto Press, 1983
Carew Hunt R.N. *The Theory and Practice of Communism*, Penguin, 1950
Hoffman J. 'The Life and Ideas of Karl Marx', *Social Studies Review*, November 1985
McClellan D. *Karl Marx*, Macmillan, 1973
McClellan D. *Marx*, Fontana, 1975
Ruis *Marx for Beginners*, Unwin Paperbacks, 1986
Simon R. *Introducing Marxism*, Fairleigh Press, 1986
Worsley P. *Marx and Marxism*, Tavistock, 1982

FURTHER READING

Althusser L. *For Marx*, Penguin, 1965
Blauner R. *Alienation and Freedom*, University of Chicago Press, 1964
Braverman H. *Labor and Monopoly Capital*, Monthly Review Press, 1974
Marcuse H. *One Dimensional Man*, Routledge & Kegan Paul, 1964
Marx, K. *Gründrisse*, Penguin, 1973
  A Contribution to a Critique of Political Economy, Lawrence & Wishart, 1971
  Das Kapital, Lawrence & Wishart 1970
  Paris Manuscripts, quoted in Bottomore and Rubel eds, 1961
Marx K. and Engels F. *The Holy Family*, Progress Publishers, 1956
  The German Ideology, Lawrence & Wishart, 1965
  'The Communist Manifesto', in *Selected Works*, Lawrence & Wishart, 1968
Seeman M. 'On the Meaning of Alienation', *American Sociological Review* Vol 33, 1959, pp 46–62

EXAMINATION QUESTIONS

1 Assess the different ways in which sociologists have explained alienation in industrial societies. (AEB June 1988 Paper 2)
2 'Alienation is the product of social structures not of individuals.' Discuss. (Cambridge Local Examinations Syndicate June 1987)
3 'The most important source of alienation at work is the way in which work itself is designed and controlled.' (G. Salaman: *Class and Corporation.*) Explain and discuss.
4 Assess Marx's theory of alienation in the light of subsequent research on work. (AEB November 1989 Paper 1)

28

ELTON MAYO *and*
HUMAN RELATIONS

THE AUTHOR

Elton Mayo (1880–1949) was born in Australia, the son of a doctor. He was educated at the University of Queensland where he studied psychology and lectured. During the First World War he was involved in the treatment of shell-shocked soldiers. He emigrated to America in 1922 and took up a post as a researcher at the University of Pennsylvania, studying industrial organisation and discipline. In 1927 he became consultant to the Western Electric Company's Personnel Division and became heavily involved in the Hawthorne studies. His work helped publicise this research programme and, in turn, made him quite famous during the 1930s.

Mayo went on to lead research into productivity in the American arms industry during the Second World War, and after the war worked for the British Labour Government, advising on labour relations in British industry. He died in England in 1949.

His key works were:

■ *Human Problems of an Industrial Civilization* (1932)
■ *Social Problems of an Industrial Civilization* (1949)

THE IDEA

The idea of 'human relations' has had a profound influence on the sociology of organisations and on personnel management theory and practice. This concept originated from Mayo's researches into industrial relations and productivity at the Western Electric Company's Hawthorne plant in Chicago (1927–32). The dominant theory in the field at this time was F.W. Taylor's concept of scientific management (see page 287), the view that:

■ Workers' primary motivation is economic.

■ Men work essentially as individuals rather than as part of a social group or team.

The key to raising productivity levels, therefore, argued Taylor, was to encourage individual workers to maximise output by offering them financial incentives. Workers are motivated more by financial considerations than social ones, he claimed. Mayo's researches and theories were to turn this view of man as essentially an economic animal on its head.

Mayo and his team initially began their research on the basis of scientific management's assumptions that the main determinants of productivity were the physical conditions of the work environment, the aptitude of the worker and financial incentives. A variety of experiments were set up to establish causal relationships between such variables as the levels of lighting and heating, bonus payments, rest periods and productivity. However, the results proved inconclusive and, at times, contradictory. For example, in one experiment not only did changes in lighting not appear to have a direct effect on productivity, but at one point a gradual dimming of the lights led to workers working harder and producing more, rather than less, as any 'scientific' hypothesis might have predicted. It appeared that the workers involved were responding more to social factors than to physical conditions, were working harder because they were being watched, rather than because the lights were getting low. The presence of the researchers made the workers feel that, at last, the management was taking an interest in them as people, not just as factors of production.

Another study, of the Bank Wiring Room, revealed that, far from men working as individuals, they operate as part of a social group, and that such informal work groups are a greater influence on productivity than either the ability or motivation of any individual. The Bank Wiring study involved observing a team of wiremen connecting wires to banks of terminals. Tests relating output to the men's intelligence or dexterity produced no positive relationship, nor did the group incentive scheme appear to have a dominant influence. Rather, everyone seemed to work towards a uniform weekly rate of production, rather than maximising their own individual output, and so, pay. The worker's output, it appeared, was determined not by bonus schemes, but by an informal norm established by the work group as a whole. In this way, the group ensured that all its members achieved a reasonable bonus and, most especially, prevented the management raising productivity targets on the basis of the ablest workers' output – a tactic which would have saved the company money, lost most workers bonus payments, and possibly led to the sacking of weaker workers. These groups norms and sense of solidarity against management were reinforced by such informal social controls as sending 'deviant' workers to 'Coventry', disrupting their work, or even using threats of verbal/ physical intimidation to bring them into line.

Such results led Mayo and his chief researchers, P.J. Roethlisberger and W.J. Dickson, to conclude that social factors are far more important than economic ones, that man is essentially a 'social being' rather than an 'economic animal'. Thus, argued Mayo, the poor output and resistance to supervision evident in the Hawthorne plant and factories elsewhere in America were due to the impersonal treatment created by the management techniques of scientific management. Workers felt as though they were merely cogs in a giant industrial machine, felt alienated in factories where teamwork and social collaboration were frowned on. Drawing on Durkheim's ideas of anomie and social harmony, Mayo and his researchers proposed a radically alternative approach to scientific management, that of the human relations school of management. Roethlisberger and Dickson argued that, to achieve industrial harmony and maximise output, managers must pay far greater attention to:

■ Social and personal factors: fulfilling workers' social needs for friendship, status, recognition and group support; releasing workers' talents and creativity rather than suppressing them; making the factory or workplace a social unit as well as an economic one.
■ Industrial relations: establishing consent and co-operation between management and workers, and so overcoming the present divisions and conflict between 'us' and 'them'.

THE IDEA IN ACTION

Mayo's ideas blossomed into the Human Relations School of Industrial Relations, and even into a social movement which has had a profound effect on western capitalism. It even influenced personnel management in socialist societies, and led to the development of personnel work as a specialist area of modern management; it encouraged major firms to alter radically the basis of their industrial relations. Such harmony and staff care has become the by-word of such leading British firms as Marks & Spencers and Sainsburys. Many industrial organisations and mass production factories, especially in Scandinavia, began radically to re-think their organisational structure, to abandon their 'assembly lines' and austere environments in favour of teamwork, job rotation and enrichment schemes, worker participation, social clubs and friendlier, more pleasant surroundings. The social needs of the worker – job satisfaction, good staff relations and a 'happy family' atmosphere – began to take precedence over immediate profits.

Academically, the idea of human relations inspired a whole series of experiments and researches into group dynamics, social psychology, leadership styles and social factors, not least at Chicago University's own School of Human Relations. However, it was also extensively criticised:

■ Research into the application of human relations techniques produced inconsistent results. Coch and French's study of the introduction of new production methods and piece rates in a pyjama factory showed that where the workers were actually involved in the change-overs, rather than merely being informed of them, then productivity rose accordingly, with minimum staff upset. Similar studies, however, produced different or inconclusive results.

■ Goldthorpe and Lockwood (1968) criticised the human relations approach for failing to look beyond the factory gate out into society at large, for factors influencing workers' attitudes and motivations. Their study of 'affluent workers' in Luton (see **Embourgoisement**) showed that workers' needs vary and depend as much on the culture of society and the individual's place in the social structure as on anything that goes on in the workplace. Different workers have different needs. Their affluent workers were motivated primarily by financial reward. They neither sought nor expected any intrinsic satisfaction at work, be it group solidarity or job satisfaction. They had come down to Luton simply for the money. Their social needs were satisfied at home.

More radical critics went further, castigating human relations ideas:

■ For being pro-management and anti-union, for being a new, subtle form of worker manipulation and control.

■ For assuming that, at heart, there is no conflict of interest between management and workers; that by simply re-organising social relationships within organisations, treating workers as human beings, industrial discord can be eliminated and harmony established. Marxist writers, in particular, reject such an assumption. For them, there is a fundamental conflict between employers and employees in a capitalist society which can only be eliminated when the class structure and ownership of the means of production are radically altered. Personnel work and worker participation are merely more subtle forms of social control and indoctrination. The end result is still the same – profit and exploitation.

Whilst the Human Relations movement enjoyed its heyday in the 1940s and 1950s, by the late 1960s it had been severely undermined academically. It still, however, enjoys some prominence in both industrial theory and practice as major corporations continue to espouse and use new techniques of worker–manager groupings and collaboration, continue to try and involve or win over the workforce, aided in the 1970s and 1980s by the threat of mass unemployment.

SEE ALSO

☐ Scientific management

SUGGESTED READING

Mayo E. *Human Problems of an Industrial Civilization*, Macmillan, 1932
Mayo E. *Social Problems of an Industrial Civilization*, Routledge & Kegan
   Paul, 1949

FURTHER READING

Goldthorpe J.H. and Lockwood D. *et al. The Affluent Worker*, CUP, 1968

EXAMINATION QUESTION

'Scientific Management and Human Relations are different approaches to the study of organisations but they share the same aim of controlling the workforce.' Discuss. (AEB June 1988 Paper 1)

29

GEORGE HERBERT MEAD *and* SYMBOLIC INTERACTIONISM

THE AUTHOR

George Herbert Mead (1863–1931) was born in South Hadley, Massachusetts. His father was a Congregational minister, his mother a college President. He was educated at Oberlin College (1879–83) and attended the Universities of Harvard, Leipzig and Berlin. He taught initially at the University of Michigan (1891–3) where he was influenced by John Dewey, and then spent the rest of his academic career at the University of Chicago during its heyday in the early 1900s. He was a leading figure within the school of philosophy known as pragmatism and a major critic of the traditional form of behaviourism in psychology.

Although primarily a philosopher and social psychologist, he is generally seen in sociology as the founding father of symbolic interactionism, a sort of micro-sociology that falls between the grand theories of Marx and Parsons and psychology itself. This is reflected in the titles of his major works: *Mind, Self and Society* (1934), *The Philosophy of the Act* (1938) and *The Philosophy of the Present* (1959). In fact he himself published nothing, but his students, especially Herbert Blumer, translated his lectures and introduced them into sociology.

THE IDEA

Whilst most sociological theories attempt to analyse and explain society in terms of its overall structure, symbolic interactionism is more concerned with the everyday worlds we all live in and how, through symbols and communication, people create order and meaning out of their daily interactions. Whilst many sociological theories have attempted to adopt the scientific methods of cause and effect analysis from the natural sciences, symbolic interactionism has merely tried to describe social reality from *within*, simply aimed at interpreting the views, feelings and actions of those involved in a given situation or lifestyle.

George Herbert Mead laid the foundations for this perspective with his interpretation of the workings of the human mind. According to Mead, what distinguishes man from the rest of the animal kingdom is this unique mental mechanism which enables man:

■ To plan consciously and adapt his behaviour according to the situation in hand or the goals he has set himself.
■ To communicate with others through a wide variety of symbols, the most important of which is language, and interpret the meaning behind what they say, do or indicate in reply.
■ To be self-conscious; to be aware not only of his own feelings, motives and views but those of others; to be able to take the 'role of the other' and imagine how other people might interpret a particular act or situation and even to imagine how he looks to other people. We all therefore have a self and a 'self-image'.

It is this capacity that allows man to have some control over his behaviour and over his environment. Therefore, in Mead's view, human behaviour is not predetermined either by instincts or by external social forces. Rather we are thinking, conscious beings, capable of pursuing a wide variety of aims and objectives and capable of communicating with each other in order to create some sort of social order and structure. We are capable not only of conveying meaning but of interpreting the words and actions of others and such meanings are neither fixed nor absolute. They vary from situation to situation, context to context. Consider, for example, the wide variety of possible meanings behind the word strike or the situation where two people are alone in a room. A strike could refer to an industrial dispute, a baseball game or the lighting of a match; two people alone in a room could be involved in an interview, a tutorial, or something more secretive or sexual. Humans are therefore in a continual process of negotiating over the definition of a particular situation or relationship and out of this process of daily interaction arises our 'social world'.

However, social order does not only arise out of direct communication, out of people talking to one another, but out of common expectations. We are usually already aware of what is expected of us in a particular situation. We have learnt through socialisation and role play how we ought to behave. As children grow up they learn through instruction, imitation and, in particular play, the roles of mummy and daddy, doctors and nurses. As they grow older and their minds mature, such social guidelines are 'internalised' and used as a means of both responding to and even manipulating others. Such control is especially evident when children play games and have to use the rules to interpret and predict the behaviour of others in order to win. As adults we act out a wide variety of fairly well-defined social roles, from being a husband and father through to being a foreman, friend and local sportsman. But in Mead's analysis none of these roles is fixed. They are simply general outlines within which individuals improvise according to their own images, motives and abilities.

Mead further distinguished between the 'I' and the 'me', between a person's real 'inner' self and his public front, the social image people put on in front of others. Every individual has his own private desires and wants but, because we are able to imagine what others think of us, we dare not act in an entirely selfish way. There is therefore a constant battle between the 'inner' I and the 'outer' me and this, argues Mead, is the basis of what we call self-control, the means by which we try to get our minds to govern our bodies and keep our emotions under control, though sometimes such self-restraint breaks down. However, it would be impossible to predict accurately the expectations of every other person we ever met, especially as most of them are not known to us personally. So we generalise, we create a *generalised other,* an image of what we think other people would think of us if, for example, we started singing on a bus or laughing at a funeral. But we do not religiously conform to others' expectations. As Mead emphasised, we have minds of our own and often defer only to the pressure of *significant others,* people who are especially important to us.

Thus for Mead man is essentially a social being and society is the world he has created about him, one that is in a constant state of flux, a continual process of creation and recreation, interpretation, negotiation and definition. We are both individuals and social beings. We both shape our society and are shaped by it. We all live in a wide variety of miniature 'worlds' – from the home to the office, the golf-club to the local pub, and yet are part of a broader and shared human culture. Each of these 'worlds' has an essential structure but may at any time change or collapse as, for example, when a factory closes or a family experiences divorce.

Thus at the centre of Mead's analysis is not the class struggle or the division of labour but the individual and his mind and its ability to communicate and interpret. Symbolic interactionism has no real vision of society at large but is more an analysis of group interaction and psychology, more an interpretation of the 'internal' dynamics of man's social behaviour than of broader social trends.

Students of Mead extended and refined this analysis. Herbert Blumer, for example, sought to develop the methodology to put such ideas into practice, arguing that sociologists should study society from the inside, from the participant's own viewpoint, within 'natural' situations so as to understand why people act as they do, rather than from the 'outside' using artificial laboratory experiments or simplistic 'cause and effect' analyses. Everett Hughes developed the concept of a *career* not only to explain the common features of a range of jobs but also to outline the stages people pass through to become a criminal, a mental patient and a variety of other lifestyles.

THE IDEA IN ACTION

Mead's work influenced a wide variety of fields from psychology to philosophy. Within sociology this emphasis on the individual and his free will became the basis of numerous studies by the Chicago School in America in the 1920s and re-emerged in the 1960s and '70s as a major critique of the determinism of structural functionalism – its picture of society as a thing above and beyond ordinary people, its portrayal of the individual as a puppet; its abstract theory and jargon. Symbolic interactionism spawned a whole tradition of empirical analyses rich in detail and involvement and with a particular concern for the 'underworlds' of such deviant groups as delinquents and the insane. It produced such offshoots as labelling theory, ethnomethodology, phenomenology and dramaturgy. It contributed to debates on socialisation, role play and the nature of social knowledge.

However, symbolic interactionism has been criticised for failing to get beyond analysing small group behaviour. It offers no picture or explanation of society at large, no grand theory of social change or the distribution of wealth or power. It seems at times to portray society as merely something in people's heads. It is a very 'American' view of the freedom of the individual and the limited role of society. Some of this criticism is unfair or based on extreme versions of Mead's ideas. Mead recognised the importance of social structure, of social institutions, but simply rejected the idea that they determined human behaviour.

Secondly, by definition, symbolic interactionism sees no social reality beyond that created by human interpretation and so rejects the possibility of explaining society at large.

Thirdly, the concept of power is integral to such analyses, if not always explicitly stated. It is an essential part of human interaction, of the ability of some to control how a situation is 'defined'. In fact such writers often argue that their studies concentrate on the 'underdogs' of society precisely because the powerful in society are already well able to make their voices heard.

Since the 1970s, however, symbolic interactionism seems to have lost steam and fragmented into a variety of directions as more powerful and critical perspectives like Marxism have gained prominence – and dominance.

SEE ALSO

☐ **Phenomenology** as the parent theory to this form of interpretative sociology.
☐ **Labelling** and **Stigma** as examples of the development of symbolic interactionism.

SUGGESTED READING

Miller D.L. *George Herbert Mead*, University of Texas Press, 1973 – an overview of Mead's life and work.
Rock P. *The Making of Symbolic Interactionism*, Macmillan, 1979 – assesses the contribution of symbolic interactionism to modern sociology. Interactionism has contributed enormously to such fields as deviance and education.
'George Herbert Mead', *Social Studies Review*, Vol 4 No 5, May 1989, p 200

FURTHER READING

Mead G.H. *Mind, Self and Society*, Chicago University Press, 1934
Mead G.H. *The Philosophy of the Act*, Chicago University Press, 1938
Mead G.H. *The Philosophy of the Present*, Chicago University Press, 1959

EXAMINATION QUESTIONS

1 Evaluate Mead's contribution to our understanding of the nature and development of the self. (WJEC June 1987)
2 'The main deficiency of the interactionist perspective is that it tends to ignore social structure.' Discuss making reference to *one* area of sociological investigation. (London University January 1987)
3 'The central problem in sociological theory is explaining the interrelations between social structure and social action.' Explain and evaluate this view. (Oxford Delegacy May 1987)

30

ROBERT K. MERTON *and*
SOCIOLOGY OF SCIENCE

THE AUTHOR

Robert K. Merton (1910–   ) was born in Philadelphia, the son of an immigrant family from Eastern Europe. Despite his poor background he was an avid reader and an outstanding student. He won a scholarship to Temple University and then went on to do graduate study at Harvard University under such leading lights in social science as Talcott Parsons and Pitrim Sorokin. He lectured at Harvard and Tulane Universities before moving to the Department of Sociology at Columbia University in 1941, where he remained until his retirement in 1979. He rose to become a full professor and, alongside Paul Lazarsfeld, Associate Director of the Bureau of Applied Social Research. This 'Columbia School', as it came to be known, produced generations of outstanding sociologists.

Robert Merton was an outstanding academic, highly acclaimed both within and outside sociology. He held numerous presidencies, awards and honorary degrees, including the highly prestigious MacArthur Prize Fellowship. His academic output has been equally prodigious and includes twenty-three books he wrote or edited, 125 articles and 120 book reviews.

His key works include:

■ *Science, Technology and Society in Seventeenth-Century England* (1938)
■ *Social Theory and Social Structure* (1949)
■ *A Reader in Bureaucracy* (1952)
■ *The Sociology of Science* (1973)
■ *Contemporary Social Problems* (4th Edition 1976)

Robert Merton has been one of the key figures in modern American sociology, ranking alongside Talcott Parsons. One of his biographers, Charles Crothers (1987) has divided his contribution to modern sociology into four main areas:

■ Theoretical sociology, especially the refinement of structural functionalism by such concepts as manifest/latent functions and dysfunctions and his concept of middle-range theories.
■ Social and cultural sociology (e.g. anomie, bureaucracy).
■ Sociology of knowledge.
■ Sociology of science.

Merton's range of sociological interests has been enormous. He sought to combine theoretical analysis with empirical research. His other biographer, Piotr Sztompka (1986), has called him the 'last classical sociologist' and H.M. Johnson has claimed that Merton 'is the most frequently cited living sociologist'. In Peter Hamilton's view (Introduction to Crothers, 1987), Robert Merton 'stands at the crossroads between the great sociologists of the late nineteenth century and early twentieth century, and the professional or institutional sociology of the present day'.

THE IDEA

Traditionally and academically, ever since the scientific revolution of the seventeenth century, scientific knowledge has been something of a world unto itself. Almost by definition, scientific knowledge has been considered to have a depth and reliability beyond any other academic discipline. It deals with the 'real' world; its scientific method has proved capable of both discovering and measuring facts and figures, and from them producing theories and laws capable not only of explaining, but of predicting the natural world. Natural scientists form an academic and social elite whose authority and impartiality is unquestioned. It was this 'secret kingdom' of modern 'magicians' that Robert Merton sought to penetrate, sought to expose to sociological analysis, sought to show that even natural scientists are not oblivious to the social forces that so obviously govern the rest of us in our everyday lives. In so doing he laid the foundations of the sociology of science.

Merton's sociology of science was two-fold: an analysis of both the external and the internal workings of the scientific community.

EXTERNAL ANALYSIS – THE EMERGENCE OF MODERN SCIENCE

Merton's argument here was that no scientific community exists in isolation. Rather, it depends for its existence on the material and cultural support of the rest of society. In his doctoral thesis, Merton used Weber's idea of the Protestant ethic (see page 297) to argue that modern science did not emerge until the seventeenth century because it was not until the Industrial Revolution that it was socially and economically needed and so had a social 'function'. The Protestant ethic created the cultural and ethical ethos so vital to the development of experimental science (and so, ironically, the rejection of religious faith). Merton cited numerous key scientists of this period from Newton to Boyle who made an explicit connection between their Puritan beliefs and their scientific work. In contrast to Catholicism, which on occasions outlawed scientific ideas (e.g. Galileo), aesthetic Protestantism actively encouraged scientific experimentation, actively supported 'rational' study and analysis of the natural world, as a way of appreciating more fully the power and goodness of God, the beauty of the natural world he created. In particular, it encouraged practical research of benefit to all in preference to mere theorising and speculation. This religious or ideological support for scientific study was reinforced in this period by both the military's demand for increased firepower and businessmen's desire to increase productivity. Merton's analysis of the emergence of modern science thus combined Weber's emphasis on cultural factors with Marx's on economic and military ones. Science emerged to fulfill the industrial needs of modern capitalist society.

Merton was now able to fit the sociology of science into a structural functionalist analysis, to highlight the social functions performed by science and the way it only emerged when supported by the social consensus of the time. Should science at any time threaten that consensus, should its researches seriously challenge society at large and its underlying values – for example by the creation of nuclear power or artificial life – then it, too, would be under threat. Similarly, whilst sceptical criticism of traditional ideas and values is at the heart of scientific method, such questioning of authority can lead to either the suppression of the scientific community (as in Nazi Germany) or its reorganisation into an arm of the state, producing only that research required by and supportive of the government (as in totalitarian societies).

INTERNAL ANALYSIS – THE EMERGENCE OF
THE SCIENTIFIC COMMUNITY

Having outlined the social background to the establishment and acceptance of modern science, Merton went on to analyse in detail the underlying ethos and internal workings of the scientific profession – what is it that makes scientists a separate community, almost a breed apart? In his 1942 study, Merton outlined the following key scientific values or, as he called them, institutional imperatives:

Universalism – the evaluation of new knowledge solely in terms of objective, impersonal criteria and the career advancement of scientists solely in terms of talent.

Communism – the common or public ownership of scientific knowledge. No individual scientist 'owns' any particular knowledge beyond those rights of authorship and academic recognition. Secrecy is forbidden and publication to promote the development of knowledge is a professional duty.

Disinterestedness – whilst being intensely involved in their work, scientists are also meant to be objective and detached. Over-involvement, cheating or exaggeration are considered professional suicide because they threaten the sanctity of public faith in scientific knowledge.

Organised scepticism – no aspect of the real world is regarded as sacred, beyond the scope of scientific analysis.

Such values form the basis of the scientific value system, its 'normative structure' or what Merton called its paradigm, its rules of the game. It is this ethos which binds the scientific community emotionally as well as professionally. It is these principles:

That bind this body of people (and minds) irrespective of where they are working throughout the world.

That form the basis for socialising young students into the scientific community.

That provide the basis for public support for scientific research as a legitimate, professional and responsible social activity.

That underlines our faith in the product of scientific study – a body of tried and tested rational knowledge.

Such values, therefore, underlie not only the scientific consensus but the social one. They represent a moral commitment as well as a professional function.

In a Presidential Address of 1957, Merton went deeper into an analysis of the 'reward' system of the scientific community, into a study of what motivates scientists at work. In contrast to the material and financial rewards of many other professions or careers, scientific rewards are primarily symbolic. Few scientists earn great wealth, or even achieve public recognition for their work. Most are primarily motivated by peer group acclaim, by achieving academic rewards and recognition in the form of professional appointments (e.g. professorships) and/or academic prizes such as the Nobel Prizes. Young scientists build up their professional reputations by the quality of their research and the quantity of their publications in the form of books and/or articles in leading scientific journals. The highest rewards, the greatest prestige, goes to those scientists who produce the most original research, who achieve scientific breakthroughs and so promote the advance of scientific knowledge. The highest reward, according to Merton, is an *eponymy*, having one's name attached to a particular field of study or scientific discovery, be it Boyle's Law or Newtonian physics. Those scientists who deviate from or violate such norms and mores are subject to intense professional and moral indignation because they threaten the heart of this scientific reward system: fair play. Equally, Merton's analysis helps explain why disputes as to the authorship of any new scientific discovery are so bitterly fought within the scientific community, and why they are so feared, because they threaten the unity and spirit which binds scientists world-wide together.

In the 1960s the Mertonian School went on to develop a Mertonian model, a functional model of the stratification system or meritocracy within the American scientific community, and tested this against the actual hierarchy of modern scientists and their academic posts or prestige. The aim was to test whether such a stratification and reward system produced a scientific hierarchy that served the 'objective' interests of science and society at large in the best possible way.

Thus Merton laid the foundations for a functionalist analysis of the sociology of science, a model which linked its functional imperatives both to society at large and to the internal workings of the scientific community. Merton linked its normative system to its system of rewards, motivations and social controls, and highlighted the links between the consensus in society at large and that within the scientific community. It is precisely because the scientific community appears so pure and professional, so untainted by 'worldly' rewards and personal profit, so objective, detached and socially concerned that it has earned the depth of public support and respect that it has. It is because scientific knowledge is so ideal and yet so real, so theoretical and yet so practical that it is able to command such enormous financial and material resources, be it for new cures or space travel, new foodstuffs or test-tube babies.

THE IDEA IN ACTION

Robert Merton is often referred to as the founding father of the sociology of science. His analysis opened up the previously 'secret garden' of scientific study to sociological scrutiny and laid the foundations for a new sociological sub-discipline which has, in turn, contributed significantly to the sociology of knowledge.

Merton's functionalist model inspired, in the 1960s, a range of studies into the scientific community, their work and motivation, and laid the basis for the Mertonian School of scientific study. Merton's model, however, has been criticised at two levels.

FOR BEING TOO PURE

His ideal type model of the scientific community has been seen as too pure, even inaccurate:

■ Mulkay and Mitroff, for example, have both challenged Merton's view that conformity to institutional norms is an essential feature of modern science. They both cite studies where new discoveries or theories which challenged the scientific orthodoxy of the day were met, not with rational criticism, but with emotional, even personal, abuse. Similarly, they cite examples of scientists being over-involved in their research, biased and secretive. They both argue that scientists' prime commitment is not to Merton's institutional imperatives but to the dominant scientific orthodoxy of the time, what T.S. Kuhn called the normal scientific 'paradigm' (see page 162).
■ Studies of today's scientific community by Ravetz (1971) and others have further undermined the Mertonian image of the scientific community as a loose body of 'free thinking' individuals working on their own individual projects, by showing the shift to an industrialisation of science, to modern scientific projects being increasingly organised on the basis of large-scale teams financed by big business or government and organised along industrial lines. This is a sort of scientific mass-production assembly line with an extensive division of scientific labour, an administrative and managerial hierarchy whereby junior scientists are left with the repetitive and tedious task of mass testing whilst senior

scientists direct and make policy decisions. Thus, far from modern scientific research being internally inspired and controlled, as Merton claimed, much of it is now externally sponsored and directed.

■ Radical and Marxist writers have taken this point even further, arguing that, far from being independent and detached, modern science is yet another servant of the ruling class, serving the private interests of capitalist profit or military power rather than the public interest at large. Pure research is increasingly being replaced by applied scientific projects, funding for public research is minute in comparison with military and space research.

■ Authors like Lesley Doyal (1979) have highlighted the way industrial research by, for example, the drug companies, is not aimed primarily at discovering new cures, but at producing duplicate drugs to maintain a particular company's share of the market. Governments like those in Britain and France have directed energy research into nuclear power, virtually to the exclusion of other sources of energy.

Such radical critiques thus see Merton's model as highly idealistic and conservative, as failing to recognise that, within a capitalist society, science, like all forms of economic production, is geared ultimately towards producing profit; reproducing the class system of a nonmanual elite and a subordinate manual class of exploited workers; and reinforcing the dominant capitalist ideology. The otherworldly ethos of the scientific community, its image of public service, helps hide the extent to which scientific research actually serves private profit and promotes elite privilege and power.

Recent studies in the sociology of science have tended to use a phenomenological approach, have tended to involve detailed microscopic studies of actual research situations, of how scientists actually work together: negotiate, interpret and evaluate findings and so create what we call scientific knowledge.

FOR BEING TOO LIMITED

His model of the sociology of science was seen as too limited. It only covered the social, economic and political factors influencing the scientific community. It tended to ignore the social influences on what the scientific community produced – scientific knowledge. It tended to assume that such knowledge is real and objective rather than relative and socially constructed.

■ The key study within the sociology of science which sought to link the scientific community with scientific knowledge was Thomas Kuhn's concept of paradigms. This theory was that scientific knowledge does not evolve naturally and gradually, but in fact progresses in leaps and bounds via 'scientific revolutions' whereby new theories and new generations of scientists overthrow existing orthodoxies and hierarchies, whereby a new paradigm or theoretical framework comes to dominate and direct scientific research. Kuhn's thesis not only highlighted the internal 'politics' of the scientific community, but the relative nature of scientific knowledge and its dependence on a particular theoretical framework, rather than being merely the discovery of existing facts about the nature of reality (see Kuhn, page 162).

This modern view of scientific research as theoretically and culturally dependent, as relative rather than objective, has tended to supplant the positivist assumptions that lay behind much of Merton's functional analysis and so made it look outdated. Although, as Charles Crothers (1987) has argued, much of this criticism is more of Merton's earlier work than his later, more mature analyses, which recognised many of these new trends. In fact, Merton superseded many of Kuhn's ideas, but he used the concepts of paradigms and normal science to refer more to the scientific community than to scientific knowledge. Moreover, whatever the strength of such criticisms of Merton's model, it was he who inspired and founded this sociological sub-discipline, he who 'opened the door' to the sociological study of science.

SEE ALSO

☐ **Paradigms** and
☐ **Falsification** for alternative strands in the sociology of science.

SUGGESTED READING

Crothers C. *Robert K. Merton*, Tavistock, 1987 – a stimulating and thoughtful overview of Merton's life and work
'Robert Merton' *Social Studies Review*, Vol 4 No 5, May 1989, p189

FURTHER READING

Doyal L. with Pennell I. *The Political Economy of Health*, Pluto, 1979
Johnson H.M. in Kuper A., Kuper J. (eds) *The Social Science Encyclopedia*, Routledge & Kegan Paul, 1985

Merton R.K. *Science, Technology and Society in Seventeenth Century England*, Harper Row, 1938

Merton R.K. *Social Theory and Social Structure*, Free Press, 1949, 1968

Merton R.K. *A Reader in Bureaucracy*, Free Press, 1952

Merton R.K. *The Sociology of Science*, University of Chicago Press, 1973

Merton R.K. and Nisbet R. eds. *Contemporary Social Problems*, 4th ed. Harcourt Brace Jovanovich, 1976

Ravetz J.R. *Scientific Knowledge and its Social Problems*, OUP, 1971

Sztompka P. *Robert K. Merton. An Intellectual Profile*, Macmillan, 1986

EXAMINATION QUESTIONS

1 'Whether we consider sociology to be scientific or not depends on which definition of science we choose.' Explain and discuss. (AEB June 1988 Paper 2)

2 'The use to which any knowledge is put is a profoundly moral issue which sociologists like other scientists must not evade.' What does this mean? What consequences should an acceptance of this view have for social research? (Cambridge Local Examinations Syndicate June 1987)

31

ROBERT MICHELS *and*
IRON LAW OF OLIGARCHY

THE AUTHOR

Robert Michels (1876–1936) was born in Cologne in Germany, the son of parents with a mixed German-French-Belgian background. He studied at the Universities of Halle, Marburg and Turin where he became friends with Gaetano Mosca and later gained the patronage of Max Weber. Initially he was an active socialist and member of the German Social Democratic Party but he became increasingly disillusioned with the gap between its revolutionary statements and its cautious policies. Through the guidance of Weber he moved from radical action into an academic career becoming Professor of Economics in Basel (1914), a lecturer in political sociology at the University of Rome (1926), a visiting professor in the United States and then Professor of Economics at the University of Perugia. Thus he shifted in ideas from revolutionary syndicalism to becoming a critic of socialism, and especially Marxism, and their claims to be able to liberate the masses, to becoming an apologist for fascism as he lost faith in revolutionary zeal and in the masses.

His major work was *Political Parties* (1911) in which he outlined the 'iron law of oligarchy'. He also wrote about nationalism, fascism, the role of intellectuals, elites, social mobility and sexual morality.

THE IDEA

Robert Michels' key idea is known as the iron law of oligarchy, the thesis that in all societies and all organisations, at all times, there is an inevitable tendency towards oligarchy, towards rule by the few in the interests of the few.

Like fellow-theorists Pareto and Mosca, Michels was writing at the turn of the century, at a time when mass democracy seemed to be sweeping Europe, when socialist and communist ideas were all the fashion, and when many were proclaiming the advent of true democracy – government of the people, by the people, for the people. But like Pareto and Mosca, Michels increasingly came to see such democracy as impossible and oligarchy as inevitable. The basis of his thesis was that there is a fundamental contradiction in mass democracies between the need for organisation ('democracy is inconceivable without organisation') and the inbuilt tendency of large-scale organisations to become oligarchical ('Who says organisation, says oligarchy'). In a mass democracy, the individual on his own is powerless. Only by joining others in organisations can he make his voice heard, and this is especially true for the working classes who lack the education, money and connections to pull political strings. However, within such mass organisations not everybody can be involved in making decisions so delegates have to be elected 'to represent the masses and carry out its will'. Moreover, to be efficient such organisations need full-time officials and an administrative hierarchy of rules and regulations. Amongst both officials and the organisations' leaders, however, oligarchical tendencies soon develop.

■ Increasingly officials begin to use their expertise and power over information to influence decision making. Increasingly a career structure develops within bureaucracies and amid 'the mania for promotion' deference to one's superiors soon counts for more than simple ability. Individuality and criticism are thus soon excluded or crushed and the power of those at the top increased.

■ Increasingly, those at the top of such organisations become more interested in maintaining their own powers and privileges than in promoting the causes of the organisation. The organisation becomes an end in itself rather than a means to an end; the policies of the organisation become increasingly conservative for fear that radical actions will lead to its destruction; the leadership dominates all decision making and appointments, dismantles any checks on its power and, where possible, votes itself into office for life.

■ Increasingly, the ordinary members find themselves excluded from the organisation, from decision making. They find the rules, procedures and jargon of meetings and documents incomprehensible and react by not attending, not participating and so increasing the power of the leadership. Those at the top of organisational structures begin to adopt an elite lifestyle and so find it very difficult to even consider returning to the shop floor. They come to believe in their own omnipotence, come to accept mass adulation as natural, come to see themselves as invincible and to believe in their own propaganda that they alone know what is best for the organisation, for the 'people'.

To support his thesis Michels made a detailed analysis (1911) of the German Social Democratic Party and the trade union movement organisations which in the 1900s seemed to epitomise radical policies and true democracy. They claimed mass democracy: they claimed to represent the working classes. They claimed to be organisations designed to overthrow capitalism and establish socialism. But, in practice, their actions and policies were reformist rather than revolutionary and conservative to the point where the leaders of the SDP became part of the German 'establishment'. Thus in Michels' view, just as democracy inside organisations is bound to fail, so democracy in society at large is doomed and this is true whatever type of society is involved, capitalist or communist. Democratic leadership is simply a new type of elitism and socialism a new form of ideology to be used to control the masses. The rise of totalitarian governments in both fascist and communist countries in the 1930s only confirmed his theory. Initially Michels had hoped that such an analysis would inspire the rank and file to seize back control of socialist parties and trade unions and force the leadership into radical action. However, in later years he came to the conclusion that the masses were inept and apathetic, that they had a psychological need to be led and that decisive leadership was to be admired: 'leaders never give up their power to the mass but only to the other, new leaders'. Hence his esteem for the new fascist regimes of Hitler and Mussolini and his shift from analysing power in terms of organisational features to an analysis of its psychology, the charisma of leadership and the deference of the masses.

THE IDEA IN ACTION

The vast majority of studies of organisational power have supported Michels' thesis:

■ Philip Selznick's study (1966), for example, of the Tennessee Valley Authority set up as part of the New Deal in America during the 1930s depression, found that though this organisation was established to represent and promote the interests of ordinary people in the area, it quickly came under the control of the wealthier white farmers. Only by accepting such a takeover, such 'goal displacement', argued Selznick, could the TVA survive, because to have opposed the farming establishment would have meant its death. Robert McKenzie's study of British political parties (1964) used Michels' thesis to argue that, despite their enormous ideological differences, once in power the British Labour and Conservative parties adopt very similar policies.

■ Studies of socialist and communist societies from Stalin's Russia to present-day China show the same tendency to oligarchy, and Eva Rosenfeld (1974) found this even in the highly democratic Israel kibbutzim.

■ Today in Britain the struggle for control between the rank and file and the party leadership has been a major feature of the recent furore in the Labour Party – the change in its rules over elections to the leadership and reselection of MPs, the debate over the purity of the manifesto and the need to regain power after the defeats of the 1979, 1983 and 1987 elections.

■ Similarly, Mrs Thatcher's attacks on the trade unions and the new laws on secret ballots have struck a chord in the hearts of many trade unionists who feel ignored and poorly represented by their leaders.

The only major study to identify real democracy in a mass organisation was Lipset, Trow and Coleman's study (1956) of the International Typographical Union (ITU), a craft printers' union in America which ensures active mass membership and prevents oligarchy by numerous elections, referenda and a two-party system. However, as Lipset *et al.* themselves concluded, the ITU is rather exceptional. It has a long tradition of very active membership politically and socially and it is highly unlikely that such a structure of internal democracy could be transplanted to other unions or organisations: their leaders at least would oppose such a threat to their powers.

The other main criticism of Michels' analysis, though, is his failure to distinguish between different types of oligarchy. At least in western democracies there is some possibility of accountability as the electorate has a choice of parties; in dictatorships no such popular power exists save through revolution.

Thus, unlike most sociological theories, Michels' thesis has stood the test of time exceptionally well and stimulated a wide variety of studies. Whether it has yet achieved the status of being a 'sociological' let alone an 'iron' law is another question.

SEE ALSO

☐ Elite theory
☐ Power elite

SUGGESTED READING

'The Crowther Hunt Report' (*see under* Kellner and Crowther Hunt (1980) in the Bibliography)

McKenzie R. *British Political Parties*, Mercury Books, 1964

Michels R. *Political Parties*, Free Press, 1911 – Michels' own study of oligarchy.

Sedgemore B. *Secret Constitution*, Hodder & Stoughton, 1980 – modern-day example.

FURTHER READING

Lipset S.M., Trow M. and Coleman J. *Union Democracy*, Free Press, 1956

Mosca G. *The Ruling Class*, McGraw-Hill, 1896

Pareto V. *Mind and Society*, Dover, 1916

Rosenfeld E. 'Social Stratification in a Classless Society', in Lopreato & Lewis, 1974

Selznick P. *TVA and the Grassroots*, Harper, 1966

EXAMINATION QUESTIONS

1 To what extent do studies of different types of society support the argument that 'power in society will always lie in the hands of a minority'? (London University June 1986)

2 'Whoever says organisation means oligarchy.' Consider the relevance of Michels' statement to an understanding of power in the modern world. (London University June 1987)

3 'All organisations are oligarchies.' Examine the arguments and evidence for and against this view. (AEB June 1989 Paper 1)

32

C. WRIGHT MILLS *and*

POWER ELITE

THE AUTHOR

C. Wright Mills (1916–62) was born in a middle-class Catholic family in Waco, Texas. He gained his degrees at the Universities of Texas and Winsconsin and after an assistant professorship at the University of Maryland moved to Columbia University. However he did not gain a full professorship here until 1956 due to certain political opposition. Such obstacles duly reflect Mills' highly controversial career. He was a rebel, even against the social science establishment in America, and whilst he attracted critics as well as admirers, many would agree with Irving L. Horowitz that he was 'the greatest sociologist the US has ever produced'.

C. Wright Mills was a man of action as much as an intellectual, more at home with men of business, politics or the military than his fellow academics. He believed that the task of sociology was to confront and critically analyse the key issues of his time not, as he felt many social scientists did, run away from them. His aim was to reform society as much as explain it, to popularise sociology and develop a sociological imagination amongst the American public. He led a very varied career teaching in such institutions as the US Air War College and the William A. White Institute of Psychiatry. He travelled not only to Europe and Latin America but, at a time when the Cold War was 'hotting up', to Russia, Poland and even Castro's Cuba. Mills believed that American liberalism had lost its critical edge, had gone flabby and complacent, and so he turned for inspiration to the conflict theories of Weber and increasingly Marx. But he never lost his 'liberal' and humanist instincts, never uncritically followed any theoretical vein and always insisted on highlighting the importance of ethical values in social science. He often spoke of the 'moral uneasiness of our times' on both sides of the Iron Curtain, of the failure of contemporary intellectuals to continue providing moral leadership at a time when the masses were increasingly under the control of political and social elites and of the inadequacy of both theory and method in modern social science. He hoped, however, that through knowledge all men could be set free and the good society achieved.

His key works were:

  White Collar (1951)
  The Power Elite (1956)
  The Sociological Imagination (1959)
  The Causes of World War III (1958)
  Listen Yankee (1960)
  The Marxists (1962)

THE IDEA

Power was the focal point of most of his analyses and, whilst he believed that in the past power had been fragmented, what had oc-curred in the twentieth century was a massive concentration of deci-sion-making in all spheres by elites increasingly unaccountable to the ordinary people. The concept of a 'power elite' is nothing new. Such an idea could be traced back to such classical writers as Mosca, Pareto and Michels. What was original about his concept was that he analysed elite power in terms of institutions rather than individuals and focused specifically on American society in the 1950s, a society that had just fought two world wars against dictatorships, was intensely involved in a Cold War against communism and saw herself as the 'statue of liberty'. To publicly claim that the very home of democracy was itself controlled by a power elite was not only courageous but, in the era of McCarthyism, positively dangerous.

In *The Power Elite* (1956) Mills identified three key institutions in American society – the major corporations, the military and the federal government – and argued that, though the elites of each of these organisations appear to be separate, in fact they tend to come together to form a single unified elite integrated by what he called 'institutional proximity'. Modern American capitalism, he believed, was increasingly a military economy as the arms industry became big business and as the politicians were increasingly pushed into huge defence budgets by a spiralling arms race. The power elites' unity was further reinforced by the similarity of social and educational background of its top personnel (white Anglo-Saxon Protestants from upper-class backgrounds and Ivy League universities) and by the extensive interchange of top personnel between these three institutions. Thus this power elite not only shared a similar view of American democracy, opposed radical change and sought to preserve inequality and privilege, but moved quite easily from top jobs in business to those in military or political circles. President Eisenhower, formerly Commander-in-Chief of the Allied Forces, was a classic example of this elite mobility. In Mills' view this elite governed primarily in its own interests and for him the classic example of its unaccountability to the mass of the American people was the bombing of Hiroshima. The party political conflict of the Republican and Democratic parties he saw as a sham offering the electorate no real alternative and providing no real check on the elite's power. Through the mass media and affluence of modern capitalism the masses were managed and manipulated, excluded from power, directed into the everyday concerns of family and career so that the power elite could pursue power and self-aggrandisement in peace.

However, in Mills' view there was hope. The basis of such power was institutions. If the American people could seize back control of such bodies, if the intellectuals could provide the moral leadership to expose such elite power, then society could be changed.

THE IDEA IN ACTION

Whilst such a description of mass control fitted the American people's image of Stalin's Russia, it was a devastating view of their own society and inevitably inspired a massive counter-attack. At an intellectual level critics argued that Mills' idea was purely circumstantial. He had simply revealed the existence of elites at the top of American society, shown that they had the potential for mass manipulation but he had produced no proof that they had conspired together against the American people, no evidence that they had ruled in the strongest sense of the word. Only an examination of key decision-making could substantiate such a claim. So began what has come to be known as the 'pluralist–elitist debate' over the distribution of power in advanced industrial democracies.

Whilst pluralists like Robert Dahl (1961) and Arnold Rose (1967) in America and Chris Hewitt (1974) in Britain claimed that their analyses of decision-making at the local and national level revealed not a centralised structure of power but a highly fragmented, diverse and competitive one, elitists moved on from analysing the common backgrounds and values of top decision-makers to highlighting 'non-decision making', the idea that key decisions are not made (and certainly not debated) in public or in the political arena of Congress or Parliament but are made behind closed doors or simply never raised. Issues such as inequality, racism and nuclear weapons are so much a part of modern capitalism that the establishment takes them for granted and, through its control of the media, excludes debate or criticism.

One attempt to actually identify the American power elite, to name names, has been by Thomas R. Dye (1979). He actually identified 5416 individuals involved in controlling America's key institutions and resources, highlighted the power of such key families as the Rockefellers and Kennedys, their common background and outlook, the exclusion from elite power of women and Blacks and the way political controversy rages merely over means not ends, as the agenda is set before debate begins. However, he also found evidence of social mobility into such elite circles, conflict between the various elites as well as consensus, and some limited influence on decisions by the mass of American people. Thus Dye concluded that the power elite is neither as coherent as Mills portrayed it nor as competitive as pluralists believe but rather an oligarchy requiring further examination. Therefore, as yet, Mills' idea has been neither proved nor disproved but, as he hoped, it has inspired a major debate throughout the western world and awakened ordinary people to the dangers of elite power in modern society.

SEE ALSO

☐ **Iron law of oligarchy**
☐ **Elite theory**
☐ **Corporatism** and
☐ **Relative autonomy** as alternative and complementary theories of the structure of power.

SUGGESTED READING

Bottomore T. and Brym R. (eds) *The Capitalist Class*, Wheatsheaf Press, 1989 – an update on the Pluralist–Elitist debate.
Eldridge J. *C. Wright Mills*, Tavistock, 1983 – a short readable overview of Mills' life and times.
Mills C.W. *The Power Elite*, OUP, 1956 – though dated, still worth reading.

FURTHER READING

Dahl R.A. *Who Governs?*, Yale University Press, 1961
Dye T.R. *Who's Running America?*, Prentice Hall, 1979
Hewitt C.J. 'Elites and the Distribution of Power in British society' in Stanworth
  P. and Giddens A. *Elites and Power in British Society*, CUP, 1974
Mills, C.W. *White Collar*, OUP, 1951
Mills C.W. *The Causes of World War III*, Simon & Schuster, 1958
Mills C.W. *The Sociological Imagination*, OUP, 1959
Mills C.W. *Listen Yankee. The Revolution in Cuba*, McGraw-Hill, 1960
Mills C.W. *The Marxists*, Dell, 1962
Rose A. *The Power Structure*, OUP, 1967

EXAMINATION QUESTIONS

1 How useful is the concept of 'power elite' in explaining the politics of
modern society? (London University June 1987)
2 How relevant is the concept of 'political elite' to the study of British politics?
(Oxford Delegacy May 1985)
3 There has been a long-standing debate among social scientists about the
form of the national power structure in contemporary Western industrial
societies. Evaluate the main positions taken in this debate. (AEB June 1983
Paper 1)
4 Assess the strengths and limitations of pluralist theories of the nature and
distribution of political power. (AEB June 1982 Paper 2)

33

THE AUTHOR

Ray Pahl was born in London in 1935. He read geography at Cambridge, and his first piece of research – on commuter villages in Hertfordshire – was carried out for his doctorate at the London School of Economics.

In 1965 he went to Kent University as a lecturer in sociology, and in 1972 took up a personal chair in sociology. He is now Research Professor of Sociology at Kent. In the late 1960s, he acted as consultant to the South-East Joint Planning Team, which in 1970 produced the strategic plan for the southeast of England.

Ray Pahl's best known books are:

- *Urbs in Rure* (1965)
- *Patterns of Urban Life* (1970)
- *Whose City?* (1975)
- *Divisions of Labour* (1984)

THE IDEA

During the late 1960s the cities of America and western Europe exploded into orgies of aggression and destruction amid the violent protests of American negroes, students, women's groups, housing tenants and environmental groups. Underlying such powerful pressure-group activity, such violent unrest, was a fundamental dissatisfaction with the distribution of power and resources in the urban centres of western capitalist societies. People felt alienated, felt isolated, felt unable to influence the way their cities were being run. No one seemed to be in control, there seemed to be no institution on which they could focus their dissatisfaction. Rather, western cities seemed to be run by hidden forces beyond the control of ordinary citizens. Traditional theories in urban sociology could not explain such social unrest, such hidden power, so many turned instead to the conflict theories of Marx and Weber. One such important attempt was R.E. Pahl's thesis of urban managerialism.

Using Max Weber's thesis about the power of bureaucracy in advanced industrial societies, Pahl argued that today's cities are not controlled by hidden natural forces, but rather are run by the impersonal power of faceless bureaucrats. These 'urban managers' control the distribution of such urban resources as housing and education. They plan our cities and organise its transport systems. They decide what rates are levied and what they are spent on, choosing between parks and play-schools, leisure centres and shopping precincts. As cities grow in size and complexity so the need for urban management, for bureaucracy, increases – and with it an increase in people's sense of alienation, of powerlessness and of losing control of their environment. Though, officially, we elect local politicians and political parties to run our cities, decide policy and make key decisions, in practice, as Weber pointed out, real power lies with their officials, the faceless men who control information, give advice and control resources at the ground level, allocating (or withholding) council houses or school places, school meals or parking places. It is these small administrative decisions that, each in their different way, so crucially affect the lifestyle, environment and futures of individual families. Such officials by their planning decisions have the power to create and destroy whole communities, be they in the inner city or the new town, the suburb or the housing estate. They have the power to alter the distribution of urban wealth by, for example, increasing the rates on home-owners in order to increase public spending on council housing or on public transport. Equally, planning permission for a new shopping complex may attract major corporations but it is also likely to destroy many small businesses and dramatically alter the shape and character of the city centre.

But the management of the urban environment and its resources is not just under the control of public officials; private managers also have power. Building society managers control the allocation of mortgages and so significantly influence home ownership; bank managers similarly affect consumer spending and business investment by their lending policies and interest rates. It is these public and private local managers, these 'urban gatekeepers', argued Pahl, who are the real power in our cities today, not some hidden 'market' forces.

By identifying such bureaucratic power, Pahl hoped to provoke detailed studies of urban management, of local decision-making and its effect on the local distribution of wealth, on the shape of our cities. In particular he hoped to highlight the ideologies, the values underlying such allocation, such an ordering of priorities, why one section of the community or city gained more favourable treatment than another. What assumptions, for example, lie behind the allocation of council houses or free school meals, why is a new ring road more likely to go through a council estate than a middle class suburb? By such analyses Pahl hoped to lay the basis for a new 'political' theory of urban sociology:

Thus there can be a sociology of the organization of urban resources and facilities: the controllers, be they planners or social workers, architects or education officers, estate agents or property developers, representing the market or the plan, private enterprise or the state all impose their goals and values on the lower participants in the urban system. We need to know not only the principles of access to scarce resources and facilities for given populations but also the determinants of [their] moral and political values. (Pahl, 1968)

THE IDEA IN ACTION

Such a 'political' analysis of the allocation of urban resources contrasted starkly with ecological and functional theories about the hidden hand of the market or natural forces of urban evolution. Instead the thesis of urban managerialism sought to expose the individuals, in particular the officials and bureaucrats, who run our cities and control our daily urban lives by their decisions and underlying values/ideologies as to how a city should look, about which groups should get priority, which be listened to and which ignored. This thesis equally sought to explain the growth of urban protest movements that sprang up in the late 1960s and 1970s, angry and frustrated at such impersonal decision-making but unable to identify who the key decision-makers were. Though local politicians were the obvious target for such pressure group activity, Pahl sought to show that real power lay behind the political scenes with the ever-growing army of officials and managers attempting to control the ever more complex 'urban jungle'.

Urban managerialism inspired a wealth of highly detailed and very fruitful studies into urban bureaucracy and decision-making. Ironically, it was these very studies that revealed the limitations of Pahl's idea, in particular that this thesis concentrated far too much on the 'middle dogs' of the urban power structure, middle-managers in local government departments, banks and insurance companies and so ignored the 'top dogs', the real decision-makers who laid down policy from the top – the company chairmen, the national politicians and civil servants. It is they who lay down policy guidelines, who decide the amount of resources available. Pahl's urban managers merely carry out such instructions, merely work within this predetermined framework so their power over the city is in fact quite limited. Pahl's thesis failed even to identify those within the ranks of urban managers who were more influential on people's lives – the departmental manager laying down general policy or the clerk at the counter handling individual cases.

In recognition of this criticism Pahl attempted to broaden his idea to include such 'top dogs', to raise his 'searchlight' further up the urban decision-making hierarchy by proposing the 'corporatist thesis', a theory about the power of top civil servants and national bureaucracy (see page 220).

However, even these key officials do not work in isolation, their power is constrained and limited. And again, Pahl's thesis offers little guidance as to the really key decision-makers. As Peter Saunders (1981) argued:

Quite simply, Pahl's recent work leads empirical research into the familiar problem of the receding locus of power; the actions of urban managers can be understood only in the context of national state policy; national state policy can be understood only in the context of the operation of a complex mixed economy; the operation of the economy can be understood only in the context of the crisis of the capitalist world; and so on. Thus the researcher who starts out by attempting to understand, say, the patterns of housing inequalities in Birmingham ends up by trying to analyse the oil policies of the Middle Eastern states or the impact of American fiscal policy on the international balance of trade.

SEE ALSO

☐ Collective consumption
☐ Housing classes
☐ Human ecology
☐ Urbanism as alternative analyses of today's urban crisis.

SUGGESTED READING

Pahl R.E. *Whose City?*, Penguin, 1975
Slattery M. 'Urban Sociology, Section 2' in Haralambos M. ed. *Sociology New Directions*, Causeway Press, 1985 – An overview of the whole topic of urban sociology.

FURTHER READING

Pahl R.E *Urbs in Rure*, Weidenfeld & Nicolson, 1965
Pahl R.E. *Readings in Urban Sociology*, Penguin, 1968
Pahl R.E. *Patterns of Urban Life*, 1970
Pahl R.E. *Divisions of Labour*, Blackwell, 1984
Saunders P. *Social Theory and the Urban Question*, Hutchinson, 1981

EXAMINATION QUESTION

Examine sociological explanations of zones of high deprivation in urban areas.
(AEB November 1988)

34

RAYMOND E. PAHL, JACK WINKLER and
CORPORATISM

THE AUTHORS

The concept of corporatism cannot be traced back to any one single author but rather has its roots in the authoritarian regime that existed in Italy and Germany in the 1930s and in the feudal systems of the Middle Ages. This idea was resurrected in the 1970s as a major explanation of the changing nature of political and economic decision-making in advanced industrial societies like Britain. The boom period of the 1950s and 1960s was giving way to economic slump and the growth of mass unemployment. The traditional post-war methods of managing advanced capitalism proposed by John Maynard Keynes – demand management and deficit budgeting – no longer seemed to work. So governments found themselves increasingly having to intervene more directly in the economy and they did this primarily through agreements with organised labour and big business. A new tripartite system of government seemed to be emerging in which the CBI and TUC not only influenced government but were partners in a new style of corporate state. Economic planning seemed to be replacing parliamentary government.

Whilst a wide variety of writers contributed to the development of this thesis, notably the European sociologist Phillipe Schmitter, Alan Cawson and the historian Keith Middlemas, one of the clearest and most influential expositions of this idea was by Ray Pahl and Jack Winkler in their article in *New Society* (10 October 1974), 'The Coming Corporatism', which Winkler extended and developed in his piece in the *European Journal of Sociology* (Vol 17, pp 100–36). For a useful overview of this thesis see Wyn Grant's article 'Corporatism in Britain' in *Social Studies Review* (Vol 2 No 1, September 1986, pp 36–40).

THE IDEA

In liberal democratic capitalist societies political and economic decision-making and control are separate. Political decision-making is organised through elections, pressure groups and parliament, and economic decision-making is governed by 'market forces' and the private ownership of industry. In socialist and communist societies political and economic decision-making is integrated through a centrally-planned economy and one-party dictatorships. Corporatism, according to Jack Winkler (in Scase R. ed. 1977), is an alternative system that combines elements of both capitalism and communism:

Corporatism is an economic system in which the state directs and controls predominantly privately-owned business according to four principles: unity, order, nationalism and success.

These four principles represent the underlying philosophy of corporatism – the belief that society is essentially one organic body or 'corpus' in which every part is interdependent; that there is a fundamental national interest underlying every society that will be best achieved by co-operation rather than competition; that social and economic order is not only the path to national prosperity but a moral obligation. The worker has a duty to work, the employer to employ and the role of the state is to enforce such economic discipline even, if necessary, at the expense of individual rights and the rule of law. Hence corporatism's associations with dictatorship, with fervent nationalism and the expansion of state power. All such restrictions are justified by the goal of economic success, and the idea that the national interest comes before individual freedoms or profits. The market economy is seem as wasteful and unstable, the centrally-planned one as bureaucratic and inflexible.

The key difference therefore, in Winkler's view, between the economic role of a capitalist state and a corporatist one is that there is a distinct shift from 'supporting' the economy to *directing* it, from merely encouraging and stimulating private business to actually telling it what it 'must do and may not do'. The state establishes national goals, controls the allocation of resources, co-ordinates key industries and regulates the distribution of rewards. The extent of such state control may vary but essentially it involves 'control over the internal decision-making of privately-owned business' by establishing limits over the choices available to capitalist owners and managers.

Similarly, the key difference between the political role of a communist dictatorship and a corporate state is that the latter controls and directs the economy in a far more flexible and non-bureaucratic way. It uses discretionary laws, voluntary agreements and financial inducements to encourage companies in the direction it wants. It hides behind quasi-government organisations which appear to be independent but in fact are not (e.g. the Bank of England and the BBC). Decisions can, therefore, rarely be traced back to the government. It uses the courts, and creates new semi-judicial bodies such as ACAS, to actively enforce industrial discipline and settle industrial disputes. It concentrates its control on the monopoly sector of modern industrial economies, allowing the smaller firms in the market sector the freedom to compete, and where monopoly sectors do not exist the state creates them in the form of nationalised industries or cartels. Prices and incomes policies are introduced to control inflation and wages. But the prime method of establishing economic order and co-operation is the creation of agreements between both sides of industry. Such key bodies as the CBI, TUC and major professions are invited to participate with government in developing policy on such major issues as prices, wages and investments. In return such leading bodies are expected to implement voluntary agreements and keep their own members in order.

Whilst corporate decision-making therefore appears to be highly democratic in fact it is not. Parliament and elected decision-making bodies are being by-passed and a hierarchial structure of power is being created which *includes* organised labour and big business but *excludes* all others. Ironically, as Winkler points out, even this form of participation is a form of manipulation by which capital and labour think they are in control (and so become the focus of any public criticism) whilst real power still lies with the state: 'participation has always been the cunning rulers' form of social control – to make people believe they rule themselves' (Winkler 1977). And, ultimately, if all else fails to establish order, the power of the police will be extended to enforce it. Thus in Winkler's view 'corporatism is a bargaining system, not a bureaucratic one', a highly flexible system of negotiation and voluntary agreements rather than direct control. However as state control of the economy inevitably expands, both 'free enterprise' and 'free collective bargaining' diminish so the role of the state will cross the line from being supportive to being directive. Then a new type of economic system will be established: corporatism.

BRITAIN IN THE 1970s

As evidence of his general thesis Winkler used the example of post-war Britain. Britain's initial Industrial Revolution involved the minimum of state intervention but by the early twentieth century the government had to increase its role as advanced capitalism seemed unable to regulate itself. The growth of giant monopolies and powerful unions, two World Wars, the Great Depression and responsibility for both the welfare state and full employment forced modern governments to take a more direct role. Initially this was achieved by indirect management of the economy using the ideas and techniques of John Maynard Keynes, but by the late 1960s and 1970s this was obviously not enough as the economy again slumped. Winkler traces the trend to corporatism in Britain to 1960 (though others like Keith Middlemas go back further to the 1920s). In that year the Conservative Government set up the National Economic Development Organisation and thereafter both the Labour Governments of 1964–70 and 1974–9, and the Conservative administration of Ted Heath sought to 'incorporate' big business and organised labour into its economic management procedures by a wide variety of devices. Harold Wilson set up the Department of Economic Affairs and the NEDC, the Ministry of Technology, and the Industrial Reorganisation Corporation. His administration introduced incomes policies, legislation such as the 1968 Industrial Expansion Act and the 1968–9 White Paper *In Place of Strife*. National Plans were drawn up to establish tripartite agreements between Government, industry and the unions. After an initial attempt to revert to 'free market' forces the Heath Government did a 'U-turn' back to corporate management when it introduced the 1972 Industry Act to rationalise industry, reorganise investment and support ailing or 'lame-duck' firms. ACAS and the Manpower Services Commission were created to improve industrial relations and employment. And in 1972–3 a full-blown incomes policy was introduced.

The 1974–9 Labour Government continued such policies, climaxing in the introduction of the 'Social Contract' with the unions to restrain wages, and of a Prices Commission to control prices. There thus grew up in the 1960s and 1970s a network of economic controls, quasi-government institutions and a new 'tripartite' structure of economic policy-making *outside* Parliament that appeared actually to incorporate big business and organised labour into the state machinery. So strong were these trends that Pahl and Winkler predicted the establishment of full-blown corporatism by the 1980s.

THE IDEA IN ACTION

As Leo Panitch (1980) has pointed out, the concept of corporatism developed almost into a growth industry as a vast array of writers in a variety of subjects subscribed to this general thesis. As the 1970s progressed it did seem to be an increasingly accurate analysis of the direction both Conservative and Labour Governments were taking in Britain.

However, by the late 1970s and early 1980s, this whole idea, and Jack Winkler's version of it in particular, came under increasing attack:

WHAT WAS CORPORATISM?

As Leo Panitch has argued (1980) there was a 'profound lack of agreement on what the concept [of corporatism] actually referred to'. Some writers concentrated on economic developments alone, others focused on the structure and role of the state, whilst others used it to distinguish between different types of pressure group activity.

OPPOSITION TO CORPORATE GOVERNMENT

As writers like Dearlove and Saunders (1984) have argued, beneath the apparent industrial harmony in the 1970s lay a hotbed of unrest and opposition to corporate government:

■ Whilst the trade union leadership may have been incorporated into the state machinery, the rank and file membership was not. It resented such pay restraint agreements as threatening ordinary workers' standard of living and an explosion of wildcat or unofficial strikes broke out in this period.
■ Whilst big business may have benefited from pay and productivity deals, the small businessman did not and he found himself being choked to death by ever-increasing price controls and 'red-tape'.
■ Whilst politicians and civil servants basked in the glory of industrial peace, there grew up amongst the general public a growing resentment against such cosy arrangements between the privileged and the powerful, and against the growth of anonymous bureaucratic control at both the local and national level. The 1970s saw the rise of a vast array of pressure groups representing women, Blacks, consumers, local communities and nationalist aspirations, all demanding *inclusion* in the political process. People wanted more say in government, not less, and they resented the power of the corporate barons, especially that of the union bosses.

A NEW FACE OF CAPITALISM

Whilst Weberian writers like Pahl and Winkler saw corporatism as a new form of economic and political system, Marxists like Panitch saw it simply as a new face of capitalism, a new strategy for trying to overcome capitalism's inherent contradictions and recurring crises of overproduction, falling profits and ailing industries. For Marxists corporatism was merely a short-term attempt to paper over the underlying class conflict, a new way of restraining the power of the working class, of restricting pay and strikes in the interests of profitability.

FAILURE OF THE CORPORATE STRATEGY

Most especially, the corporate strategy failed. Such 'consensus politics', such prices and incomes policies, failed to stem spiralling inflation, economic decline or the growth of mass unemployment and instead bred the underlying discontent and industrial strife that bedevilled the 1970s and exploded in the Winter of Discontent of 1978–9.

ELECTION OF MRS THATCHER

The final nail in the corporatist coffin though, the one event that sunk Winkler and Pahl's thesis and prediction, was the election in 1979 of Mrs Thatcher. Far from extending the structure of the corporate state, she was swept to power on a wave of resentment against it and her prime task ever since has been to dismantle it. She has attempted to return to the *laissez-faire* government of nineteenth-century capitalism, to cut back state interference and control of the economy and liberate 'market forces'. She has restored the power of government and severely cut that of the unions, cut government subsidies and let 'lame ducks' die, encouraged competition and used mass unemployment to discipline the workforce.

Thus, as Panitch (1980) argues, corporatism was a temporary not a permanent feature of modern British government. Winkler's thesis provided important insights into a new form of policy-making, to the growing power of certain economic groups *outside* Parliament, but it was too pure and too partial a thesis. It only explained economic policy-making and so missed the growth of conflict, of pressure group politics on such non-economic issues as race, local government and abortion. It was a limited theory of a limited period in post-war British politics, with little applicability elsewhere.

SEE ALSO

☐ **Power elite** and
☐ **Relative autonomy** as alternative views of modern power structures and the role of the state.

SUGGESTED READING

Pahl R.E. and Winkler J. 'The Coming Corporatism', *New Society*, 10 October 1974
Winkler J. 'Corporatism' in Scase R. ed. *Industrial Society: Class, Cleavage and Control*, Allen & Unwin, 1977

FURTHER READING

Cawson A. *Corporatism and Welfare*, Heinemann, 1982
Dearlove J and Saunders P. *Introduction to British Politics*, Blackwell/Polity Press, 1984
Middlemas K. *Politics in Industrial Society*, Deutsch, 1979
Panitch L. 'Recent Theorizations of Corporatism', *British Journal of Sociology*, Vol 31, 1980, pp 159–87
Schmitter P. 'Still the Century of Corporatism?' in Schmitter P. and G. (eds) *Trends Towards Corporatist Intermediation*, Sage, 1979
White Paper, *In Place of Strife*, HMSO, 1968–9
Winkler J. 'Corporatism', *European Journal of Sociology*, Vol 17, 1975, pp 100–36

EXAMINATION QUESTION

What have sociologists identified as the role of the state in advanced industrial societies? (AEB June 1985 Paper 1)

35

VILFREDO PARETO, GAETANO MOSCA *and*

ELITE THEORY

THE AUTHORS

Vilfredo Pareto (1849–1923) was born in Paris, the son of an Italian political refugee and a Frenchwoman. The family returned to Italy in 1958. Vilfredo studied engineering at the the Polytechnic Institute in Turin and then worked as an engineer and manager of a railway company for twenty years. He developed a growing interest in social science, particularly economics and politics, and became heavily involved in the Italian Free Trade Movement of the 1880s. On receiving a sizeable inheritance he took up the study of mathematical economics full time. In 1893, at the age of forty-five, Pareto was appointed Professor of Political Economy at Lausanne. After 1900 he became something of a recluse, living alone in Switzerland, though appointed a member of the Italian Senate by Mussolini shortly before he died in 1923.

The considerable range of influences in Pareto's background – his engineering work, his mathematical and scientific training, his fluency in both Italian and French, his knowledge of ancient history, his intense interest in economics, all came to bear on his writings and ideas. He sought to apply the techniques of natural science to social studies and, in particular, sought to apply the concept of 'equilibrium' to both his economic and political theories. His overall aim was to try to establish a systematic theoretical analysis of the whole social system, to interrelate such social sciences as economics, politics and psychology, to draw attention to the non-rational elements of human behaviour. In particular he distinguished between:

■ 'Residues' – the fundamental sentiments behind human action; the subjective factors based on man's innate drives and instincts, and
■ 'Derivations' – the intellectual justifications or ideologies used by men to provide some semblance of rationality to their actions. Concepts such as these lay behind both his political analysis of 'circulating elites' and his key contributions to modern economics (Pareto's Law, the Pareto optimum in welfare economics and his theory of economic equilibrium).

His key work was:

■ *Mind and Society* (1916)

Gaetano Mosca (1858–1941) was born in Palermo, Sicily. He trained as a constitutional lawyer and lectured at the Universities of Palermo and Rome. He then became editor of the *Chamber of Deputies Journal* for ten years. He resumed his academic career in 1896 as Professor of Constitutional Law at Turin University and in 1923 was appointed Professor of Political Institutions and Doctrines in Rome.

Mosca was also very active politically and, from 1908 to 1919, he served as a conservative member in the Chamber of Deputies. Between 1914 and 1916 he served as Undersecretary for the Colonies and in 1919 was made a Senator. It was this combination of academic study and political experience that so illuminated his major work, *The Ruling Class* (1896).

THE IDEA

Vilfredo Pareto and Gaetano Mosca are usually paired together as the founding fathers of modern elite theory, partly because their ideas have acted as a bridge between classical and modern elite theory, partly because their analyses of political power are so similar. Though working separately, both writers analysed political elites more in terms of personal qualities than in terms of the structure of power as, for example, in Marxian analyses. In fact, both theories developed partly as a rejection of Marx's prediction of a future society in which everyone would be equal and there would no longer be any rulers and ruled.

Both Pareto and Mosca argued that elite rule – the rule of the few – was inevitable in all societies; that we are all, to an extent, born to be either a ruler or a follower, that revolution merely replaces one elite with another. The basis of elite rule, they argued, is the personal qualities of the ruling group or class and their unity and organisation, compared with fragmentation, disunity and apathy of the masses. They are occasionally referred to as the 'New Machiavellians'.

Vilfredo's theory of political elites rests essentially on a psychological distinction between different types of ruling group, the way they circulate and the way they rule the masses. He identified two key types of elite: 'lions' and 'foxes'.

■ Lions rule by force. They are direct, decisive and ruthless (e.g. military dictatorships).
■ Foxes rule by stealth. They are cunning, manipulative and diplomatic (e.g. European democracies).

These elites reflect both distinctly different personal qualities and different styles of political leadership – force versus persuasion. Major changes in society, argued Pareto, occur through a circulation of elites, by lions replacing foxes or *vice-versa*. Ultimately, all elites have a tendency to decadence, decline and corruption; all have to face the problem of elite replacement. Whilst some elites pass the reins of power on to their sons and daughters, others seek to recruit 'new blood' from the lower ranks. Whilst both methods help perpetuate power, both types of elite identified by Pareto contain inherent weaknesses which will ultimately bring them down. Lions lack imagination and cunning, so they recruit foxes to think for them. Once 'inside', foxes quickly begin to take over power. However, foxes too have their weaknesses. They lack the ability to act forcefully, to take decisive action, and so are open to a seizure of power by a group of determined and organised young 'lions'. History, according to Pareto, is an endless story of circulating elites, 'a graveyard of aristocracies'. Power ebbs and flows until a new political equilibrium is established. He rejected the idea of democracy being a radically new form of government, a more progressive and representative distribution of power. He saw it merely as a new form of elite rule, a new ideology 'derived' by foxes to disguise their control. For Pareto, the masses are always too inarticulate and apathetic to assume the responsibilities of government.

Gaetano Mosca's thesis is essentially the same as Pareto's, that rule by the few is an inevitable feature of all societies; that in all history there are only two classes of people, 'a class that rules and a class that

is ruled'. Like Pareto, Mosca believed that the ruling class is superior to
the rest of society, intellectually, materially and morally, and that the
essence of elite power is the unity and coherence of the rulers compared
with the disorganisation of the masses. Whilst he, too, emphasised the
psychology of power, Mosca differed from Pareto in arguing that the
qualities necessary for elite rule vary from society to society, from time
to time. Whilst, in some societies, during some historical epochs, military prowess is the key to power, in others diplomatic skills or great
oratory are paramount.

Mosca further distinguished between intellectual and moral forces,
such as cultural traditions and religious beliefs, and material or economic forces. He argued, in true Machiavellian style, that human
beings prefer submission to abstract principles rather than to people.
The key to effective rule, therefore, is to combine control of the major
economic and political institutions with ideological control, to base
authority on ideological grounds as well as on force and/or economic
power. Thus, for example, feudalism was based not only on the
ownership of the land and military force, but on the concept of the
divine right of kings; the French Revolution was based on the rights of
man; and modern democracy is based on the rule of law.

By such an analysis Mosca sought to identify the underlying laws of
political organisation and power, to highlight the complex interplay of
political power, ideas and personality. In his view, the political stability
of the ruling class of any particular society depends on the balance
between the controlled and uncontrolled forces flowing through the
political system, on the ability of the ruling class to channel and control
such forces to their own advantage. Here Mosca distinguished
between:

■ Politicians – skilled in manipulating power, and
■ Statesmen – capable of sensing the undercurrents of social change
and of responding to them in new and imaginative ways.

It is this mixture of social forces and elite response that determines the
different character of each society's ruling class.

Mosca went on to argue that stable government requires an effective
and fair judicial system and as wide a representation of society in
government as possible. He therefore recommended fluid balances

■ Between the 'aristocratic tendency' of the ruling class to perpetuate
itself from within and the 'democratic tendency' to perpetuate itself
from without.

■ Between the 'autocratic tendency' of rule from above and the 'liberal' one of power to the people.

Modern 'princes', argued Mosca, must be sensitive to such balances if they are to retain power. He had little faith in popular government, arguing that elite rule was the only way to civilised government and society.

Every generation produces a certain number of generous spirits who are capable of loving all that is, or seems to be, noble and beautiful, and of devoting large parts of their activity to improving the society in which they live, or at least to saving it from getting worse. Such individuals make up a small moral and intellectual aristocracy which keeps humanity from rotting in the slough of selfishness and material appetites. (Mosca, 1896)

Whilst Mosca developed a more favourable view of democracy in his later writings, he always opposed universal suffrage, always argued for elite rule, even through representative government. In this way he hoped to outline not only a 'scientific' analysis of political regimes, but a theory of elite rule and a political programme for preserving the ruling class.

THE IDEA IN ACTION

Pareto's ideas were very popular in the USA in the 1930s and his concept of equilibrium even influenced such leading sociologists as Talcott Parsons. His psychological analysis of elite rule is evident in Robert Michels' 'iron law of oligarchy' and even C. W. Mills' 'power elite'. His concept of circulating elites is still quite widely used, especially in analysing one-party states like the Soviet Union. However, the rest of his theory is now largely considered outdated. It is too dependent on psychological qualities and ignores important structural factors. He simply 'lumped together' all types of political system, even those as dissimilar as western democracies and eastern dictatorships. For Pareto they are all merely varying forms of elite rule. Moreover, he failed to provide any clear psychological analysis as to why lions and foxes were inherently superior to the masses below.

Mosca's thesis, however, has proved more enduring, more clearly provided a 'founding footstep' to modern elite theories, precisely because he ventured beyond simply a psychological analysis. *The Ruling Class* established Mosca as the founding father of Italian political science, though its somewhat Machiavellian tone led to charges that it was a justification for fascism. Mosca was, in fact, quite critical of both Mussolini and Hitler. His belief in the superiority of elite rule in terms of moral leadership as well as its civilising influences was more a reflection of his nineteenth-century liberal principles than his support for mere dictatorship.

Whilst both Pareto's and Mosca's ideas now seem dated and simplistic in terms of the complexities of modern political power structures, they both highlighted the fact that, even in an age of apparent mass democracy, elites still rule. Their ideas founded the tradition of elite analysis which is as vital now as it was when they lived – if not more so.

SEE ALSO

☐ Iron law of oligarchy
☐ Power elite
☐ Corporatism
☐ Relative autonomy
☐ Hegemony and
☐ Legitimation crisis for more recent analyses of these classic theories.

SUGGESTED READING

Meisel J.H. ed. *Pareto and Mosca*, Prentice Hall, 1965

FURTHER READING

Bottomore T.B. *Elites and Society*, Penguin, 1966
Mosca G. *The Ruling Class*, McGraw Hill, 1896
Pareto V. *Mind and Society*, Dover, 1916
Parry G. *Political Elites*, Allen & Unwin, 1969

EXAMINATION QUESTIONS

1 Examine the similarities and differences between pluralist and elitist theories of the nature and distribution of political power. (AEB June 1988 Paper 1)
2 'Social order is dependent upon the unequal distribution of power in society.' Indicate what evidence you would use to demonstrate this unequal

distribution of power in society and outline some of its consequences. Briefly comment on the adequacy of this explanation of social order. (JMB June 1987)
3 With reference to pre-literate, developing and industrial societies, how would you identify the social groups who have gained power in society? (London University January 1988 Paper 3)
4 Outline elite theories of the distribution of political power and examine the major criticisms of these theories. (AEB November 1989 Paper 2)

36

ROBERT E. PARK *and*
HUMAN ECOLOGY

THE AUTHOR

Robert Ezra Park (1864–1944) was an American sociologist who created, led and held together the Chicago School of Sociology which flourished in the 1920s and early 1930s. Park was born in Harveyville, Pennsylvania, but his family moved soon afterwards to Red Wing, Minnesota where his father was a businessman. He was educated at the Universities of Minnesota and Michigan where he studied under and was heavily influenced by John Dewey. He married Clara Cahill, daughter of a leading Michigan lawyer in 1894 and for eleven years worked as a newspaper reporter in Detroit, Denver, New York and Chicago. It was this occupation that taught him how to sniff out news, the importance of detail, and gave him an appreciation of the colour and vitality of city life. Park returned to academic life as a student of William James at Harvard and then Georg Simmel at the University of Berlin. For nine years he worked as secretary to the American negro leader Booker T. Washington, gaining an intimate insight into America's race problem and then at the age of fifty he joined Albion Small and W.I. Thomas at the University of Chicago's department of sociology. Under their leadership and inspiration this Chicago School of Sociology blossomed and dominated American sociology for the next twenty years. Park retired in 1929, travelled and lectured extensively abroad and then worked at Fisk University, a negro institution in Nashville, USA, from 1936 until his death in 1944.

R. E. Park's influence on American sociology was immense. Fascinated by the ebb and flow of urban life at a time when America's cities, especially Chicago, seemed to be overwhelmed by floods of immigrants from south-eastern Europe, he and his students established the distinct discipline of urban sociology. He introduced the ideas of such European thinkers as Durkheim, Darwin and Simmel into American sociology in an attempt to explain how, out of the urban chaos before him, America's cities not only survived but adapted and grew successfully, assimilating into the 'American way of life' a multitude of ethnic groups and races. He inspired his students to go out into the streets of Chicago and see for themselves the rich detail of a society in transition. His emphasis on detailed empirical research led to the development of new sociological techniques, notably participant observation, and though his ideas are often associated with the theory of structural functionalism he equally influenced such leading symbolic interactionists as Everett Hughes, Herbert Blumer and Howard Becker. Park collaborated with Ernest Burgess on a major textbook *Introduction to the Science of Sociology* (1921) but most of his writings were through occasional articles, reviews and essays, later published in three volumes by one of his students, Everett Hughes.

THE IDEA

When you study any city or large urban area certain distinct patterns of housing and residency emerge. Most cities can be divided up into distinct neighbourhoods or areas each with its own territorial boundaries, character and sense of community (or lack of it): the inner city slums and ghettoes of the poor, rootless and ethnic groups, the leafy suburbs of the middle class and the country mansions of the wealthy. Such neighbourhoods often appear to 'breed' their own distinctive way of life and pattern of behaviour. Some seem to be highly stable, others to be in a constant state of flux as new people move in and existing residents move out to the next neighbourhood or zone. Modern cities thus seem to be involved in a complex process of change and stabilisation, of adaptation and evolution, as their characters change and their boundaries grow. But what causes and directs such urban development; how does order emerge from such apparent chaos?

To answer such questions, Park and Burgess developed the theory of human ecology. From biology they borrowed the concept of ecology – the study of plant and animal lifestyles in relation to their environment, the web of life or ecosystem created by each species living in a particular area from which develops a balanced and interdependent way of life or community. Over time this natural community develops from simple to more complex forms through a sequence of stages called succession, by which each habitat is invaded by a new species. A state of disequilibrium or flux exists until a dominant species emerges in control of the environment and a new era of community and balance reigns until the next evolutionary invasion. Park combined such Darwinian ideas as natural selection, competition and struggle for survival with Emile Durkheim's concept of societies being governed by an underlying cultural and moral consensus and his idea of anomie (see page 63), that there is an inbuilt tension between the individual's need for freedom and society's need for social control. Thus human ecologists came to perceive the city as a sort of organism, a 'social jungle' with a life of its own, within which people continually adapt to their environment in a complex process of struggle for survival and competition for territory in which the strongest dominate and the weakest get left behind in the inner city. However, as in nature, once a period of territorial competition has abated, people, like plants, settle down into a particular neighbourhood, grow roots and develop a sense of community. A new era of invasion and succession develops as new groups invade the inner city, pushing existing residents out to invade their nearest neighbourhood with a ripple effect across the whole city. In time a new balance and equilibrium emerges with a new pattern of urban settlement, a new balance of urban power. One of Park's students, Roderick McKenzie, summed up this process of urban evolution as follows:

Just as in nature one species succeeds another as the dominant life form in a particular area, so too in the human community the pattern of land use changes as areas are invaded by new competitors which are better adapted to the changed environmental conditions than the existing users. Such a process of invasion and succession is reflected in the human community in changes in land values with the result that competition for desirable sites forces out the economically weaker existing users (e.g. residents) who make way for economically stronger competitors (e.g. business). Following a successful invasion, a new equilibrium is then established and the successional sequence comes to an end. (McKenzie, in Saunders, 1981)

And Ernest Burgess proposed his famous theory of concentric urban zones (1925). He noted the tendency for most cities to spread outwards like ripples on a pond with each zone tending to be inhabited by a particular 'class' of people. He conceived of five main urban zones arranged in a pattern of concentric circles. In the city centre there tends to be a central business district (CBD) surrounded by a zone of transition, followed by a belt of working men's housing, a residential area of high class apartments and finally a commuter zone of suburban areas in satellite towns. Whilst the well-to-do can afford to live out of the city, the poor and ethnic groups have no choice but to live in the polluted and slum areas of the zone of transition. As the population of the city grows, as industry expands, so, by a process of invasion and succession, the inhabitants of each zone move ever outward forming new patterns of urban settlement, new patterns of social segregration and community.

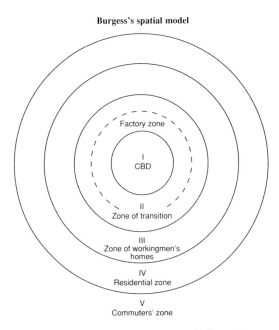

Figure 1   Burgess's Concentric Urban Zones

THE IDEA IN ACTION

The theory of human ecology seemed to explain many of the processes evident in Chicago and other major American cities in the early twentieth century; in particular:

■ The settlement patterns created by waves of immigrants and early industrialisation and the development of urban communities and segregation.
■ The lifestyles of such urban ghettoes as Little Sicily and Chinatown in the zone of transition.

Park and Burgess's theories spawned a wealth of mapping exercises tracing such zones and inspired a multitude of 'natural' histories of both slum and affluent neighbourhoods such as Zorbaugh's *The Gold Coast and the Slum* (1929). Much of this analysis focused on the zone of transition and its apparent disorganisation, its lack of social and moral order, its constant state of flux. It was seen as the least stable area, the one most likely to breed crime and deviance. Hence the mass of studies in this period of juvenile gangs, prostitutes, drug addicts and ethnic groups. The essence of human ecology was its attempt to explain city life in terms of distinctly separate urban laws of evolution, competition and market forces. This theoretical framework not only 'bred' a whole generation of urbanologists but left a legacy of concepts that are still popular today – the ideas of immigrants 'invading' a neighbourhood, of inner city areas breeding crime. It inspired Louis Wirth's classic essay 'Urbanism As a Way of Life' (1938) and the whole tradition of community studies.

However by the 1930s criticisms of this theory were growing, partly, ironically, as a result of the very empirical studies it had initiated:

■ Attempts to apply Burgess's zonal model to other cities did not always work. Its emphasis on competition, on a struggle by all for the same favourable locations, ignored cultural and personal influences on where and how people live. Firey's study (1945) of the residents of Beacon Hill in Boston and of an Italian slum showed how people were reluctant to move for sentimental reasons.

■ The major criticism of this approach, however, was its portrayal of urban development as something natural, the result of impersonal market forces which somehow produce a fair and equitable distribution of housing. To more radical writers such a conservative analysis seemed to justify the present inequalities of wealth and power and, most especially, to ignore the power of certain key groups (businessmen, planners, politicians) to control the life and futures of our cities by their decisions on investment, employment and housing. Various attempts were made to refine the theory of human ecology – by Hawley (1950), Duncan (1932), Schore (1965), and Mann (1965), but by the mid-1960s both it and its sister tradition, community studies, were being rejected in favour of theories based on conflict and power. Like their parent paradigm they were essentially conservative theories, good at explaining social consensus but weak in explaining rapid social change and conflict. They had no explanations for the riots and rebellions that swept western industrial cities in the 1960s as the urban environment exploded in waves of Black power, civil and women's rights and student rebellion. Urban sociology underwent a sort of paradigm revolution as the theories of Park and Parsons were overthrown in favour of the radical conflict perspectives of Marx and Weber.

Though now out of favour, the idea of human ecology still ranks as a founding theory in the development of urban sociology and Park's techniques of participant observation and 'fact finding' continue to inspire such potent modern-day studies of inner city life as Gerald Suttles of Chicago (1968) and Ken Pryce's of St Paul's, Bristol (1979).

SEE ALSO

☐ Urbanism
☐ Collective consumption
☐ Housing classes
☐ Urban managerialism for alternative views of how the city lives and breathes.

SUGGESTED READING

Matthews F.H. 'Quest for an American Sociology: R.E. Park and the Chicago School', quoted in *Student Encyclopaedia of Sociology*, Macmillan, 1977
Slattery M. 'Urban Sociology' in Haralambos ed. *Sociology New Directions*, Causeway Press, 1985 – a useful overview of urban sociology.
Smith D. 'The Chicago School', *Social Studies Review*, Vol 4 No 4, March 1989

FURTHER READING

Burgess E. 'The Growth of the City' in Park R.E. and Burges E. *The City*, University of Chicago Press, 1925
Park R.E. and Burgess E. *Introduction to the Science of Sociology*, University of Chicago Press, 1921
Pryce K. *Endless Pressure*, Penguin, 1979
Suttles G. *The Social Order of the Slum*, Chicago University Press, 1968
Wirth L. 'Urbanism as a Way of Life', *American Journal of Sociology*, Vol 44, 1938, pp 1–24
Zorbaugh H.W. *The Gold Coast and the Slum*, University of Chicago Press, 1929

EXAMINATION QUESTIONS

1 Assess the contribution of the Chicago School to the development of sociological theory and practice. (WJEC June 1986)
2 Evaluate the observation that cities may create crime. (London University January 1987)

37

TALCOTT PARSONS *and*
STRUCTURAL FUNCTIONALISM

THE AUTHOR

Talcott Parsons (1902–79) is generally acknowledged as the founding father of structural functionalism, the school of sociology that dominated American, and to a lesser extent British sociology in the 1940s and 1950s. He was born in Colorado Springs, USA, the son of a Congregational minister and a college teacher. He did his first degree at Amherst College (1920–4) and post-graduate work at the London School of Economics (1924–5) and Heidelberg University (1925–6) where he was influenced by the famous anthropologist Malinowski and the 'Weber Circle' respectively. In 1928 he was appointed as a lecturer at Harvard University and there he remained for the rest of his academic career, inspiring a whole generation of post-graduate students that included Robert Merton, Kingsley Davies, Neil Smelser and Harold Garfinkel. He wrote over 150 books and articles.

His key works include:

- *The Structure of Social Action* (1939)
- *Towards a General Theory of Action* (1951)
- *The Social System* (1951)
- *Societies: Evolutionary and Comparative Perspectives* (1966).

His overall aim was nothing less than a complete synthesis of the major ideas in sociology and the social sciences generally, from Durkheim and Malinowski through to Freud and Weber, into one complete theoretical framework capable of explaining not only the structure of society but the behaviour of the individual.

THE IDEA

The sociological perspective called 'Functionalism' did not originate with Parsons – that claim dates back to Comte, Spencer and especially Darwin. What Parsons did was to put the structure into functionalism, to make this rather general theme that society is a living entity with a life and structure of its own, above and beyond those of its members, theoretical and scientific. The usual analogy used by functionalist writers to explain how society works is that of a living organism which, to survive in an ever-changing environment, has to adapt and evolve, maintain its 'equilibrium' and ensure that every part of its body is 'functioning' properly (see Durkheim page 63).

Parsons however used a systems approach. He viewed all societies as distinct and self-sufficient systems made up of a wide variety of sub-systems, all interconnected and interdependent. Thus, for example, the economic system depends on the education system for its supply of skilled workers, schools depend on the family for their supply of future pupils. Each of these sub-systems contributes towards four key functional imperatives or basic needs that a society must fulfil in order to survive: 'A.G.I.L.', as discussed below.

ADAPTION

Every society has to feed, clothe and shelter its members and so it needs an economic system to produce and distribute its resources and adapt to the external environment.

GOAL ATTAINMENT

Every society has to set goals for itself, make decisions and create organisations and so needs a political system.

INTEGRATION

Every society has to create a sense of belonging, of community and common identity. It has to prevent the development of social divisions and conflict or it will disintegrate. It therefore needs systems for establishing codes of behaviour (religion), communication (media), and social control (the law, the courts, police and prisons).

LATENCY

Like all species, every society seeks to perpetuate itself even though individual members are constantly dying and being born. It seeks to pass on its rules, customs and culture from one generation to the next and such pattern maintenance, in Parsons' theory, depends primarily on the kinship system, on the family socialising its offspring. This process is reinforced by such other social institutions as schools, the media, the church and the law. Not only must society at large fulfil these four imperatives but the sub-system (and sub-sub-system) must too, if it is to function properly.

Strongly influenced by Durkheim, Parsons saw the 'heart and life-blood' of a stable and efficient social system as its central value system: its code of values and set of norms which, if properly established, would not only ensure perfect synchronisation of all the various sub-systems but ensure the integration of the individual so that everything and everyone is in perfect harmony, ticking over perfectly. But how do societies integrate, harmonise and motivate, often millions of people, each with their own personality, ambitions and desires, into working hard towards a set of common goals along certain social guidelines? According to Parsons this is achieved by socialisation, social control and role performance. Every individual has to perform a wide variety of social roles – as a parent, a worker, a citizen – and although other people's expectations pressure the individual into effective role performance and the system of social control can force him/her to carry out these duties, real efficiency comes from people being committed to the social system. Such 'internal' motivation comes from effective socialising, from parents bringing up their children properly, teaching them the prevailing norms and moral values of society to the point where they are internalised and become a part of the child's own consciousness, even conscience. Like Durkheim, therefore, Parsons emphasised the importance of morality in the central value system. Whilst his study of Freud and behaviourism led him to see children as empty vessels into which the culture of society could be poured, he saw human behaviour and personality as open to moulding, particularly by parents, through punishment and reward, love and affection, teaching children how to fit into society. Deviant behaviour was thus portrayed as primarily due to inadequate socialisation, necessitating the use of the institutions of social control (the police and courts) to restrain or isolate such unhealthy and anti-social behaviour.

Parsons went on to divide social norms and values into two main categories:

■ Those like particularism, affectivity and collective orientation that are essentially expressive or emotional ones.
■ Those like achievement, self-discipline and individualism that are instrumental or task-orientated.

Such pattern variables, Parsons argued, represent different levels of integration and equilibrium and reflect different types of society. More advanced societies, for example, rely on instrumental values for efficient functioning, whilst small-scale societies are more personal and expressive. Similarly, different social institutions rest on differing values. The family, for example, is essentially expressive, an 'emotional haven', whilst factories are usually impersonal and mainly concerned with results.

Such a distinction is very similar to Durkheim's idea of mechanical and organic solidarity (see page 55). Parsons further claimed that, by analysing a society's norms and values, sociologists could pinpoint sources of conflict and tension, areas where there was a lack of 'fit' between the values and norms of one sub-system and another, and suggest ways to improve integration, to help the transition of the individual from one social institution to another. Schools, for example, could prepare youngsters better for the changing world of work. The essence therefore of Parsons' social system is equilibrium, integration and consensus. All forms of conflict are generally seen as a threat to the stability and functioning of society and must be eliminated. He sought to show how society at large functions as a complete unit and how the individual fits into it.

THE IDEA IN ACTION

From this framework, Parsons produced some excellent empirical studies of, for example, the nuclear family and the sick role. He inspired a generation of functionalist studies like Davis and Moore's (1967) analysis of social stratification and, even today, functionalist ideas are a major source of sociological debate.

However, by the late 1960s, as even the consensus in American society was breaking down, with riots over Black power, Vietnam and civil rights, criticisms of structural functionalism grew and grew:

■ Parsons' view of human nature was criticised as overdeterministic, as making man seem like a 'puppet on a string' without any personality or free will of his own. Certainly this was the picture Parsons painted in his later works, but initially he had been heavily influenced by Weber's emphasis on social action, choice and meaning, on Freud's idea of tension between individual free will and society's need for control. However by the time of *The Social System* (1951) such 'subjective' understanding (*verstehen*) had given way to descriptions of people as cogs in the social machine.

■ His theory over-emphasises social consensus and order. It ignores the influence of power and is unable to explain rapid, especially revolutionary social change. In response to such criticisms Parsons did introduce 'evolutionary' ideas into his theory, arguing that societies, like nature, grow and mature through certain stages of evolution, and he did make some analysis of power but as an aid to collective action rather than a source of conflict.

■ It is a very 'conservative' approach. It assumes that all agree on the goals and values of society; it assumes consent and not only explains how the existing social order works but justifies it, arguing that whatever social institutions exist, must do so because they have a function to perform. It thus ignores the 'power' of some to impose their goals and values on society at large and offers no real framework for reforming or criticising the existing social systems.

■ It is a very 'American' approach, assuming that their system, their free enterprise economy and liberal democracy is naturally the best.

■ His writings are often tortuous to read, full of 'scientific' jargon and abstract theory and much of his argument is teleological, explaining an effect as a cause, explaining all social institutions by their function.

Attempts by students of Parsons, such as Robert Merton (and his notions of manifest and latent functions, and dysfunctions) and Lewis Coser (conflict as an integrating force) only temporarily stemmed the decline of structural functionalism and, today, the more radical and conflict-orientated approaches of Marx and Weber are more in sociological fashion in Britain and Europe (though less so in America).

Though in today's conflict-ridden and divided world structural functionalism seems a highly conservative, even archaic and less relevant sociological explanation, it was a major step in establishing sociology as a separate and scientific discipline and it still has tremendous value as an explanation of social order and integration.

SEE ALSO

☐ Positivism
☐ **Social Darwinism** and Durkheim's ideas on **Social solidarity** as background material to this modern version of functionalism.

☐ **Phenomenology** and its offshoots
☐ **Ethnomethodology** and
☐ **Symbolic interactionism** for very different interpretations of social structure and change.
☐ **Historical materialism** and its offshoots
☐ **Structural Marxism** and **Critical theory** represent a further alternative based on conflict rather than consensus.

SUGGESTED READING

Hamilton P. *Talcott Parsons*, Tavistock, 1983 – an introduction and overview.

FURTHER READING

Coser L. *The Functions of Social Conflict,* Free Press, New York, 1956
Davis K. and Moore W.E. 'Some Principles of Stratification', in Bendix R. and Lipset S.M. eds. *Class, Status and Power*, Routledge & Kegan Paul, 1967
Parsons T. *The Structure of Social Action* McGraw-Hill, 1939
Parsons T. *The Social System*, Free Press, 1951
Parsons T. and Shils E.A. eds. *Towards a General Theory of Action*, Harvard University Press, 1951
Parsons T. and Shils E.A. eds. *Social Structure and Personality*, Free Press, 1964
Parsons T. and Shils E.A. eds. *Societies: Evolutionary and Comparative Perspectives*, Prentice Hall, 1966
Parsons T. and Shils E.A. eds. *Sociological Theory and Modern Society*, Free Press, 1967
Parsons T. and Shils E.A. eds. *The System of Modern Societies*, Free Press, 1971
Parsons T. and Shils E.A. eds. *The Evolution of Societies*, Prentice Hall, 1977

EXAMINATION QUESTIONS

1 'An essential task of sociology is to explain the functioning of society and to explore the relations between the parts and the whole and among the parts themselves.' Discuss and illustrate. (WJEC June 1987)
2 It has been argued that 'there are, in fact, *two* sociologies: a sociology of social system and a sociology of social action. One type of sociology views action as deriving from the system, the other views the social system as deriving from social interactions.' Using illustrations from any area of sociology with which you are familiar, explain what you understand by this statement. Comment briefly on whether you see these two approaches as contradictory or complementary to one another. (JMB June 1987 Paper 1)

3 'The central problem in sociological theory is explaining the interrelations between social structure and social action.' Explain and evaluate this view. (Oxford Delegacy May 1987)

4 'Functionalist accounts of the family underestimate the extent of strain and exploitation in family life.' Discuss. (AEB June 1989 Paper 2)

38

KARL POPPER *and*
FALSIFICATION

THE AUTHOR

Sir Karl Popper (1902–   ) was born in Vienna, the son of a prosperous lawyer and a talented musician. After the First World War he studied for nearly ten years at the University of Vienna, receiving his doctorate in 1928 and qualifying as a secondary schoolteacher in mathematics and physics in 1929. In 1934 he published his first major work *The Logic of Scientific Discovery* and so began his career as a philosopher. He emigrated to New Zealand in 1937 but later (1945) returned to take up a post at the London School of Economics where he remained as Professor of Logic and Scientific Method until his retirement in 1969. He and his wife took out British citizenship and later he was knighted (1965) and made a Companion of Honour (1982).

Popper's lectures and writings have inspired generations of students to ponder the philosophical secrets of the universe and in particular those discovered by modern science. Equally, although an enthusiastic Marxist in his youth, Popper became a major critic of this and various other political dogmas that he feared threatened 'open' democracy. Sir Peter Medawar, a Nobel Prize Winner, described Popper as 'incomparably the greatest philosopher of science that has ever been'.

His key works include:

- *The Logic of Scientific Discovery* (1934)
- *The Open Society and its Enemies* (1945)
- *The Poverty of Historicism* (1957)
- *Conjectives and Refutations* (1963) and
- *Objective Knowledge* (1972).

THE IDEA

The traditional view of scientific discovery and knowledge is that of a process of *verification*. The scientist observes the results of carefully controlled experiments from which an idea, hypothesis or theory emerges about the behaviour of a particular type of matter. The scientist searches by further experiments for evidence to verify his hypothesis which, if successful, grows in stature into a scientific theory or law upon which he and other researchers can not only accumulate further knowledge about the wonders of nature but can actually 'predict' its behaviour. This process of accumulating fresh facts, this constant searching for new ideas by observation and experiment is known as induction, and this method is seen as the dividing line between scientific and non-scientific knowledge.

In *The Logic of Scientific Method*, Sir Karl Popper pointed out two key flaws in this traditional picture of scientific method and knowledge:

■ Firstly that, in reality, many of the major scientific discoveries had resulted not from systematic observation and analysis but from wild speculation, inspiration and chance.

■ Secondly, that no matter how scientifically arrived at, no theory can be totally verified, absolutely correct. Rather as the eighteenth-century philosopher, David Hume, argued there is always the possibility that sometime in the future it will be 'falsified', proved wrong. All it takes is one or two contrary examples. It only takes the observation of one black swan (as has occurred in Australia) to refute the thesis that all swans are white. Equally, whilst we can predict that the sun will rise tomorrow we cannot prove it until it happens. Thus, in Popper's view, all scientific hypotheses are only temporal and as yet unrefuted: all scientific knowledge is provisional, workable and the best available so far.

Popper therefore proposed that the real essence of scientific method was not and could not be verification but was and should be falsification, that good science would involve a process of trial and error or conjecture and refutation by which scientists were actively encouraged to develop bold new ideas and hypotheses and then set up tests and experiments, not to prove them correct but to refute or falsify them. In this way weak and inadequate theories could be swiftly eliminated and only the strongest ideas would survive for future testing and form the basis for some temporary advances in scientific knowledge and understanding.

A good scientific theory for Popper therefore is one that is falsifiable, one that makes definite claims and predictions about the natural or social world that can then be put to the test. Newton's theory of gravity fulfilled such a criterion by making a wide variety of highly testable claims which survived examination for over a century, and so became the basis for major advances in scientific knowledge. Falsification, however, gradually eroded its authority and opened the way for Einstein's grandiose and spectacular theory of relativity which, so far, has survived the tests of the twentieth century. A bad scientific theory is one that is not empirically or rationally testable, one that is so general and wide-ranging that there is nothing definite to test, or one whose supporters ignore such criticism and simply keep amending it whenever its predictions prove false. Popper was especially scathing here about Marxism and psychoanalysis, both of which he regarded as pseudo- or 'untestable' sciences.

In some of its earlier formulations [Marxist] predictions were testable and in fact falsified. Yet instead of accepting the refutations the followers of Marx reinterpreted both the theory and the evidence in order to make them agree. (Popper, 1963)

Thus, for Popper, what distinguished science from non-science was the falsifiability of its ideas and knowledge and, though this meant that we could never absolutely prove any scientific theory, such continual testing did bring us gradually nearer to the truth, slowly peeling away the many layers of reality. More important, for immediate, practical purposes it gave us 'relatively' solid ground upon which to base our technology and social policies.

THE IDEA IN ACTION

Popper's idea of science as a process of falsification rather than verification has been widely accepted as an accurate description of what scientists actually do and should do. Such a thesis supports the popular view of scientific method as highly rational and objective, and of scientific knowledge as being tried, tested and true compared to the untestable claims of such 'disciplines' as religion and mysticism. The distinguished mathematician and astronomer Sir Hermann Bondi declared: 'There is no more to science than its method and there is no more to its method than Popper has said.'

Others, however, have severely criticised Popper's model of scientific discovery.

■ Firstly, it is in practice very difficult to falsify a theory. Although a particular experiment many disprove an hypothesis, its author could rightfully claim that the experiment was at fault not the idea; that under different conditions the hypothesis would have stood up. More important, whilst a theory may seem false now, with the development of more accurate scientific techniques it may well be proved correct sometime in the future. As A. F. Chalmers (1982) points out, if falsification had been strictly adhered to some of the now most respected of scientific theories would never have been developed, including Newton's gravitational theory and Bohr's theory of the atom.

■ Secondly, writers like Kuhn (1962) and Feyerabend (1975) have argued that far from scientific discovery being a process of rational, critical and open-minded enquiry, scientists are in fact a very closed and conservative community very opposed to outside criticism. Feyerabend criticises the sloppiness, secretiveness and lack of imagination of modern scientific method and calls for a far more speculative and 'abandoned' approach. T. S. Kuhn has argued that during any one period of 'normal science' scientists are locked into a particular theory or paradigm (see page 162) which is taken for granted and from which alternative ideas are excluded or rejected. Only when this dominant paradigm reaches a 'crisis' point, when the evidence against it is so overwhelming that it cannot be ignored does a 'scientific revolution' take place and a new paradigm (and with it a new generation of scientists) take control and reanalyse all existing scientific knowledge. Thus, whilst Popper accepts that existing knowledge is relative and provisional, he does believe that ultimately we will discover an objective reality and truth. However, for writers like Kuhn all knowledge, even scientific knowledge, is relative, depending for its existence and meaning on the theoretical framework through which it is interpreted.

Despite such criticisms Popper's thesis of falsification has been a major advance in the philosophy of science and still has a lot of popular appeal, not least because it recognises the limitations and fallibility of human understanding and because it proposes a gradual and critical improvement in human knowledge and society rather than the all-embracing claims of some less rigorous theories.

SEE ALSO

☐ Positivism
☐ Paradigms and
☐ Sociology of science

SUGGESTED READING

Magee B. *Karl Popper*, Fontana, 1973

FURTHER READING

Chalmers A.F. *What is this Thing Called Science?*, OUP, 1982
Feyerabend *Against Method*, New Left Books, 1975
Kuhn T.S. *The Structure of Scientific Revolutions*, Chicago University Press, 1962, 1970
Popper K. *The Logic of Scientific Discovery*, Hutchinson, 1934
Popper K. *The Open Society and its Enemies*, Routledge & Kegan Paul, 1945
Popper K. *The Poverty of Historicism*, Routledge & Kegan Paul, 1957
Popper K. *Conjectures and Refutations. The Growth of Scientific Knowledge*, Routledge & Kegan Paul, 1963
Popper K. *Objective Knowledge. An Evolutionary Approach*, Clarendon Press, 1972

EXAMINATION QUESTIONS

1 'Sociologists may be unable to use the methods of natural scientists; nevertheless sociology can still be scientific.' Discuss. (Oxford Delegacy May 1985)
2 Examine the similarities and differences between sociology and natural science. (AEB November 1988)

39

NICOS POULANTZAS *and*
RELATIVE AUTONOMY

THE AUTHOR

Nicos Poulantzas (1936–79) was born in Athens, the son of a Professor of Forensic Science and a leading figure in the Greek legal establishment. A very bright child and an outstanding student, Poulantzas was educated at an experimental school attached to the University of Athens, and at the University itself, from where he graduated with a degree in law in 1957. From an early age he acquired an intense interest in philosophy, especially existentialism, socialism and Marxism, becoming an active member of the Greek Communist Party and United Democratic Left. On graduating he entered the Greek navy as a translator and then gained a licence to practice law. He wanted to go to Germany to do his doctorate but, with the growth of Nazism, he moved to Paris, becoming immersed in the French intellectual circle which included Sartre, Simone de Beauvoir and Merleau-Ponty. He became deputy editor of the French legal journal *Archives de philosophie du droit* and from 1966 to 1972 worked as legal researcher to the National Centre of Scientific Research. He married Ann Leclerc in 1972.

Increasingly influenced by Althusser, Gramsci and British Marxists, Poulantzas moved towards Eurocommunism and away from the rigid Marxism of Stalinism. He split with the Greek Communist Party over the Soviet invasion of Czechoslovakia and Russian support for the Greek military dictatorship. He stood as a candidate for the breakaway Greek Communist Party in the 1977 election. He was profoundly influenced by both the Greek generals' military coup (1967) and the May revolution in France (1968). He obtained a lectureship in sociology at the University of Paris and collaborated with Louis Althusser on such major theoretical and strategic issues as the nature of class and the role of the state in post-war capitalism. He returned to Greece in 1974 after the collapse of the Greek junta to advise the transitional government on educational matters. He continued teaching at Vincennes and at the post-graduate School of Advanced Studies in Social

Science and continued with his involvement in left-wing politics in Greece and France. He suddenly committed suicide in October 1979 at the age of forty-three.

Poulantzas is generally considered a leading Marxist intellectual of the 1970s.

His major works include:

- *Political Power and Social Classes* (1973)
- *Fascism and Dictatorship* (1974)
- *Classes in Contemporary Capitalism* (1975)
- *The Crisis of Dictatorships* (1975)
- *State, Power, Socialism* (1978)

THE IDEA

A key issue in recent Marxist analyses and debates has been the role of the state in advanced capitalist societies; a state that has taken many forms from the liberal democracy of western countries to the fascist model of the 1930s and many Third World countries today. Traditional Marxism tended to view the state – which comprises not only the government but all the associated organs of state control such as the army, police, courts and civil service – as merely the organ of the ruling class, and tended to see political activities simply as a reflection of underlying economic changes. Thus, for example, under feudalism the ruling class, the aristocracy, not only owned the means of production (land) but actually sat in government and directly ran the civil service, army and courts, and so were able to suppress the peasantry and maintain their own interests. However, in the twentieth century (in an age of mass democracy) such direct class rule is difficult to sustain. A variety of people from a variety of social backgrounds now hold office, and non-capitalist, even socialist parties now get elected into government. So how does advanced capitalism continue to control the state? One answer proposed by writers like Sam Aaronovitch (1961) and Ralph Miliband (1969) is that the modern state is 'manned' by the capitalist class and constrained by the capitalist system; that most top political posts are held by those from public school and upper middle-class backgrounds and that, even when socialist parties get into power as, for example, with the British Labour governments of the 1960s and 1970s, ultimate power lies with big business and the city financiers.

Nicos Poulantzas, in a famous and long-running debate with Miliband, rejected such an individualistic approach in favour of a more structural analysis based on the concept of *relative autonomy*. He puts far greater emphasis on the capitalist system and considers the individuals in power as relatively irrelevant. In an attempt to draw up an ideal model of the capitalist system and capitalist state, Poulantzas argues that the capitalist mode of production comprises three key levels or sub-systems – the economic, political and ideological which, though inter-related, also have some measure of autonomy or independence. Thus, whilst the economic system significantly influences the political and ideological, it is equally possible for political and ideological events to influence the economy and/or develop a momentum of their own.

Amid this complex interaction the role of the modern capitalist state is to regulate the system as a whole, protect the long-term interests of capitalism, maintain bourgeois rule and healthy profits and keep the proletariat under control – by force if necessary, by ideology if possible. In particular, it has to regulate the class struggle, an underlying antagonism between capital and labour that cannot be eliminated but which can be controlled to prevent actual class revolution breaking out. And the way to do this in an age of mass democracy and liberal freedoms is not by direct suppression, but by indirect control, by the state having 'relative autonomy' from the ruling class. In this way the government, police and judiciary can 'appear' to be independent of any one class and so gain the support and consent of all classes in society. Moreover, an 'independent' state can better protect the long-term interests of the capitalist system than can the capitalist class itself, which is highly fragmented and divided into a variety of 'fractions' or competing interests which range from large landowners and big business to high finance and the multinationals. By having relative autonomy, the government can mediate between the various fractions of the capitalist class and between the bourgeoisie and the proletariat, thus giving the ruling class vital unity and leadership and preventing outright class conflict. Such autonomy allows the government to grant short-term concessions to the working class such as increased welfare provisions, and even allows it to introduce restrictions against capitalist 'fractions' or groups such as speculators, whose greed threatens to upset the whole system or the reputation of capitalism. The capitalist state is thus able to discipline the ruling class and fragment the working class, protect the long-term interests of capitalism and preserve its appearance of neutrality. Such neutrality is a vital element in modern class control. By 'appearing' to represent all the people and all social classes, the modern state can rule by consent rather than by force as in the past. Such ideological control is far more effective than military might and direct suppression.

But how is such a delicate balancing act achieved? How does the state know when or how to respond to the ever-changing balance of power between capital and labour? For Poulantzas the key mechanism is the 'class struggle' which at all times is reflected in the state apparatus – in parliament, government, the civil service, etc. – as a balance of power between workers and capitalists, one that ebbs and flows as each side grows in strength or weakens. When, for example, the unions are strong, as in the early 1970s in Britain, the government will grant concessions in the form of wage rises, welfare benefits or new laws against landlords or employers. When the working class is weak or disunited, or when key interests of capitalism are threatened, then the government will stamp down on the unions, restrain wages, cut taxes and boost profits rather than jobs, as in the Britain of the 1980s. And it does not really matter which party is in power. Both monetarism and trade union restrictions, key aspects of the Conservative Government of Mrs Thatcher, were originally initiated by Labour Governments in the late 1960s and 1970s. For Poulantzas the class background of top politicians, judges, etc. is irrelevant. What is crucial is the fact that the structure of capitalist society forces the state to act in the long-term interests of capitalism, whoever occupies the seats of power. Its autonomy, however, is always relative and limited. The state could never be used to destroy or undermine capitalism, so severely restricting the potential for a socialist party in western capitalist society to democratically achieve power and effect a peaceful transition to socialism. The form that this class control takes, be it military rule, fascism or liberal democracy, will depend on particular national political developments, but the more disguised this rule is, the better. 'The capitalist state best serves the interests of the capitalist class only when members of this class do not participate directly in the state apparatus, that is to say when the Ruling Class is not the politically governing class' (Poulantzas, 1973).

THE IDEA IN ACTION

According to his biographer, Bob Jessop (1985), 'it is no exaggeration to claim that Poulantzas remains the single most important and influential Marxist theorist of the state and politics in the post-war period'. His ideas have had influence as far afield as Latin America and Scandinavia and his concept of relative autonomy continues to be a major contribution to both the theory and practice of the modern capitalist state, of how the ruling class continues to rule, and of strategies by which that rule might be undermined by stimulating struggles between the various fractions of the capitalist class *within* the state as well as by encouraging outside revolution by the working class.

However, the concept of relative autonomy has also been subject to serious criticism both over its vagueness and the difficulty of finding evidence of it at work. Exactly how relative is relative autonomy? How autonomous and constrained is the state? Dearlove and Saunders (1984) have identified four particular weaknesses of this theory:

■ Poulantzas' argument is circular, that the only way to gauge the strength or weakness of the working class is by the amount of concessions it is granted. However, it could equally be argued that even when the working class is weak it may gain state benefits, especially if the Labour Party is in power.

■ It is tautologous. The idea of relative autonomy is untestable. It can be used to explain everything and nothing because Poulantzas fails to provide any criteria for testing it empirically.

■ It is too narrow. It only includes the class struggle, so ignoring the rise of many other groups and interests in post-war society which cut across class lines – feminism, Blacks, gays, environmental groups, etc. Poulantzas' attempts to subsume all such pressure groups under a class analysis is inadequate.

■ It is incomplete. It ignores the influence of individual personalities, groups and factions, offering only a mechanical analysis which implies that it makes no real difference whether Margaret Thatcher or Tony Benn, the National Front or Militant Tendency are in power.

This is the essence of the alternative Marxist view of the workings of the modern capitalist state proposed by writers like Ralph Miliband (1969) in his long-running debate with Poulantzas. Miliband argues that members of the capitalist class actually staff the modern state, steering it through the periodic crises that are endemic to capitalism and using it to suppress the class struggle. Miliband's approach is more flexible and less deterministic than Poulantzas', dependent more on people and personalities than the underlying structure and logic of the system, but it, too, suffers from problems of actually measuring such a balance of power, and of proving that a concession was a concession, not a reform. Neither approach clearly answers the key practical question of whether a socialist or labour party can transform capitalism into socialism – though neither is optimistic.

In his final work (*State, Power, Socialism*, 1978) and in research notes published after his death, Poulantzas himself was moving away from the idea of relative autonomy. Nevertheless, it has stimulated a major debate within modern Marxism and brought to the forefront of sociological theory the role and functioning of the modern state.

SEE ALSO

☐ **Structural Marxism** as a parent theory of this idea.

SUGGESTED READING

Jessop B. *Nicos Poulantzas*, Macillan, 1985 – as overview of Poulatzas' life and work.

Lukes S. *Power: A Radical View*, Macmillan, 1974 – a superb summary and development of the whole debate on power today.

Miliband R. *The State in Capitalist Society*, Weidenfeld & Nicolson, 1969 – an easy read of an alternative view of the structure of the modern state.

Urry J. and Wakeford J. eds. *Power in Britain*, Heinemann, 1973 – summarises the Miliband–Poulantzas debate

FURTHER READING

Aaronovitch S. *The Ruling Class*, Lawrence & Wishart, 1961

Dearlove J. and Saunders P. *Introduction to British Politics*, Polity Press, 1984

Poulantzas N. *Political Power and Social Classes*, New Left Books, 1973

Poulantzas N. *Fascism and Dictatorship*, New Left Books, 1974

Poulantzas N. *Classes in Contemporary Capitalism*, New Left Books, 1975

Poulanztas N. *The Crisis of Dictatorships*, New Left Books, 1975

Poulantzas N. *State, Power, Socialism*, New Left Books, 1978

EXAMINATION QUESTIONS

1 'Despite increased social mobility and the expansion of the education system the British power structure has remained fundamentally unaltered since the nineteenth century.' Discuss. (Cambridge Local Examinations Syndicate June 1986)

2 'What have sociologists identified as the role of the state in advanced industrial societies?' (AEB June 1985)

40

JOHN REX, ROBERT MOORE *and*

HOUSING CLASSES

THE AUTHORS

John Rex (1925–   ) was born in South Africa and educated at Rhodes University College. He took his doctorate at Leeds University and lectured there from 1949 to 1962. After two years at Birmingham University Rex was appointed Professor of Social Theory and Institutions at Durham University (1964–70) and from 1970 to 1979 he was Professor of Sociology at Warwick University. He became Director of the SSRC Unit on Ethnic Relations at the University of Aston and is currently Research Professor on Ethnic Relations at Warwick University.

His major works include:

- ■ *Key Problems in Sociology* (1961)
- ■ *Race Relations in Sociological Theory* (1970)
- ■ *Colonial Immigrants in a British City* (1979)
- ■ *Race, Community and Conflict* (1967).

Robert Moore (1936–   ) was born in Kent. After eight years in the Royal Navy, he read sociology and social administration at Hull University. He lectured at Durham University between 1965 and 1970, then moved to Aberdeen University, where he is now Professor of Sociology.

THE IDEA

The late 1950s and early 1960s saw the emergence of race relations as a major social problem. The Black and ethnic groups of America and Europe rose up in protest against poverty, discrimination and prejudice. The cities of Harlem, Detroit and Watts in the USA exploded in orgies of violence and destruction as Black power took to the streets. The Notting Hill riots of 1958 raised fears of a 'race war' in Britain too and Enoch Powell's famous 'Rivers of Blood' speech in 1965 thrust the issue of immigration to the forefront of British politics. The traditional perspectives in urban sociology of human ecology and community studies could not explain such conflict and confrontation, so sociologists of this period increasingly turned to the more radical theories of Marx and Weber.

At the forefront of this academic revolution was Rex and Moore's book *Race, Community and Conflict* (1967) and their theory of housing classes. Their aim was to try and explain the distribution of housing in the cities of advanced industrial societies, to explain in particular why ethnic groups always seemed to end up trapped, isolated and segregated in the ghetto areas of the inner city. They sought to show the link between housing and racial conflict. They chose as the basis of their study the Sparkbrook area of Birmingham, an apparently typical 'immigrant colony' in the twilight zone of a city that regularly attracted thousands of Asians and West Indians, anxious to share in the British dream of a secure job and a home of their own.

Like the human ecologists before them (see page 234), Rex and Moore noted that housing in Birmingham followed a circular pattern comprising an inner ring of the central business district and a zone of transition, surrounded by three further rings each with a different type of housing, 'class' of resident and type of lifestyle – the cramped terraces of the working class in the inner zones, the semi-detached houses of the middle classes in the suburbs and the detached mansions of the very wealthy out in the country. Whilst the white classes occasionally moved up the housing hierarchy, black immigrants remained trapped in the delapidated Victorian slums of the zone of transition. To try and explain such racial segregation Rex and Moore devised the concept of housing classes. Instead of using occupation or the ownership and non-ownership of the means of production as the basis of their 'class' analysis, as traditional and Marxist sociologists did, Rex and Moore adopted Weber's view that social class is based on a wide variety of 'market' situations and that a person's lifestyle and status depends not only on their job and income but also on their control of such key sources of power and wealth as housing. They argued that everyone, from the homeless and the council tenant through to the home-owner and the lord of the manor, belongs to a housing class according to their position on the housing hierarchy. 'Membership of a housing class is of first importance in determining a man's associations, his interests, his lifestyle and his position in the urban social structure' (Rex and Moore, 1967). Such housing classes are involved in a 'class struggle' for that most scarce and valued of resources – a home in the suburbs. Inevitably, in such a struggle, there are winners and losers and, whilst the more powerful groups achieve this suburban ideal, the weaker ones have to accept inferior housing on council estates or in the inner city: 'there is a class struggle over the use of houses and this struggle is the central process of the city as a social unit' (Rex and Moore, 1967).

However, this part of their thesis on its own does not explain why Black groups in particular end up in the twilight zone and are unable to move out. Such racial segregation is caused, argued Rex and Moore, not only by their poverty and by the racialism of the host white society, but also by the way the rules and regulations of the housing markets, both public and private, work. Blacks are not offered mortgages by the building societies because they lack secure employment. They cannot get on to council house waiting lists because they have not lived in the area long enough. Both these public and private bureaucracies have an 'inbuilt bias' towards 'respectable' white workers. Hence the ease with which the middle classes get mortgages and the skilled working classes get on to good council estates. Thus Rex and Moore's definition of a housing class included not only the type of housing possessed but a group's ability to satisfy the rules and regulations of either the building societies or the local authority. On this basis they identified five main housing classes, a list they later extended to seven.

1   The outright owners of large houses in desirable areas.
2   Mortgage payers who 'own' whole houses in desirable areas.
3   Local authority tenants in houses built by the local authority.
4   Local authority tenants in slum houses awaiting demolition.
5   Tenants of private house owners.
6   House owners who must take lodgers to meet repayments.
7   Lodgers in rooms.

Like Park and Burgess (see page 234), Rex and Moore saw the continuous outward growth of the city as a sort of 'urban leapfrog' as all classes tried to achieve the ideal of a house in the suburbs. Left behind in the zone of transition and ignored by the building societies and housing departments, the only way immigrants can house themselves is to buy up a tenement at high rates of interest and let out as many rooms as possible. Such multi-occupation leads to a further deterioration in inner-city housing, to increasing complaints about 'Rachman-like' landlords and so the local authority introduces new laws to stop such landlordism and delapidation spreading. Thus residents blame the immigrants for lowering the tone of the neighbourhood and racist stereotypes about overcrowding become widespread. Immigrants thus become both the victims and the scapegoats for the discriminatory policies and inadequate housing provision of the housing authorities. Equally, trapped in ghetto housing by white racism, the Black community's own alienation and frustration festers. As Rex and Moore so profoundly predicted:

Any attempt to segregate the inhabitants of this area permanently is bound to involve conflict. The long term destiny of a city which frustrates the desire to improve their status by segregationist policies is some sort of urban riot. (Rex and Moore, 1967)

THE IDEA IN ACTION

Rex and Moore's theory of housing classes was a brilliant and original exposé of the real forces underlying the distribution of housing in our cities today and the way this distribution of such a key source of wealth and power is intimately linked to social inequality and racial conflict. It highlighted the way the policies and practices of housing officials, rather than any natural 'market forces', were creating both housing shortages and the inner city ghettos, were laying the foundations for race riots in Britain just as explosive as those in the USA. The riots of the 1980s showed just how accurate their predictions were to be as first St Paul's, Bristol, and then Brixton, Toxteth and later Birmingham's own Handsworth district exploded in violence and destruction. Their thesis inspired a series of studies into Britain's other inner cities and into local authority housing policies. A recent study of Hackney Council in London, for example, clearly revealed the way racial prejudice often underlies the allocation of council housing.

Ironically, such studies also revealed severe weaknesses in Rex and Moore's thesis. Firstly, as Rex later accepted, Sparkbrook was not a typical inner-city immigrant area. Neighbouring Handsworth with its mixture of West Indians, Asians and poor white, mainly elderly, residents was a much better example. Secondly the whole idea of housing classes underwent severe criticism:

■ As R. Haddon (1970) argued, Rex and Moore seemed to have confused cause and effect. The house you own or occupy is not the *cause* of your position in the social hierarchy, but the effect. If you are rich you can buy a big house but buying a big house does not make you rich. The unequal distribution of housing in society is the result not the cause of the unequal distribution of wealth. Moreover, home ownership is part of the lifecycle and changes not only through changes in income but changes in need. Thus a young couple with young children might need a large semi-detached house whereas an elderly couple prefer a bungalow. It is your occupation or income rather than your house that determines your class position and lifestyle.

■ Since no two individuals are ever exactly in the same position in the housing market, Rex and Moore's list of housing classes can be added to *ad infinitum*. They themselves added to it twice. They offered no criteria for identifying specific housing classes and their thesis was more a description of struggles *within* housing classes than between them. Generally the middle classes compete against each other in the private housing market whilst the working classes compete for council housing on good or bad estates.

■ A variety of studies have shown that not all social groups aspire to a house in the suburbs. Some positively prefer to live in the inner city. Many immigrants may prefer such areas because they are cheap (and so they can send more money home to their families in India and Pakistan) and because living with fellow countrymen allows them to continue practising their own culture and provides a form of self-protection and mutual aid. Similarly Davies's study in Newcastle (1972) showed that lodging-house landlords often bought tenement housing, not as a last resort but as a way of making money.

■ Despite all the obstacles, some immigrant groups have moved out of their inner city ghettoes and successfully integrated into more middle-class suburban areas (Ratcliffe, 1981).

In the face of such criticism Rex eventually gave up the idea of housing classes in favour of describing the position of Blacks in Britain as an 'underclass' (Rex and Tomlinson, 1979). Nevertheless Rex and Moore's theory of housing classes was a major contribution to debates in the 1960s and 1970s on race relations and social conflict. It deservedly ranks as a major inspiration behind the radical new approaches to urban sociology that poured forth in this period.

SEE ALSO

☐ Collective consumption
☐ Human ecology
☐ Urbanism
☐ **Urban managerialism** as alternative theories of urban development and conflict.

SUGGESTED READING

Rex J. and Moore R. *Race, Community and Conflict*, OUP, 1967
Slattery M. 'Urban Society' in Haralambos ed. *Sociology New Directions*, Causeway Press, 1985 – provides a short overview of the topic.

FURTHER READING

Bottomore T.B. *Classes in Modern Society*, Penguin, 1965
Davies J. *The Evangelistic Bureaucrat*, Tavistock, 1972
Haddon R. 'A Minority in a Welfare State Society', *New Atlantis* Vol. 2, 1970
Moore R. *Pitmen, Preachers and Politics*, CUP, 1974
Moore R. *Racism and Black Resistance in Britain*, Routledge & Kegan Paul 1975
Moore R. *The Social Impact of Oil – The Case of Peterhead*, Routledge & Kegan Paul, 1982
Rex J. and Moore R. *Race Relations in Sociological Theory*, Weidenfeld & Nicolson, 1970
Rex J. and Moore R. *Race, Colonialism and the City*, Routledge & Kegan Paul, 1973
Rex J. and Tomlinson S. *Colonial Immigrants in a British City*, Routledge & Kegan Paul, 1979

EXAMINATION QUESTIONS

1 'Racism is the major explanation for the disadvantages experienced by ethnic minorities in industrial societies.' Explain and discuss. (AEB November 1988)
2 Examine sociological explanations of zones of high deprivation in urban areas. (AEB November 1988)

41

ROBERT ROSENTHAL
LEONE JACOBSON *and*

SELF-FULFILLING PROPHECY

THE AUTHORS

A wide variety of writers have contributed to the development of the idea of a self-fulfilling prophecy, not least Professor J. W. B. Douglas in his classic study of educational achievement *The Home and The School* (1964). However, the first detailed study of this thesis is generally attributed to a series of experiments at Oak School in California by Robert Rosenthal and Leone Jacobson and outlined in their book *Pygmalion in the Classroom* (1968). Both were educational psychologists and Rosenthal is best known for his work on 'experimenter effects', especially through his book *Experimenter Effects in Behavioural Research* (1966).

THE IDEA

Rosenthal and Jacobson developed their thesis from the fairly commonplace observation that 'people more often than not do what is expected of them'. So strong is this tendency that it is often possible to prophesy how a person will behave in a given situation even if you have never met them before. The accuracy of this prediction, however, increases if you have met them before, not only because you know more about them but because such knowledge affects the way you treat them and so in a sense you are creating the very behaviour you are expecting. In other words, how you treat people not only has a self-fulfilling effect but can create a self-fulfilling prophecy – an idea developed by George Bernard Shaw in his classic play *Pygmalion*:

You see, really and truly, apart from the things anyone can pick up (the dressing and the proper way of speaking, and so on), the difference between a lady and a flower girl is not how she behaves, but how she's treated. I shall always be a flower girl to Professor Higgins, because he always treats me as a flower girl, and always will; but I know I can be a lady to you, because you always treat me as a lady, and always will.

Drawing on insights into this idea by the sociologists Robert Merton and Gordon Allport, the famous Hawthorne studies and a variety of experiments on animals and their trainers, Rosenthal and Jacobson sought to apply this thesis to education; to test the hypothesis that teachers' expectations not only had an influence on pupil performance but actually created *Pygmalions in the Classroom*.

Oak School was a public elementary school with a below-average record of achievement in a poor part of a Californian city. Pupils were divided into three streams according to academic ability and, although Mexican children were a minority in the school, they tended to be in the majority in the bottom stream. In the spring of 1964 Rosenthal and Jacobson tested all the school's pupils with a non-verbal test of intelligence called the 'Harvard Test of Inflected Acquisition'. The teachers were told that this particular test had the capacity to pick out those pupils with the potential for intellectual 'blooming' or spurting. The following school year the researchers gave the teachers the names of 20 per cent of their pupils from all three streams with such potential. In fact this IQ test was simply a standard one and far from the test picking out these 'spurters', the researchers had done so using a table of random numbers. Thus no real difference actually existed between the special children and the ordinary children. It was all 'in the mind of the teacher'.

Nevertheless, in subsequent testing these special children achieved remarkable increases in their IQ scores compared to pupils in the control group. Nearly half the experimental group increased their IQ score by twenty points compared with only 20 per cent of the control group. The most dramatic increases were initially amongst younger pupils though this advance subsequently fell off. Older pupils were less easily influenced by increased teacher expectancy initially, but over time they too improved and such gains tended to be maintained later, even when taught by teachers who had not been told that they were special. There was little difference between the sexes though boys tended to bloom more in verbal IQ and girls in reasoning. Most important, it was not the pupils in the bottom stream who developed most from increased teacher expectations (as the researchers had expected) but those in the middle band, and this advance was sustained over the next two years of tests. Gains by Mexican children, however, were significant. Even those who merely looked like Mexicans did better from the more positive attitudes of their teachers: a sort of inverse 'halo effect' because teachers were so surprised at any Mexicans doing well in the initial test.

Thus the Oak School experiment showed just how powerful an influence teacher expectation is on pupil performance and that once set in motion a self-sustaining cycle of improvement is capable of feeding on itself.

'Teachers may not only get more when they expect more; they may also come to expect more when they get more' (Rosenthal and Jacobson, 1968). The researchers had deceived the teachers by their fake test into believing that certain pupils had hitherto unrecognised talent. The teachers' attitudes and expectations of such pupils radically changed and in the face of this more positive teaching and higher standards the pupils involved responded by doing much better, so creating a self-fulfilling prophecy. How such teacher–pupil interaction actually worked was not clear from this experiment. Possible teachers encouraged these special children more, gave them and their work more attention or simply by facial expressions, postures and even touch communicated their higher expectations to them. Whatever 'language' was used pupils' motivation, standards and self-concept all rose significantly. The aim of future research, argued Rosenthal and Jacobson, must be to find out how teacher expectations are transmitted and/or to devise programmes for selecting out those teachers with special powers of positively motivating pupils. Such special teachers should be set to work with disadvantaged children because what this experiment also implied (though it did not directly test) was the inverse thesis that low teacher expectations can equally create a self-fulfilling prophecy of failure, setting in motion a downward and self-sustaining spiral of under-achievement that pupils cannot break out of.

THE IDEA IN ACTION

Obviously, such a dramatic finding about the relationship between teacher attitudes and pupil performance had a major impact on educational research. It inspired a host of replica studies and, although Rosenthal claimed that many of these supported his findings, other researchers were more sceptical both of his claims and the methods he used:

■ William L. Claiborn (1969), for example, repeated Rosenthal and Jacobson's experiment as closely as possible, but found no gains in his special children and a resistance by teachers to expectation statements. As Marten Shipman (1972) has suggested, possibly 'Rosenthal, the virtuoso in detecting experimenter effect' was 'introducing some himself'.
■ Others criticised Rosenthal and Jacobson on ethical grounds for deliberately misleading the teachers involved – and in so doing putting the 80 per cent of non-special children at a disadvantage in terms of

teacher attention. In some ways the researchers recognised part of this problem and instead of testing the effects of both favourable and unfavourable teacher expectations they only tested the former.

Such technical and professional criticisms, however, were rather limited to the world of educational psychologists. What distinguished this particular experiment was its widespread impact throughout the educational field, reinforcing similar ideas or inspiring new ones.

J. W. B. Douglas's major longitudinal study (1964) of the respective influences of home and school on educational achievement had similarly identified the power of a self-fulfilling prophecy, but this time through that institutionalised form of teacher expectations – streaming. His study showed that those pupils who were put into the lower streams in school significantly deteriorated and those in the upper stream improved in terms of their test scores. He argued that those pupils who were put into the lower stream tended to see this as a sign of failure. This sense of rejection and inadequacy was reinforced not only by being in a class with others labelled as being of low ability but by the attitudes of their teachers. Teachers tend to assume that low-stream pupils are 'thick' and so they set them less-demanding work and expect poor results. In contrast upper-stream pupils tend to be pushed harder, given more attention and resources, on the assumption that they are bright. Often, however, the tests or evidence used to allocate pupils to streams is weak or inadequate, yet, 'once allocated the children tend to take on the characteristics expected of them and the forecasts of ability made at the point of streaming are to this extent self-fulfilling' (Douglas 1964). Moreover, as Douglas's study found, streaming by ability often reinforces social selection as children from more middle-class homes 'stand a better chance of getting into the upper streams than their measured ability would seem to justify'. However once there they are likely to stay and to improve in performance so apparently justifying their initial selection.

A range of studies by other educationalists and sociologists – Hargreaves (labelling, 1975), Keddie (ideal pupil, 1973), Nash (halo effect, 1973), Sharp and Green (stereotyping, 1975) – all similarly highlighted the self-fulfilling influence of teachers' attitudes on pupil performance and self-image.

Thus the concept of a self-fulfilling prophecy has had a considerable impact on educational thinking and even practice. It has helped the shift in British schools away from rigid streaming and made teachers more aware of the effect of stereotyping and labelling. It has also had an impact in other fields of study, notably research into deviancy and crime.

SEE ALSO

☐ Labelling theory
☐ Stigma

SUGGESTED READING

Douglas J.W.B. *The Home and the School*, MacGibbon & Kee 1964, Panther, 1968
Hargreaves D. H. *et al. Deviance in Classrooms*, Routledge & Kegan Paul, 1975

FURTHER READING

Claiborn W.L. 'Expectancy Effects in the Classroom. A Failure to Replicate', *Journal of Educational Psychology*, Vol 60, 1969, pp 377–83
Keddie N. *Tinker Tailor*, Penguin, 1973
Nasha R. *Classrooms Observed*, Routledge & Kegan Paul, 1973
Rosenthal R. *Experimenter Effects in Behavioural Research*, Century-Crofts, 1966
Rosenthal R. and Jacobson L. *Pygmalion in the Classroom*, Holt, Rinehart & Winston, 1968
Sharp P. and Green A. *Education and Social Control*, Routledge & Kegan Paul, 1975
Shipman M. *The Limitations of Social Research*, Longman, 1972

EXAMINATION QUESTIONS

1 Assess sociological explanations of the influence of teachers' expectations on the educational performance of pupils. (AEB June 1987)
2 Assess the extent to which educational achievement is influenced by labelling processes and pupil subcultures in schools. (AEB November 1988)

42

WALT WHITMAN ROSTOW *and*
MODERNISATION THEORY

THE AUTHOR

W. W. Rostow (1916–   ) was born in New York City. He was educated at Yale University and won a Rhodes scholarship to Balliol College Oxford (1936–8). He had a very distinguished war record during the Second World War, serving as a Major in the O.S.S. (1942–5) and was decorated with the Legion of Merit and the OBE. After the war he resumed his academic career, teaching American history at both Oxford and Cambridge Universities. In 1950 he was appointed Professor of Economic History at Massachusetts Institute of Technology but also served as an adviser to the President on national security. During the 1960s he became special adviser to Presidents Kennedy and Johnson on economic affairs and foreign policy, acquiring a reputation as something of a 'hawk'. He has since returned to academic life and is at present Professor of Political Economy at the University of Texas.

Walt Rostow has produced a wealth of books and articles on economic policy and foreign affairs, the most famous of which was *Stages of Economic Growth – A Non-Communist Manifesto* (1960).

THE IDEA

W. W. Rostow is seen as a leading exponent of a theory of development called modernisation theory. However, modernisation theory is not one man's thoughts but an amalgamation of a wide variety of ideas about how societies grow and develop. It was particularly influenced by the functionalist theories of Emile Durkheim and Talcott Parsons that societies, like natural organisms, even like human beings, grow by stages, maturing gradually from infancy through childhood to adult-hood via some sort of internal dynamism.

True maturity only occurs when such physical (or in society's case economic) development is accompanied by appropriate psychological (or cultural) development. Just as we often talk of a child being imma-ture, even retarded, when its mental development doesn't match its physical growth, so too we talk of underdeveloped even backward societies, of Third World countries held back by illiteracy, ignorance and superstition. They have failed to develop what Max Weber called the Protestant or work ethic (see page 297) and David McClelland called the achievement factor – the 'culture of enterprise', the drive and ambition that seems to us so vital in getting economic progress, indus-trialisation, off the ground.

Walt Rostow's contribution, both as an economist and a Presidential adviser, was to outline in detail the five main 'stages of economic growth', through which all societies must pass:

STAGE ONE: TRADITIONAL SOCIETY

Here he lumped together all pre-industrial societies because, whatever their differences, they are all basically agricultural societies with low output, ancient technology and poor communications. The social struc-ture is highly traditional and hierarchial and there is little social mobil-ity. It is based on strong family and kinship networks and value systems geared to traditional religions and 'long-run fatalism'. Political power is highly centralised but the local landlord rules his own roost.

STAGE TWO: PRECONDITIONS FOR TAKE OFF

Gradually change occurs, triggered by some internal mechanism or outside stimulus, such as a foreign invasion which 'shocks' traditional society, sows the seed of an idea of economic progress and sets in motion the growth of trade and the establishment of infant industries. A new breed of businessmen emerges, 'men of enterprise ready to take risks in the pursuit of profit and modernisation' (Rostow, 1960) and a new political elite arises determined to overthrow the traditional landed classes (or colonial government) and lead the people into the 'modern' world.

STAGE THREE: THE TAKE OFF

A period of about twenty years during which, as the economy gathers pace, as traditional obstacles and practices are overthrown, as industry begins to replace agriculture as the core of the economy, so a country 'takes off economically and industrialisation becomes a self-generating force'. 'Market forces', supported by the state, sweep away traditional economic, political and social structures. Investment grows to at least 10 per cent of national income and economic activity spreads into the development of new technologies and the exploitation of previously untapped natural resources. Agriculture is commercialised, the economy shifts from an agrarian to an industrial base, and the people move from a rural to an urban environment and lifestyle. Britain was the first country to 'take off' (1783–1803) followed by countries like America (1843–60), Japan (1878–1900) and Russia (1890–1914).

STAGE FOUR: THE DRIVE TO MATURITY

This stage covers a period of about forty years during which a country both consolidates and builds on such progress. Investment grows to between 10 and 20 per cent of national income, technology and science spread to all branches of the economy and the economy becomes part of the international economic system.

STAGE FIVE: THE AGE OF HIGH MASS CONSUMPTION

As the economy matures and prospers the population can start to enjoy the benefits of mass consumption, a high standard of material living and, if it chooses, a welfare state. There is a shift in the economic structure from primary and secondary industries to services and, in the stage 'beyond consumption' society will have to choose between 'babies, boredom, three-day weekends, the moon and the creation of new inner human frontiers'.

Rostow's dynamic theory of economic development is essentially an evolutionary one based on the assumption that all societies must progress through a set of 'fixed' stages – there are no 'leaps' or short cuts in his model – driven by an underlying 'internal' dynamic. However, he does allow for some choice in economic strategies and for a distinction between the self-generating Industrial Revolutions of the First World and the Third World's need for outside help. In fact, as the sub-title of his book indicates, *Stages of Economic Growth* is not merely a theoretical treatise but a manifesto of the way western aid (especially American) should be organised to fight off the threat of communism, the 'disease of transition' as he called it. Such aid should not only be economic, in the form of technology, investment and expertise, but political, supporting non-communist elites, democracy and pluralism against one-party dictatorships. Thus he helped influence American foreign policy in the 1950s and 1960s in its fight against communism in Asia and Latin America.

THE IDEA IN ACTION

Walt Rostow was therefore in the highly unusual position of being able to put his theory of development into practice. As American foreign policy and aid programmes in the 1960s and 1970s fell increasingly into disrepute after the war in Vietnam and more recently after charges of American 'imperialism' in Latin America, so too did Rostow's ideas. Criticism of his thesis fell into two main types:

ECONOMIC ANALYSIS

His idea that industrialisation can only occur through one pre-determined pathway has been heavily criticised. As Alexander Gerschenkron argued, late developing countries can quite easily learn from the mistakes of the West, borrow western skills, technology and expertise and so leap a stage or two. Secondly, though Britain and America may have 'taken-off' through their own 'steam', most of the rest of Europe did so under state control and planning. Thirdly, if the Third World also begins to industrialise, the strain on the world's resources may well prove intolerable. Finally, although the First World nations may well have faced an 'open market' when they industrialised, the Third World countries today face an international economic system firmly under western control. If they restructure their economies they face the danger of not only being unable to compete on the world market (and so going bust) but of losing their capacity to feed their own people as land is given over from food production to industry or 'cash crops'. If, however, they are successful then the West may suffer not only a loss of supplies of cheap food and raw materials but of jobs, as the cheap labour industries of the East make western ones redundant.

WESTERN, ESPECIALLY AMERICAN, BIAS

He tends to assume the only true model of industrialisation is the western one, so ignoring the success in the East of a variety of communist models. Secondly, whilst promising freedom and democracy, western aid all too often has involved 'propping up' corrupt dictatorships and allowing western multinationals to dominate and exploit Third

World economies. His theory has been criticised as simply an ideological justification for American imperialism and as totally ignoring conflict, not consensus, over the distribution of wealth both *within* nations and between the First and Third Worlds.

Such criticisms reached their peak in the critique of modernisation theory by dependency theorists. A. G. Frank (see page 94) is especially severe in his criticism arguing that Rostow's various stages are largely 'fictional' and highly deterministic. His first stage 'traditional society' totally ignores the enormous variety and diversity of pre-industrial societies. To assume that they were all initially as undeveloped as the Third World today is historical nonsense. More important, Frank totally rejects this idea of *internal* economic development. Rather, the West, in his view, developed by colonising and exploiting poorer countries and it now uses the world capitalist system not to help the Third World develop but to keep it underdeveloped. A chain of dependency and exploitation was set up from the cities of the West (the Metropolis) to the capitals of the East down to the villages of the Third World (the satellites) by which the First World expropriates the surplus of the poorer countries, locks their economies into supplying the West with cheap food and raw materials and, far from aid helping them, it increases Western control and burdens them with intolerable debt. Therefore, in Frank's view the dynamism of development is not an internal one but the world capitalist system which once helped the West 'take off' but which now keeps the Third World poor and dependent.

Despite such criticisms and though now overtaken by newer variants on modernisation theory, Rostow's contribution was significant. Whilst less influential as an economic theory, it still has an influence on western development policy.

SEE ALSO

☐ Dependency theory

SUGGESTED READING

Foster-Carter A. 'The Sociology of Development' in Haralambos ed. *Sociology New Directions*, Causeway Press, 1985
Goldthorpe J.E. *The Sociology of the Third World*, CUP, 1984
Harris N. *The End of the Third World*, Penguin, 1986

Harrison P. *Inside the Third World*, Penguin, 1981
Webster A. *An Introduction to the Sociology of Development*, Macmillan,
    1984
Worsley P. *The Third World*, Weidenfeld & Nicolson, 1964

FURTHER READING

Frank A.G. *Sociology of Development and Underdevelopment*, Monthly Re-
    view Press, 1971
Frank A.G. *Crisis in the Third World*, Heinemann, 1981
Rostow W.W. *The Stages of Economic Growth*, CUP, 1960

EXAMINATION QUESTIONS

1 Do you agree that the industrialised societies of the West present 'Third
World' societies with an image of their own future? (Cambridge Local Examinations Syndicate June 1987)
2 Which theory of social change best explains social change in developing
societies? (London University January 1988 Paper 3)
3 Study the extract below and answer the questions which follow:

In discussing social change, many sociologists have made use of various forms
of *evolutionary theory*. One such approach is what is termed modernisation
theory which has been put forward to explain social change in the Third
World.
    One of the characteristics of modernisation theory is the attempt to measure
'modernisation' and place nations of the world on scale of 'modernity' from
the most traditional societies at one extreme to the most modern at the other.
In its most naive form modernisation theory has tended, so to speak, to 'line
up' all societies on a unilinear scale with, say, Australian aborigines at one
extreme and the United States at the other, sometimes with the assumption
that, given time and the removal of traditional cultural barriers, aboriginal
society would one day be like that of modern America.
    A full developed economy depends on a 'modern' set of political, legal and
educational institutions and thus *a value system conducive to economic advancement*. Traditional aspects of the indigenous culture which acted as barriers to the modernisation process (for example, inappropriate religious obser-
vance, customs or traditions, kinship attachments, etc.) need to be discarded
before economic development can proceed. Thus it is suggested that the
problems of the Third World countries are largely due to their own backwardness; the possibility that these problems might have something to do with the
behaviour of the 'advanced' nations is never seriously considered.

(a) Explain what you understand by
  (i) an 'evolutionary theory' of social change [italicised above]
  (ii) 'a value system conducive to economic advancement' [italicised above]
(b) Using **one** of the examples given in brackets in the third paragraph of the passage, **or** an example of your own, explain how 'traditional cultural barriers' might be thought to inhibit development.
(c) Taking **one** social institution for illustration (e.g. family, education, religion), examine the link between that institution and wider social and economic changes in any society.
(d) Briefly outline how any **one** sociologist has contrasted 'traditional' and 'modern' societies.
(e) Using evidence from **one** society, outline a different theory of social change which offers a contrast to modernisation theory as outlined in the extract. (JMB June 1987 Paper 1)

43

GEORG SIMMEL *and*

FORMAL SOCIOLOGY

THE AUTHOR

Georg Simmel (1858–1918) was a German academic born in Berlin, the son of a Jewish businessman. He was educated at Berlin University and studied philosophy, history, psychology and Italian. Supported by private sponsorship, he became a *'privat dozent'* at Berlin University. Initially he lectured in philosophy and ethics, then began initiating courses in the new field of sociology. His academic reputation grew rapidly, but despite the support of such contemporaries as Max Weber and Edmund Husserl, Simmel was not made a full professor at Strasbourg University until 1914, and then in philosophy, not sociology. Together with Max Weber he founded the German Sociological Society in 1910, though he withdrew into academic isolation shortly afterwards.

Though Georg Simmel is primarily noted as a sociologist, in particular as the founder of the Formal School of sociology, he was in fact more of a philosopher. His academic interests were multi-disciplinary, encompassing the whole spectrum of philosophy and social science. Similarly, in contrast to the specialist and empirical structured approaches adopted by other leading sociologists of this period, Simmel's sociology was highly individualistic, subtle and philosophical. The key focus of his attention was the individual in modern mass society, struggling to survive and express himself within the 'iron cage' of growing bureaucracy, materialism, urbanisation and technology. His major works ranged from the study of money and morality to religion, the economy, modern science and life in the city.

Simmel helped pioneer modern sociology and influenced such leading thinkers as Georg Lukács, Talcott Parsons and Robert Merton, but he has always been overshadowed as a founding father of sociology by such contemporary 'giants' as Marx and Weber. Though he published twenty-five books and hundreds of articles and reviews, the very diversity and subtlety of his work has contributed to the neglect and underestimation of his contribution.

His major works included:

- *The Problems of the Philosophy of History* (1892)
- *The Sociology of Georg Simmel* (1950)
- *Conflict and the Web of Group Affiliation* (1955)

THE IDEA

Georg Simmel's approach to sociological analysis, his attempt to construct a unified and comprehensive social theory was called *formal sociology*. Like other founding fathers, he too sought to establish sociology as a separate academic discipline, as a science even. However, in contrast to the positivist approach adopted by Comte and others, Simmel's analysis focused as much on social interaction and individual interpretation as on discovering general laws of human behaviour.

Simmel's analysis starts from three key observations:

- Firstly, that individuals are motivated by a wide variety of forces which range from self-interest to compassion, and that the study of such phenomena forms the subject matter of psychology.
- Secondly, that the individual does not explain him/herself solely by reference to self, but in relation to others. The study of groups, their interrelationships and internal dynamics, forms the subject matter of social psychology.
- Thirdly, that human activities develop in *forms*, within social structures such as the family, school and church, or according to general forms of behaviour such as imitation, competition and social hierarchy. The study of social forms, argued Simmel, constitutes the subject matter of sociology.

Simmel went on to distinguish further between the *form* and the *content* of social life. Whilst forms of social interaction refer to stable, patterned aspects of social life, identifiable within very varied situations (the state, trade union or family), content refers to variable aspects of social interaction such as the interests and ambitions of the individuals involved in a particular situation. The aim of formal sociology was to analyse forms of social interaction by extracting them from their social context, and so produce sociological laws capable of describing the regularities which occur in various types of social organisation, despite considerable variations in context. Thus, for example, despite their very different social and historical contexts, the relationship between an artisan and a lord in eighteenth-century England is essentially the same as that between a peasant and landlord in twentieth-century South America, namely one of patronage.

Simmel extended this analysis by:

GEOMETRICAL ANALOGIES

Using geometry as the basis of many of his analogies, he argued, for example, that social situations vary in terms of their nature and type according to the number of people involved. A social situation involving two or three people is fundamentally different from one involving one hundred people. Equally, though, a social situation involving two or three people is at heart the same in terms of form and relationship as that between two or three nations. Number not only acts as a determinant of group organisation, but affects the likelihood and form of social conflict – compare, for example, a political debate between ten or so people and a mass rally. It further determines the nature of relationships. Whilst one person alone exists in solitude, and a couple may form relationships of profound intimacy, equality and depth, a threesome introduces new divisions which may lead to alliances of two against one. Marriage is a classic example of the way number fundamentally alters the nature of even this most intimate of relationships. Within monogamy, a married couple have only each other to consider and so are usually extremely close, until the arrival of a third person, their first child, alters this dyadic relationship fundamentally. Similarly, though polygamy is as much a form of marriage as monogamy, its content, its relationships are fundamentally different. Simmel was especially interested in the triadic form, or the way that the third person can significantly alter a relationship between two individuals, groups or countries by playing a variety of roles: ally, referee or rascal!

The key point of all this numerical analysis was to illustrate Simmel's belief that specific and relatively autonomous forms exist independently of their social context; that whatever the social or historical situation, a triad of people, groups or nations produce similar types of behaviour. In a sense, therefore, Simmel was arguing for formal sociology to be considered as a geometry of social forms.

SOCIAL TYPES

Simmel highlighted the way certain social types occur and recur through-out history and in a multitude of social situations, yet nevertheless represent essentially the same form and produce the same reaction. The stranger and the adventurer are two such social types, labelled and reacted to in much the same way whether they be found in tribal Africa or modern Europe.

Simmel, therefore, sought to extract from their social context such key concepts as conflict, differentiation and power, and analyse them scientifically just as a chemist analyses compounds or a physicist atoms. Social content, he argued, is crucial to sociological interpretation, but a clear distinction between form and content must always be maintained if a science of sociology is to be established. Individual motives, passions, feelings and ambitions are crucial, but only become concrete, only materialise, within specific relationships, within specific social forms. Daily life itself involves a succession of social forms – work, meals, social activities. Without forms there is no society. 'In every known society there exists a great variety of forms which bind us together, that is, socialise us . . . if one imagines an absence of all forms, society would not exist', argued Simmel (Frisby, 1984). Sociology, therefore, is the science which abstractly analyses social forms on the understanding that these do not merely make society, they are society.

This emphasis on scientific abstraction did not lead Simmel, however, to reify society, to see society as a 'form' above and beyond its members. Rather, society is a man-made creation, since 'it exists only where many individuals interact'.

'If society is merely a . . . constellation of individuals who are the actual realities, then the latter and their behaviour also constitutes the real object of science and the concept of society evaporates . . . What palpably exists is indeed only individual human beings and their circumstances and activities: therefore, the task can only be to understand them, whereas the essence of society, that emerges purely through an ideal synthesis and is never to be grasped, should not form the object of reflection that is directed towards the investigation of reality. (Frisby, 1984)

At heart, therefore, Simmel's formal sociology was an attempt to combine philosophical analysis and social psychology as a basis for explaining both the form and content of social life.

THE IDEA IN ACTION

Through formal sociology, Georg Simmel has been closely associated with social psychology and symbolic interactionism. He has been strongly identified with the study of small group dynamics and relationships. Whilst the ability to capture the subtleties and intimacies of social relationships in an essay form was a key characteristic of his work, Simmel also wrote extensively about social structures, social differentiation, religion, money and the nature of sociology. His contribution to sociology was as much philosophical as psychological. Simmel used formal sociology as the basis of his sociological analysis, as the means for promoting sociology's claim to being a science and as a means of distinguishing it from other social sciences. However, he failed to develop this insight into a comprehensive and systematic sociological theory capable of analysing society at large. In fact, by 1913 his interest in sociology was on the wane. Attempts have been made since to revive, refine and develop his work, the most notable being that by Leopold von Wiese, but with limited success. The fragmentary, diverse and fleeting nature of Simmel's insights, his use of images rather than empirical evidence, the very style of his essays, have made his work both highly personal and almost impossible to replicate. His ability to focus on the minutiae of daily life, on the intimacy of social relationships, rather than on the grand topics of sociology – the state, class, wealth – were both his strength and his weakness; were the reason why his impact on modern sociology has been both limited and indirect. The richness and diversity of his social analysis, which extended from women's rights to the modern Metropolis, from Goethe to Rembrandt, and his fleeting insights have often left his readers as much frustrated as enlightened.

Georg Simmel's approach was highly original and individual, a clear alternative to the positivist perspective of Comte, Spencer and Durkheim that was to dominate and drive modern sociology right up until the 1960s. As many reviewers have commented, Simmel's work deserves re-reading, revival and re-appreciation. As Bryan Turner (1985) has commented, 'Simmel laid the foundations for the discipline of sociology long before Max Weber turned to the problem of sociology as a special discipline.'

SEE ALSO

☐ **Positivism** for a contrasting view of sociology and society.

SUGGESTED READING

Frisby D. *Georg Simmel*, Tavistock, 1984

FURTHER READING

Simmel G. *The Problems of the Philosophy of History*, Free Press, 1892
Simmel G. *The Philosophy of Money*, Routledge & Kegan Paul, 1900
Simmel G. *The Sociology of Georg Simmel*, Free Press, 1950
Simmel G. *Conflict and the Web of Group Affiliation*, Free Press, 1955
Turner B.S. 'Georg Simmel' in *Thinkers of the Twentieth Century*, Firethorn
    Press, 1985

44

HERBERT SPENCER *and*

SOCIAL DARWINISM

THE AUTHOR

Herbert Spencer (1820–1903) was born in Derby, the son of a teacher. His education was somewhat haphazard. He never attended secondary school or university and was primarily self-taught. He worked initially as a railway engineer but then became a political journalist and freelance writer. He developed a strong interest in both the natural sciences and radical politics. His interest in geology and paleontology provided him with a knowledge of evolutionary ideas, his non-conformist background stimulated his involvement in the radical politics of mid-nineteenth-century England. He became a strong supporter of utilitarianism and *laissez-faire* liberal ideas of individual rights. In 1848 he became sub-editor of *The Economist* magazine. After 1865 he became a leading exponent of the school of thought known as Social Darwinism through which he acquired an international reputation and a strong academic, and even popular, following in England, Europe, America and even Russia.

Spencer's publications included:

- *Social Statics* (1850)
- *The Study of Society* (1874)
- *The Principles of Sociology* (1896)
- *Descriptive Sociology* (17 volumes, 1873–1934)

THE IDEA

Herbert Spencer is known as the founding father of Social Darwinism, the social theory that draws on the key concepts of Charles Darwin's theory of evolution, to argue that, like nature, societies have developed according to certain underlying laws of natural selection, survival and adaptation. Like biological organisms, argued Spencer, societies have evolved from simple to complex structures by a process of natural selection, have adapted to their environment by a process of internal differentiation and integration, have progressed from the homogeneous to the heterogeneous. Human societies have evolved from the simple and homogeneous tribal units of primitive man to the advanced, integrated and heterogeneous social systems of modern civilization.

Like Darwin, Spencer used the organism as the basis of his explanation. He likened society to an organism in a variety of ways:

■ Both grow in size and evolve into more complex, differentiated structures.
■ With differentiation comes specialisation. Just as the brain evolved as the biological mechanism for control and decision-making, so has government emerged as the key social institution for this task.
■ With evolution, both societies and organisms learn to adjust and adapt.

He also incorporated certain elements of contemporary physics, including the idea that there is an inherent tendency for all things to move along the line of least resistance, and the principle of the rhythm of motion. In addition, like Comte, Spencer believed that the heart of social order is an underlying social consensus, an inherent agreement about fundamental values and morality.

These ideas were blended into a final theory of social evolution based on the key concepts of:

■ Natural selection, or, as Spencer called it, 'survival of the fittest'.
■ The inherent instability of all social systems.

As in nature, argued Spencer, social order and stability require a natural equilibrium, a sense of balance. Social change occurs because of a disturbance in that equilibrium, in the balance between the various parts of the social body or between society and its environment. Following a period of instability, a new social order emerges as a new equilibrium, a fresh moral consensus, and a new relationship between increasingly differentiated social parts is established.

Thus, like species in nature, argued Spencer, human societies have evolved from simple tribal units into the complex societies of today. Those that failed to adapt, those that were unfit, died out in the face of competition from more advanced and aggressive social units. Thus the caveman gave way to the tribesman and farmer, the great empires of Rome, India and China to the European powers of Britain, Spain and Germany. Through this law of the 'social jungle' only the fittest societies survived; through this law of social evolution human society 'marched forward'.

However, not all societies evolve at the same rate or in the same way. As in nature, evolution produces variety and diversity. Different societies may evolve differently according to their particular environment, neighbouring states and their own individual characteristics, be they racial or cultural. All, however, are following the same law of social evolution, will follow the same evolutionary stages, or will die out. Here Spencer distinguished between two types of society at different stages of evolution:

■ The militant, controlled and integrated from the centre, as in those societies run by the military.
■ The industrial, where social order is more organic and spontaneous, based on co-operation rather than force, or market forces rather than military might.

Thus, whilst early militant societies had to fight for survival against warring neighbours – as the Romans had to against the Goths and Vandals – more advanced industrial ones have learned to evolve peacefully through economic competition rather than war and conflict.

Finally, Spencer's theory had a psychological as well as sociological theme. Just as societies evolve, he argued, so do people. Modern man represents thousands of years of physical and psychological evolution as he has adapted to and survived his physical and social environment.

Herbert Spencer's overall aim was to unify all theoretical sciences and create a comparative sociology based on the theory and methods of Charles Darwin. He sought to combine this organic model of social development with an emphasis on individual rights. Social Darwinism offered a highly structured and apparently scientific approach to social research, stressing the value of comparing societies at different historical and evolutionary stages. Politically, Spencer's thesis represented a rejection of state intervention. Social planning and state welfare threatened to distort the natural and progressive forces of social evolution, threatened the rights of the individual. The appeal of Social Darwinism was thus as much a political doctrine as a contribution to scientific sociology.

THE IDEA IN ACTION

Herbert Spencer was an important figure in the development of modern sociology. Social Darwinism gave early sociology a strong theoretical base and extensive academic status by allying it to developments in the natural sciences. Like Comte, Spencer believed that certain underlying laws of nature govern the social world just as much as the natural one. For Spencer, that underlying law was evolution.

As one of the earliest attempts to produce laws of social order and change, Spencer's theory had a major impact on nineteenth-century social philosophy. It pre-dated and strongly influenced functionalist theories and, through William James and W.G. Sumner, had a significant influence on American sociology in the early twentieth century. It is a classic example of Victorian ideas and attitudes, and many of its key concepts are still both popular and influential today: the Thatcherite beliefs in market forces, a rejection of state intervention and survival of the fittest being but a few examples.

However, by the late nineteenth century, Social Darwinism and its underlying views of man and society were under increasing criticism:

■ Spencer's attempt to combine a holistic analysis of society with *laissez-faire* individualism produced theoretical contradictions between individual rights and freedoms and the needs of society at large to evolve and progress.

■ His use of a biological analogy was at times absurdly overstretched; his use of Darwinian concepts was often superficial, inaccurate and contradictory, arguing, for example, that whilst all societies are subject to evolutionary forces, some may skip certain stages or even regress from heterogeneity to homogeneity.

■ His ideas of natural selection have been used to support racist and anti-humanitarian views and policies. They reinforced the Victorian idea of white superiority, of the supremacy of the British Empire over its subject nations, especially black ones. Elements of this doctrine could be found in the racial policies of Nazi Germany and in the apartheid policy of present-day South Africa. The sister thesis of 'survival of the fittest' has been used to justify policies of abandoning the weak, sick, poor and criminal as biologically inferior and a threat to man's evolutionary development.

■ Social Darwinism is often seen as a conservative, even reactionary philosophy, justifying the existing order and existing inequalities as both natural and right.

■ The decline of the British Empire, the eclipsing of England as a world power by Germany and America produced a decline, too, in support for Social Darwinism. The rise of communist societies based on central planning contradicted Spencer's thesis of evolution by market forces. This thesis was further undermined by the adoption of state planning of the economy, welfare provisions and social democracy in advanced industrial societies at the turn of the century.

Thus, even by 1900, Social Darwinism had lost its popular appeal and much of its political support. It now looks anachronistic, a left-over from the Victorian era of the British Empire and white superiority. Nevertheless, it was a major contribution to establishing sociology as an academic discipline and its underlying themes have re-emerged in recent years in the form of such neo-evolutionary theories as structural functionalism, modernisation theses and cultural anthropology.

SEE ALSO

☐ Structural functionalism
☐ Modernisation

SUGGESTED READING

Peel J.D.Y. *Herbert Spencer. The Evolution of a Sociologist*, Heinemann, 1971

FURTHER READING

Spencer H. *Social Statics*, D. Appleton, 1850
Spencer H. *The Study of Society*, D. Appleton, 1874
Spencer H. *The Principles of Sociology*, Appleton, 1896
Spencer H. *Descriptive Sociology*, Williams & Norgate, 1873–1934

EXAMINATION QUESTIONS

1 How useful is the organic analogy for understanding social systems? (WJEC June 1986)
2 Outline and assess the usefulness of the analogy between society and a biological organism. (AEB June 1988 Paper 2)

45

FREDERICK WINSLOW TAYLOR *and*
SCIENTIFIC MANAGEMENT

THE AUTHOR

F.W. Taylor (1856–1915) was born in Germantown, Philadelphia, the son of a wealthy 'lawyer of leisure'. He was brought up in an atmosphere of genteel respectability, culture and social reform but from an early age Frederick's key passions were sport, mechanical inventions and an obsession with organisational efficiency which not only affected industry but also influenced the way he planned games like croquet and the layout of his own garden. He grew up and worked in one of the major centres of the American Industrial Revolution – Philadelphia.

Taylor's life can be divided into three main stages:

■ His early formative years as an apprentice, gang boss and eventually chief engineer at the Midvale Steel Company (1878–89) where he experimented with and developed a whole range of ways of improving work tasks, payment and industrial discipline such that the firm's output of pig-iron increased four-fold per man.
■ His mature years as a consultant to a wide range of engineering and manufacturing firms when he began publishing his ideas in such works as *A Piece Rate System* (1895) and *Shop Management* (1903). He also began putting his ideas into practice on a broad scale with 'Johnstown' as the first 'scientifically' managed factory in the US.
■ His 'retirement' on a large fortune when he devoted himself full-time to promoting 'scientific management' via lecture tours, his disciples 'The Boxly Pilgrims', the establishment of courses such as that on industrial management at Harvard Graduate School of Business Administration (1908) and the publication of his major work, *Principles of Scientific Management* (1911).

He became a highly controversial figure as his methods challenged the power of organised labour, upset many humanitarians and disturbed a lot of factory owners. He was a key witness in the Congressional inquiries into 'efficiency systems' (1911–15) but also joined the Progressive Movement of this period in its attacks on vested interests like the railroads. Taylor died in 1915, the father of the Scientific Management Movement, regarded alongside Henry Ford and Herbert Hoover as one of the trinity of early twentieth century technician-philosophers. Though he was not a sociologist, his 'system' has been a major part of the sociological debates on industrial management and the labour process ever since.

THE IDEA

By the turn of the century industrialisation was spreading in America with major advances in mass production techniques and the emergence of big business corporations and even multinationals. However, the organisation of production tasks *within* the workplace and factory was still very traditional and haphazard, with workers having considerable freedom to decide on their routines and speed of work. Such key decisions as hiring and firing were still left to individual foremen. The result was gross inefficiency and considerable unrest.

Taylor's objective therefore was to introduce a 'managerial revolution' to match the technical advances and to break the power of the foreman. His final system, as laid out in *The Principles of Scientific Management* (1911) can be summarised as follows:

ORGANISATIONAL

At the shop floor level changes based on the 'scientific' analysis of every single task to maximise efficiency and production were introduced; what we today might call 'time and motion studies'. Experiments and stop-watch studies were conducted in the minutest detail to find the most efficient tools, ways of doing a task, rest periods and groupings of workers. One Dutch worker called Schmidt, for example, was used to analyse such basic tasks as digging a hole or shovelling pig-iron, to find the most efficient way of holding and swinging a spade, the best size of spade head and so on. Work tasks were simplified, workers 'scientifically' selected for the job they were best suited to and trained to perform the task exactly as specified in written instructions from the management. The quantity and quality of work produced was continually checked by a system of 'systematic supervision' and discipline maintained by 'functional foremanship'.

At managerial level too the division of labour became more special-ised and decision-making more centralised. Control of both the work process and the workforce fell to management. They now had to plan production, hire and fire and co-ordinate the now-fragmented produc-tion line. Innovations here included standardising tool rooms and methods, a new accounting system and, in particular, the establishment of a separate planning department.

MOTIVATIONAL

Taylor assumed that men's prime motive for work was money and so, to maximise productivity and quality, and to overcome worker resis-tance to his methods, he experimented with various incentive schemes, especially differential piecework (payment according to the amount of work done).

IDEOLOGICAL

He believed that his methods would so increase industrial productivity and therefore profits and wages that workers and management would learn to collaborate for their mutual benefit, recognise the justice of his system of determining a fair wage and so a 'mental' revolution would occur whereby the two sides of industry would learn co-operation instead of conflict. He therefore saw little need for collective bargain-ing or personnel work.

THE IDEA IN ACTION

F.W. Taylor's rationalisation of industrial organisation became the philosophical basis of the Scientific Management Movement that swept through factories in America and Europe in the 1900s. It influenced the assembly-line production methods pioneered by Henry Ford and was acclaimed even by Lenin as the means of creating the abundance of goods necessary for a socialist society. Though only a few industrialists introduced his system wholesale, ideas like time and motion studies permeated the whole of industrial organisation and gave management the 'scientific' justification they needed for reasserting their control over the production process. In David Nelson's view (1980) he helped 'transform industrial management and to a lesser degree, industrial society between the 1870s and World War I'.

However, Taylor's system was also the subject of extensive and often bitter criticism on two main levels:

■ His assumptions that money is men's prime motive for work and that workers act primarily as individuals were severely undermined by the famous Hawthorne experiments of Elton Mayo in the 1920s (see page 186). The studies were, ironically, designed initially to improve productivity by introducing scientific management methods into a Chicago factory. They ended up showing that workers responded best when given some managerial 'attention' and that the key influence on a worker's output was not money but his workgroup and his fear of being ostracised by them. These findings laid the basis for the Human Relations School of Management which stressed workers' social as well as economic needs, the importance of the workgroup, of good industrial relations and communication. It introduced such ideas as personnel management, job enrichment schemes and worker participation – industrial management with a 'human' touch.

■ His claim that such methods would increase industrial harmony has been severely challenged by the American Marxist Harry Braverman (1974, see page 31) who argues that, far from enriching the work experience, the techniques of scientific management have deskilled, degraded and dehumanised the modern worker, shorn him of his skills, knowledge and autonomy and reduced him to the level of 'cogs and levers', a mere extension of the machine. In his view the key feature of such a system (and the chief attraction for employers) is not the increased productivity but the increase in managerial control brought about by the separation of mental from manual work, management from workers and, especially, conception from execution. Management is now a specialised skill with total control of the work process because it has seized from the workers all knowledge about a particular task. Therefore the ordinary factory worker now needs few skills, can be continually checked on and easily replaced. He is left skilless and powerless. As the techniques of scientific management have spread into all forms of work, into offices, shops and the like, so, argues Braverman, the working class generally has become more open to intense supervision, exploitation and replacement by machine. Scientific management has thus become a means of class control, a crucial weapon in the management of a capitalist society, 'masquerading in the trappings of science'.

Thus scientific management has become a key idea in the sociology of work as well as the management of business. It is still the subject of passionate debate on such diverse issues as alienation, affluent workers and class control.

SEE ALSO

☐ Human relations
☐ Deskilling and
☐ Bureaucracy.

SUGGESTED READING

Nelson D. *F.W. Taylor and the Rise of Scientific Management*, University of Wisconsin Press, 1980

FURTHER READING

Braverman H. *Labor and Monopoly Capital*, Monthly Review Press, 1974
Roethlisberger F.J., Dickson W.J. and Wright H.A. *Management and the Worker*, Harvard University Press, 1939
Taylor F.W. *Scientific Management*, Harper, 1911

EXAMINATION QUESTIONS

1. 'Scientific management and human relations are different approaches to the study of organisations but they share the same aim of controlling the workforce.' Discuss. (AEB June 1988 Paper 1)
2. Evaluate the contributions made by the theories of Scientific Management and Human Relations to our understanding of the social relations of the workplace. (AEB June 1989 Paper 2)

46

THE AUTHOR

Ferdinand Tönnies (1855–1936) was born and grew up in Schleswig-Holstein, part of Northern Germany, the son of a prosperous farmer. He studied philology, philosophy, theology, archaeology and art history at the Universities of Strasburg, Jena, Bonn, Leipzig and Tübingen where he was awarded a doctorate in classical philology in 1887. Supported by his father's wealth Tönnies pursued graduate studies at Berlin and London and then gained professorships in economics and statistics, and later sociology, at Kiel University (1913–33) until he was dismissed by the Nazis for his attacks on their ideas and their anti-semitism.

The key influences on his life and ideas were:

■ His farming background which gave him an understanding of the peasant way of life.
■ His mother's Lutheran background which inspired his interest in the idea of a new universal religion and his emphasis on morality.
■ His academic contemporaries, Weber, Durkheim and, in particular, Georg Simmel and Werner Sombart, with whom he founded the German Sociological Society. Like them he sought to establish the social sciences as a respectable academic discipline. He travelled widely.
■ His own political sympathies. Although conservative by temperament, Tönnies took an active interest in socialist and nationalist ideas, supporting the Independence Movements in Finland and Ireland and joining the German Social Democratic Party's opposition to Nazism. He was heavily influenced by both Fabian and Marxist ideas.

Such a variety of influences, plus his financial and academic independ-ence and his emotional attachment to the past – its traditions, stability and morality – were all reflected in his key work *Gemeinschaft–Gesellschaft* (1887). Like many of his contemporaries, he desperately tried to make sense of the massive changes sweeping across Western Europe and North America; in particular industrialisation and urbani-sation which he saw as marking a fundamental break with the past.

THE IDEA

Through the twin terms *Gemeinschaft* and *Gesellschaft* Tönnies sought to convey what he saw as the crucial difference between traditional societies and the new urban-industrial ones – the nature of their social relationships.

The term *gemeinschaft* is usually translated as 'community', a term that evokes romantic memories of a bygone age of harmony and stability. Tönnies, however, used the term more specifically to refer to human relationships that are highly personal, intimate and enduring, those where a person's involvement is considerable if not total as in the family, with real friends or a close-knit group. He strongly linked such communal ties with traditional village communities where there was a stable social order in which everyone knew their place, where status was ascribed, mobility, be it social or geographical, limited, and the whole way of life governed by a homogeneous culture, a strict set of values and morals based on organised religion and reinforced by the two key social controls: the family and the church. In such small-scale societies, everyone knew everyone else and were interrelated by blood or marriage. Tied to the land, kin and the rhythms of nature, few moved outside their own territory. Relationships seemed to be more natural, organic and emotional. They seemed to have more meaning than today.

The term *gesellschaft* is usually translated as 'society' or 'associa-tion'. Tönnies used it to refer to everything opposite of *gemeinschaft*, in particular the apparently impersonal, superficial and transitory rela-tionships of modern urban life. Commerce and industry require a more calculating, rational and self-interested approach to one's dealings with others. We make contracts or agreements rather than getting to know people. Our business, and even our everyday relationships are mainly a means to an end, to getting something from others. So they are fairly specific and limited. We talk to the shop assistant or bank clerk merely as a means to buying something. There is no time or place for sentiment or emotion in modern industrial life. The whole pace of life is much faster, more dynamic, competitive and large-scale as we strive towards economic progress, a higher standard of living and greater social status. Instead of one culture, there is a multitude of different ways of life with few social sanctions.

Tönnies' typology is often depicted as contrasting roles and relationships in the city with those in the village – the friendly village bobby with the urban 'cop', jovial Farmer Giles with the faceless bureaucrat, the tranquillity of the countryside with the urban 'rat race'. He also used it to compare the difference in the type and quality of relationship between, for example, a friend and an acquaintance, a family business and a modern corporation. Similarly Tönnies seems to have been deeply pessimistic, seems to have been arguing that industrialisation was destroying any sense of community and with it the broader basis of civilisation. Yet he also used these twin terms as part of a sociological analysis of organisations, culture and human 'will', intended to form the basis of an analysis of man's social evolution from primitive agrarian communism through industrial capitalism to a new socialist order in the future in which *gemeinschaft* would re-emerge. He never finished this grand scheme. Equally he never tied these two terms to any particular locality, never said that rural societies create a sense of community and urban ones destroy it, though he did strongly imply this, but rather argued that *gemeinschaft* and *gesellschaft* were two pure or ideal types. In reality there would always be a mixture of both – some *gemeinschaft* in the city; some *gesellschaft* in the village. Nor did he say that industrialisation caused the collapse of community, but rather argued that the decline of *gemeinschaft* created the conditions, the rationalism, calculative habits and contractual relationships necessary for industrial capitalism to flourish. He even used these concepts to analyse deviancy, arguing for example that as *gemeinschaft* declined, so crime and suicide increased.

THE IDEA IN ACTION

The dual concept of *gemeinschaft–gesellschaft* earned Tönnies a place in the sociological history books as the founding father of community studies and urban sociology. Though his book was not widely read until the 1930s, it (and the works of Durkheim and Simmel) inspired a mass of studies of every type of society, every aspect of community life, and strongly influenced the urban studies of the famous Chicago School in America in the 1900s. Such social scientists developed the theory of the rural–urban continuum with Robert Redfield (1930) and Louis Wirth (1938), in particular, comparing the peasant and urban ways of life as 'two poles in reference to which one or other of all human settlements tend to arrange themselves'. In other words, *where* you lived determined *how* you lived. However, such a 'search for community' was not limited to academics. It inspired such diverse movements as the 'hippy' communes of the 1960s, the new towns and garden cities so beloved by town planners and the commuter villages of the urban middle class.

As already explained, however, Tönnies' analysis of community was somewhat more subtle and complex than that above. By tying it to a particular locality, the community studies tradition produced a narrow, even distorted version of *gemeinschaft–gesellschaft* and once studies started to show the existence of tight-knit communities *within* the city (as in Young and Wilmot's study of Bethnal Green (1962), or of 'class conflict' in the country (as in Ray Pahl's study of commuter villages, 1965) then the theory of a rural–urban continuum was doomed. Raymond Williams' (1973) analysis of the traditional community as simply the 'mutuality of the oppressed', as the reaction of medieval peasants to their harsh way of life and the cruelty and oppression of the gentry, further destroyed this myth. Finally there was nothing in even the original version of *gemeinschaft–gesellschaft* that could explain the race riots that exploded in American cities in the 1960s; and so younger, more radical, urban sociologists turned to the theories of Marx and Weber to illuminate the influence of power and class conflict in determining the shape of the modern city and the behaviour of its inhabitants.

Today Tönnies has been consigned to the sociological history books rather than inspiring modern sociology in the way Durkheim, Marx and Weber continue to do. But so long as the 'quest for community' continues to inspire people, so the concepts of *gemeinschaft–gesellschaft* may still have fresh life in them.

SEE ALSO

☐ **Human ecology** and
☐ **Urbanism** as developments of this concept.

SUGGESTED READING

Slattery M. *Urban Sociology*, Causeway Press, 1985

FURTHER READING

Pahl R. *Urbs in Rure*, Weidenfeld & Nicholson, 1965
Redfield R. *Tepotzlan: A Mexican Village. A Study of Folk Life*, University of
    Chicago Press, 1930
Tönnies F. *Community and Society*, Harper Row, 1887
Williams R. *The Country and the City*, Chatto & Windus, 1973
Wirth L. 'Urbanism as a Way of Life', *American Journal of Sociology*, Vol 44,
    1938, pp 1–24
Young M. and Wilmot P. *Family and Kinship in East London*, Penguin, 1962

EXAMINATION QUESTIONS

1 Examine the contention that the difference in the character of rural and urban life can be aptly summarised in the contrast between community and association. (WJEC June 1987)

2 'Pre-industrial societies can be characterised by close personal relationships, industrial societies by impersonal relationships.' Discuss. (Cambridge Local Examinations Syndicate June 1987)

3 'A sense of community has been lost in modern societies.' Discuss the evidence for and against this statement. (Cambridge Local Examinations Syndicate June 1986)

4 'The paradox of the sociology of the community is the existence of a body of theory which constantly predicts the collapse of community, and of a body of empirical studies which finds community alive and well.' (Abrams: *Work, Urbanism and Inequality.*) Explain and discuss. (AEB June 1983 Paper 1)

5 Discuss the view that the move to the towns has led to the breakdown of community ties with regard to **either** the 'advanced' **or** the 'developing' societies. (Cambridge Local Examinations Syndicate June 1987)

6 Discuss the view that urbanisation inevitably results in a 'loss of community'. (AEB November 1989 Paper 1)

47

MAX WEBER *and*

PROTESTANT ETHIC

THE AUTHOR

Max Weber (1864–1920) was undoubtedly one of the 'Holy Trinity' of founding fathers of sociology and his ideas still
provide one of the key frameworks and
a rich source of inspiration for modern
sociologists. He was born in Erfurt,
Prussia, the son of a prominent local
lawyer and liberal politician. He attended
the Universities of Heidelberg, Berlin and
Göttingen, completing doctoral theses on
medieval trading companies and Roman
agricultural history and studying a wide
range of subjects that included law, economics, history, philosophy and music.
In 1892 he was appointed lecturer in law
at Berlin University but soon moved on
to professorships in political economy at
Freiberg and Heidelberg. His academic
career stopped short in 1898 after a serious nervous breakdown brought
on partly by a violent row with his father, who died shortly afterwards.
Wracked by guilt and remorse Weber spent the next ten years travelling
across Europe and later America. The sheer pace and variety of life in
the New World inspired him to write again and he poured forth a
stream of articles on an enormous range of topics from the Russian
Revolution to Hinduism which, in comparative scope and wealth of
detail, have yet to be equalled.

Increasingly he turned to sociology as the means of synthesising his
vast range of intellectual interests and in 1902 he became joint founder
of the German Sociological Association. In the years that followed he
produced such key works as *The Protestant Ethic and the Spirit of
Capitalism* (1905) and began his major work *Economics and Society*
which was never completed.

During the First World War he was a hospital administrator and in 1918 he took up one of his key passions, politics, by joining the newly formed German Democratic Party. He failed, however, to get the nomination as a candidate for the Frankfurt constituency. He died unexpectedly in 1920 from pneumonia but his name and spirit lived on through his wife Marianne and the 'Weber Circle' of the 1920s, and through such writers as Talcott Parsons (see page 240) and Alfred Schutz (see page 140). His style of sociological analysis formed the basis of a major part of the 'debate with Marx' both then and now, as radical perspectives have again come to the fore since the 1970s. His contribution to sociological theory has been enormous, ranging from his analysis of the modern state, and the nature of class in capitalist societies, through to debates on sociological philosophy and method (*verstehen*, social action and ideal types). Underlying his vast comparative analysis is a search for the 'spirit of the modern age', the key feature that distinguishes societies today from those in the past. This he believed was *rationality*, the chief theme of his studies of religion, bureaucracy and in particular of capitalism.

THE IDEA

The Protestant ethic is possibly the most famous of Max Weber's key ideas. Whilst other writers of the late nineteenth century, particularly Karl Marx, sought to explain the Industrial Revolution mainly in economic terms, Weber tried to show the influence of ideas on such enormous historical change, in particular the influence of religious ideas and values. In a massive comparative analysis of past and present civilisations and religions, he concluded that whilst certain religious ideas promoted, or at least did not obstruct, social change, others did. The ancient civilisations of China and India possessed the necessary economic preconditions for industrial 'take off' (cheap labour, capital, inventions, mass markets) but failed to do so – why? Similarly the Industrial Revolution took place initially, not throughout the whole of Western Europe but primarily in such northern and Protestant countries as England, The Netherlands and Germany. Weber therefore concluded that the ethics of Protestantism, in particular those of the more puritanical sects such as Calvinism, provided the vital spark that ignited the Industrial Revolution.

For Weber the key characteristic of modern capitalism was that it is rational, it is based on the circulation of market forces, the costs and benefits of such factors of production as wages and labour, on the likely returns of a given amount of investment and, in particular, on the pursuit of profit. This spirit of capitalism is not limited to a few adventurous entrepreneurs but is all-pervasive, underlying the way of life of whole societies. In his essays on early Protestantism Weber noted a strong 'affinity' between such economic values and those of the more puritanical sects that arose after the Protestant reformation – Calvinists, Lutherans and Wesleyans.

■ Whilst Catholicism taught that poverty was the pathway to salvation and that heaven was in the next world, Puritanism declared personal wealth to be a sign of God's favour, a visible symbol of the elect few who were predestined for salvation. By working hard and growing rich, Calvinists sought to convince themselves that they were the chosen few, and so profit-making became a psychological release from the fear of damnation. However, and this was crucial to the spirit of capitalism, such wealth must not be squandered but saved and invested as a means to further profits and for the greater glorification of God. In contrast to the riches and extravagance of the Catholic Church, Puritans were noted for their thrift and frugality, their strict rejection of all forms of pleasure. This desire to save rather than spend provided the spirit of investment so vital to the development of the Industrial Revolution.
■ Whilst highly structured and collectivist religions such as Catholicism and Islam subordinated the individual to the greater good of the whole, Protestantism was much more individualistic and democratic. In contrast to the authority of the papacy and the power of priests, Protestants were encouraged to seek their own salvation and to talk to God directly.
■ Whilst traditional religions rested on faith, ritual and even magic, Protestantism is much more rational, rejecting extravagant rituals and all forms of irrational explanation.
■ Whilst in medieval times work was seen as a necessary evil undertaken simply to maintain existing standards of living, and money-making was viewed with suspicion, for Puritans hard work and the accumulation of profits were the pathway to salvation.

From such comparisons Weber drew out the similarities between an ideal-type capitalist and ideal-type Protestant – their individualism and veneration of profit, their 'Puritanism', determination to succeed, and inner faith or self-confidence, involving where necessary risk-taking in pursuit of their 'calling'.

THE IDEA IN ACTION

The value of Weber's thesis was that it restored the realm of ideas to explanations of social change (and order) and re-emphasised the importance of 'individual' action at a time when sociological theories based on economic determinism relegated cultural factors to the sidelines. The thesis of the Protestant ethic has yet to be totally disproved as a major explanation of industrialisation and there are many examples, even today, of societies where the power of religion seems to be the major obstacle to modernisation – Iran, India and even Ulster.

The idea that certain values, a capitalist ethos, is as vital to industrialisation as technical factors, has profoundly influenced many western theories and policies for promoting modernisation in developing countries. The American psychologist David McClelland (1961), for example, argued that an orientation to achievement, the 'N-ACH factor', was the secret ingredient, the vital spark necessary for industrialising the Third World. He even set up training programmes to instil in local businessmen the necessary drive and determination so that they, in turn, could teach the local population the values of hard work, punctuality and motivation. Such programmes have been criticised by radical writers as ideological nonsense, blaming the lack of industrial progress in Third World countries on their own people's laziness when in fact the real cause of their backwardness is their exploitation by the First World, in particular by the giant multinationals that drain away such countries' natural resources and keep them in a state of poverty and dependence. From a socialist viewpoint it is capitalism and its market forces that is irrational and unjust and only through some form of planned economy will order be restored.

Many other criticisms of the Protestant ethic thesis, however, rest on a misunderstanding of Weber's ideas – not always that surprising given the ambiguities surrounding much of his writings:

■ He has been criticised for saying that Protestantism *caused* the Industrial Revolution. In fact he merely said that he perceived an 'elective affinity' between the Protestant ethic and the spirit of capitalism, though, as one of his biographers, Frank Parkin (1982), argues, Weber does oscillate between a weak and strong thesis, between seeing Protestantism as merely one of several influences on capitalism and seeing it as the decisive factor. Certainly his thesis fails to explain industrialisation in Catholic countries and why Scotland, one of the most puritanical of countries, failed to 'take off' in the way neighbouring England did.

■ He has been criticised for giving insufficient attention to economic and political factors in industrialisation but again this is not true. He was fully aware of the importance of technical factors, pointing out that western societies of the nineteenth century not only had the culture of capitalism but the material base and rational framework, the legal, administrative and financial institutions necessary for the flow of capital and making of contracts. He merely sought to ensure that the importance of cultural factors was also recognised. Despite his reputation as a critic of Karl Marx, he greatly respected Marx. It was the crude economic determinism of many of Marx's followers he was opposed to.

■ He has been criticised for failing to recognise the various forms of capitalism, some of which existed before the Industrial Revolution. In fact Weber did make such a distinction identifying the 'booty' capitalism of the buccaneers, the pariah capitalism of Jewish communities and the traditional capitalism of ancient civilisations. What for him distinguished modern capitalism was its 'rationality'.

■ Others have pointed out internal inconsistencies in his thesis, in particular Weber's failure to explain in detail how protestant attitudes actually influenced capitalists (and workers), why protestants invested in profits rather than churches as a way of glorifying God, how protestant attitudes arose in the first place.

Nevertheless this thesis and Weber's overall emphasis on rationality and individual action remains a key explanation of modern society and a key perspective in modern sociology.

SEE ALSO

☐ **Secularisation** as a further development within the sociology of religion.
☐ **Historical materialism** as the Marxian thesis of industrial/economic change that Weber so vehemently disagreed with.

SUGGESTED READING

MacRae D. *Weber*, Fontana, 1974
Parkin F. *Max Weber*, Tavistock, 1982 – brief but useful summaries of Weber's life and work.

FURTHER READING

McClelland D. *The Achieving Society*, Princeton University Press, 1961
Weber M. *The Protestant Ethic and the Spirit of Capitalism* (1905), Allen &
     Unwin, 1930
Weber M. *Economy and Society. An Outline of Interpretive Sociology* (1922),
     Bedminster Press, 1968
Weber M. *The Methodology of the Social Sciences*, Free Press, 1949
Weber M. *General Economic History*, Collier, 1950
Weber M. *The Religion of China*, Macmillan, 1951
Weber M. *The Religion of India*, Free Press, 1958

EXAMINATION QUESTIONS

1 Discuss the proposition that Weber's distinctive contribution to sociology
was to argue that ideas can be causal factors in social change. (WJEC June
1986)
2 Assess the view that religious beliefs can play a part in promoting social
change. (AEB June 1988 Paper 2)

48

THE IDEA

The sociological study of bureaucracy as one of the main forms of modern organisational structure is generally seen to have stemmed from Max Weber's classic analysis of an 'ideal-type' bureaucracy. This analysis embodied three of Weber's key concepts concerning the character of advanced industrial societies and the nature of sociological research:

■ His belief that the prime feature of capitalist, and communist, industrial societies is the trend towards rationalisation, towards logical, rational and calculating modes of thought, action and planning. Bureaucratisation is a classic example of this trend towards institutionalised power, towards an organisational society. As the American sociologist Amitai Etzioni (1964) has noted,

We are born in organisations, educated by organisations and most of us spend much of our lives working for organisations. We spend much of our leisure time paying, playing and praying in organisations. Most of us will die in an organisation, and, when the time comes for burial, the largest organisation of all – the state – must grant official permission.

■ His view that the basis of power in modern society is rational – legal authority, rule by laws and regulations rather than by men; power legitimised by consent and authorised by office rather than by tradition or personal charisma. Bureaucracy is a classic example of such rule by regulation, such impersonal and impartial power. Bureaucrats act without prejudice or passion, applying the rules to all, irrespective of differences in social rank or background, whilst they themselves are subject to a higher authority, the will of the people as executed by the government of the day. The power of modern-day officials rests not in themselves but in the posts they hold, be it as a civil servant, judge or policeman. Whilst in office they have the authority to issue orders, but only within limits, and only to their subordinates. Out of office, officials have no legitimate power. In office the ideal official is a faithful servant, obediently executing orders and rules from above.

His attempt to use ideal-types, model examples of key characteristics of various social, political and economic institutions, as a basis of sociological analysis and comparison.

Weber (1948) defined bureaucracy as 'a hierarchical organisational structure designed rationally to co-ordinate the work of many individuals in the pursuit of large-scale administrative tasks and organisational goals'. Though he argued that many private, capitalist organisations were becoming bureaucratic in character, the main focus of his analysis at this time was on public institutions, in particular state bureaucracies. He identified the following as the key features of an ideal-type or pure form of bureaucracy:

A specialized division of administrative labour. Complex tasks are broken down into manageable parts, with each official specialising in a particular area, be it education, finance or housing. Within each department, every official has a clearly-defined sphere of responsibility.

A hierarchy of offices and authority whereby every lower office is under the control and supervision of a higher one in a hierarchical chain of command.

Rule by regulations whereby all the operations of the bureaucracy are governed by 'a consistent system of abstract rules' and 'the application of these rules to particular cases' (Weber, 1948). Such rules both direct officials' actions and clearly define the limits of their power. They impose strict discipline and central control. They leave little room for personal initiative or discretion.

Formal impersonality is the governing characteristic of all bureaucratic action. The ideal official performs his duties without regard for persons or for his own feelings, but solely according to the rules.

Appointment on the basis of merit becomes the sole criterion for selecting and promoting officials. 'Bureaucratic administration means, fundamentally, the exercise of control on the basis of knowledge. This is the feature of it which makes it specifically rational' (Weber, 1948).

A strict separation of private and official income and life. 'Bureaucracy segregates official activity as something distinct from the sphere of private life' (Weber, 1948).

These features, argued Weber, distinguished modern bureaucratic organisation from previous forms of administration where corruption, nepotism and personal favour all abounded, producing gross inefficiency. Modern industrial societies, whether capitalist or communist, require highly efficient organisational structures to function properly. Bureaucracy, in his view, is the most efficient and technically superior form of orgnanisation precisely because it relies on rules, not men, on a hierarchy of offices, not on a network of personal relationships. In fact, the more formal and impersonal the bureaucracy, the more efficient it will be, because then, even if all the present incumbents were replaced by an entirely new set of officials, the system would continue to function as before. As Frank Parkin (1982) has commented,

On Weber's account, the behaviour of bureaucrats is fashioned by the internal logic of the administrative machine, not by the subjective meanings and perceptions of the actors. Personal motives and subjective meanings appear to be no more relevant to the conduct of Weber's typical bureaucrat than they are to the conduct of Marx's typical capitalist.

THE IDEA IN ACTION

Weber's ideal-type bureaucracy has dominated modern analyses of industrial and political organisations, be they the civil service, welfare state or such private firms as ICI. Much of the sociology of organisations has been a debate with Weber, a critique of his ideal-type as both a model of organisational efficiency and as the idea way to run a democracy. Research into real-life bureaucracies has tended to highlight their inefficiencies and to portray them as a threat to democracy and individual liberty.

BUREAUCRATIC EFFICIENCY

In contrast to Weber's claim that bureaucracy is technically the most superior form of organisation, a wide variety of writers have pointed out its administrative weaknesses. Robert Merton (1957) pointed out the features of bureaucracy he considered to be 'dysfunctional' which may even prevent the achievement of organisational goals, in particular the inefficiencies created by bureaucrats' slavish adherence to rules and regulations, their conservatism, fear of change and their cold, impersonal treatment of their clients. Many people have complained of being tied up in 'red tape', of being ignored by faceless bureaucrats. Bureaucracies are notorious for their inability to respond quickly to new circumstances, new initiatives. Bradley and Wilkie (1974) cite a classic example of bureaucratic paralysis:

The story has been told of a Soviet citizen taking a rifle into Red Square and firing a number of shots at President Mikoyan's car. Red Square at that time was saturated with security guards, but they did not dare act immediately without orders because they could not be sure that the attempted assassination was not sanctioned by an even higher authority than Mikoyan. The guards were effectively paralysed until higher 'clearance' was obtained to shoot the offender.

Peter Blau (1963) showed in his studies of both a federal law enforcement agency and an American employment agency how the 'informal' techniques adopted by employees were far more efficient than those laid down in the official rule book. Michel Crozier (1964) took this analysis further by showing how employees often ignore and bend the rules, pay lip-service to them, but in practice withhold or distort information so that their superiors do not know exactly what is going on. In an attempt to reassert control, senior managers create more rules, but in so doing only increase inefficiency and misinformation.

Alvin Gouldner's study of a gypsum mine (1954) and Burns & Stalker's of electronics firms (1966) showed that although a bureaucratic system of organisation is ideal when conditions are highly stable and predictable, a much more 'organic' structure is required in more fluid and unpredictable situations. Bureaucratic structures are totally unsuited to responding quickly to the dangers of work down a mine or the ever-changing circumstances of new technologies and new markets.

DEMOCRATIC ACCOUNTABILITY

Whilst extolling the technical virtues of bureaucracy, Weber was well aware of the power of officialdom, well aware that such institutionalised power could enslave not only its employees, but become a threat to democracy itself. He foresaw the danger of hierarchical control crushing individual initiative and creativity, of creating 'specialists without spirit', trapped in an iron cage of rules and regulations, helplessly dependent on orders from above. Equally, Weber recognised that, whilst modern democracies require bureaucracies to function effectively, there is the inherent danger of the civil servant coming to rule his elected political master: 'The political master always finds himself, *vis-à-vis* the trained official, in the position of a dilettante facing the expert.' Through their expert knowledge, secrecy and traditional anonymity, civil servants have power without responsibility. They are continually in office; politicians simply come and go. Weber saw the key to this dilemma as being control of the civil service by Parliament and regular accountability. Other writers have been less optimistic, most notably Robert Michels in his thesis about the *iron law of oligarchy* (see page 205). A wide variety of studies of modern government have highlighted the power of officials to the point where many have claimed that the British Civil Service is a form of 'ruling class' (Brian Sedgemore, Tony Benn, Crowther-Hunt Report 1980). The various techniques used by officials to keep Ministers in their place are outlined in amusing detail in the Crossman Diaries (1977) and in the television series 'Yes, Minister' and 'Yes, Prime Minister'.

Marxist writers go even further, arguing that the whole of the capitalist state – Parliament, government and civil service combined – is an instrument of class control; as Lenin put it, 'an organ for the oppression of one class by another'. Though Marx, Engels and Lenin were primarily concerned with state bureaucracies, modern Marxists like Harry Braverman (see page 31) have argued that all forms of bureaucratic structure, whether public or private, are essentially systems of control by which the bourgeouisie keep the proletariat in their place. Claims of technical efficiency are merely ideological myths to justify such oppression and exploitation.

Ironically, it is in communist societies that the bureaucratic model of centralised planning and control has reached its height, spreading its tentacles into every corner and producing a society in which the party bureaucrats and bureaucratic mentality are supreme. As Alfred Meyer (1965) has argued, 'The USSR is best understood as a large, complex bureaucracy.' Milovan Djilas (1957) goes further, arguing that the bureaucrats of the Communist Party use their powers and privilege to exploit the masses and promote their own interests and oligarchical rule. Mao Tse-Tung's attempt during his Cultural Revolution to restore 'power to the people' by giving the masses control of China's all-embracing administrative structure met with some temporary success until his death. Gorbachev's *glasnost* may achieve more permanent success in stirring the Russian empire out of its bureaucratic inertia.

Thus, in reality, bureaucy has proved far from the model of efficient planning and democratic organisation portrayed by Weber. Rather, his own very worst fears seem to have been realised the more bureaucratic the organisation or society. As Frank Parkin (1982) pointed out, it is 'the dictatorship of the officials, not of the proletariat, that is marching on'. As Weber feared, the bureaucratic lust for order and routine has tended to crush individual initiative and it is interesting to note the variety of attempts now being made by modern governments, both capitalist and communists, from Gorbachev to Thatcher, to break the power of bureaucracy and free the spirit of enterprise and individual freedom. In fact, Weber's ideal bureaucrat, untainted by human emotions, would actually emerge as little more than a mindless robot. It is somewhat ironic, therefore, that a social theorist like Weber, who put social action, individualism and subjectivity (*verstehen*) at the forefront of his sociological analysis, should have produced an ideal-type that so thoroughly eliminated such vital elements of social behaviour.

Nevertheless, whatever its weaknesses, possibly even because of them, Weber's model of an ideal-type bureaucracy has proved a major contribution both to our understanding of modern organisations and modern government, and to the underlying spirit of advanced industrial societies.

SEE ALSO

☐ Iron law of oligarchy
☐ Deskilling

SUGGESTED READING

Albrow M.C. *Bureaucracy*, Macmillan, 1970 – an overview of the topic.
Macrae D. *Weber*, Fontana, 1974
Parkin F. *Max Weber*, Tavistock, 1982 – brief but readable overviews of Weber's life and work.

FURTHER READING

Blau P.M. *The Dynamics of Bureaucracy*, Chicago University Press, 1963
Bradley D. and Wilkie R. *The Concept of Organizations*, 1974, quoted in *Society Today/New Society*, 13 May 1982
Burns T. and Stalker G.M. *The Management of Innovation*, Tavistock, 1966
Crossman R. *The Diaries of a Cabinet Minister*, Hamish Hamilton and Jonathan Cape, 1977
Crozier M. *The Bureaucratic Phenomenon*, Tavistock, 1964
Etzioni A. *Modern Organizations*, Prentice-Hall, 1964
Gouldner A.W. *Pattern of Industrial Bureaucracy*, Free Press, 1954
Kellner P. and Crowther-Hunt *The Civil Servants: An Inquiry into Britain's Ruling Class*, Macdonald, 1980
Merton R. 'Bureaucratic Structure and Personality' in Merton R. *Social Theory and Social Structure*, 2nd edition, 1957
Meyer A.G. *The Soviet Political System*, Random House, 1965
Ponting C. *Whitehall: Tragedy and Farce. The Inside Story of How Whitehall Really Works*, Sphere Books, 1986

Weber M. *The Protestant Ethic and the Spirit of Capitalism* (1905), Allen &
   Unwin, 1930
Weber M. *Economy and Society. An Outline of Interpretive Sociology* (1922),
   Bedminister Press, 1968
Weber M. *The Methodology of the Social Sciences*, Free Press, 1949
Weber M. *General Economic History*, Collier, 1950
Weber M. *The Religion of China*, Macmillan, 1951
Weber M. *The Religion of India*, Free Press, 1958

EXAMINATION QUESTIONS

1 'All institutions in the modern world are becoming more bureaucratic.'
Discuss. (Cambridge Local Examinations Syndicate June 1987)
2 'Much of the later research on organisations can be seen as a debate with
Weber. Students of organisations have refined, elaborated and criticized his
views.' (Haralambos: *Sociology, Themes and Perspectives*.) Examine **one** example of such later research and evaluate its contribution to our understanding of organisations. (AEB June 1982)
3 'There are very few circumstances in which bureaucracy is the most efficient
form of organisation.' Discuss. (Oxford Delegacy May 1985 Paper 2)
4 If bureaucratic organisations are efficient how can 'working-to-rule' be a
weapon in industrial conflict? (Cambridge Local Examinations Syndicate June
1986)
5 'Organic systems of organisation may be effective in innovative high-tech-
nology firms; they are unlikely to be effective in large-scale manufacturing
industry.' Discuss. (Oxford Delegacy May 1986)
6 Assess the extent to which informal social processes can influence the
efficiency of organisations. (AEB November 1989 Paper 2)

49

BRYAN WILSON *and*

SECULARISATION

THE AUTHOR

Bryan Wilson (1926–   ) was born in Yorkshire and, after war service, was educated at Leicester University and the London School of Economics. After gaining further degrees at London and Oxford Universities, he taught at the University of Leeds and is now Reader in Sociology at the University of Oxford.

Though he has in his time turned his attention to education, youth culture and the mass media, his main field of study is the sociology of religion – in particular, secularisation and religious sects. The work which sparked off a nationwide debate on secularisation, to which many thinkers and writers contributed, was *Religion in a Secular Society* (1966).

THE IDEA

Bryan Wilson defined secularisation quite simply as the 'process whereby religious *thinking, practice* and *institutions* lose social significance'. It is based on the theory that as societies industrialise they do not need religious organisations any longer in order to function efficiently, nor are religious ways of thinking compatible with the solving of modern problems. This thesis rests on five main arguments:

■ That there has been a decline in religious practice and participation in advanced industrial societies. This form of decline is mainly measured in terms of statistics of church attendance and membership. For example in Britain today only about a sixth of the adult population belong to a Christian church and only about 10 to 15 per cent regularly attend church on Sundays.

■ That there has been a decline in religious belief. As Wilson argues, 'religious thinking is perhaps the area which evidences most conspicuous change. Men act less and less in response to religious motivation: they assess the world in empirical and rational terms'. Such rationalism has developed from the Protestant ethic, the growth of large-scale rational organisations, the growth of scientific knowledge based on reason, and the rise of rational ideologies all of which offer practical solutions and appeal to logic rather than to faith and rewards in the afterlife.

■ That there has been a decline in the church's status and functions as a major social and political institution. Compared to its dominant role in medieval Europe, the church in western society has undergone a process of 'disengagement'. Many of the church's traditional functions have been replaced by secular organisations. Science now explains the inexplicable and has even given man control not only over nature but over the creation of life itself with the advent of test-tube babies. The welfare state now cares for those in need and educates our children whilst the mass media preaches the new gospel of materialism and progress. Although Cardinal Wolsey governed the England of Henry VIII, the present Archbishop of Canterbury has little say in affairs of state.

■ That there has been a process of 'secularisation' within the church. To survive in modern society and retain their congregations in the face of alternative competition churches today have both simplified and modernised their services. The Catholic Church, for example, now has the Mass in English rather than Latin and even involves women in its sacred rituals. Similarly some denominations are merging. As Wilson comments, 'organisations amalgamate when they are weak rather than when they are strong'.

■ That the growth in number of religious sects is further evidence of the fragmentation of religion, of the decline in power and influence of a single all-powerful church. So, instead of religion reinforcing social consensus and common values, it reflects the plurality of beliefs and truths in modern society. In Wilson's view sects are 'a feature of societies experiencing secularisation and they may be seen as a response to a situation in which religious values have lost social pre-eminence'. For him the new religious movements of the 1960s and 1970s are irrelevant, catering merely for a few dropouts and contributing nothing to the moral regeneration and unity of modern society.

Thus by drawing heavily on Max Weber's thesis that as societies industrialise so they inevitably adopt a more rational and logical way of thinking and organising and traditional sources of authority such as religion are simply swept aside, Wilson hoped to explain the apparent process of decline of religion in modern society.

THE IDEA IN ACTION

The secularisation thesis has gained widespread support and stimulated a lot of development from a variety of writers including Peter Berger (1969) and Will Herberg (1960). It has had a profound influence on both sociological theory and the sociology of religion and seemed to offer a major explanation for the fundamental shift in attitudes and values in western societies compared to the still highly religious societies of the Third World. Such ideas even influenced the attempts by organised religions to recapture people's hearts and souls by more modern methods, be it 'singalong Masses' or TV religion.

However, the thesis itself and its five key arguments have also been fundamentally challenged:

■ Firstly, the statistics on church attendance used by Wilson and others have been shown to be both unreliable and possibly invalid. Not only are such facts and figures only sporadically collected (and usually by the churches themselves) but they do not necessarily indicate a lack of faith. It is quite possible to believe in God and be personally quite religious without joining an organised religion. Whilst some religions insist on regular attendance, others do not. Similarly, attendance at church does not necessarily indicate strong religious views. Many people attend out of fear, habit or, in the case of births, marriages and funerals, for social reasons. Surveys have shown that 90 per cent of people believe in God and 60 per cent claim membership of the Church of England. Wilson himself agrees that there is 'no adequate way of testing the strength of religious commitment'.

■ Secondly, though the church today performs fewer social functions and is a more specifically religious body, this trend is only in keeping with a general movement to specialisation within all organisations in advanced industrial societies. Christian ethics still underlie the social values of most western societies; and even in Britain, one of the most apparently secular of countries, the Queen is still Head of the Church of England, Bishops still sit in the House of Lords, 80 per cent of the people of Northern Ireland are devout Protestants or Catholics and people still come to church for the key *rites de passage* of births, deaths and marriages. In other western societies – France, Italy and especially Eire – organised religion is still more powerful, having considerable influence over the national government. Similarly it has become a focal point of national unity and identity when countries are faced by an internal crisis or an external threat, as in Northern Ireland, Poland and Iran.

■ Thirdly, the growth of religious sects may be a fragmentary process but it nevertheless also reflects a revived search for truth and meaning in a highly materialistic society. It may simply reflect a turning away from traditional religions rather than a rejection of God. Thus, for example, whilst membership of the major religions in Britain has continued to decline, breakaway movements like the House Church Movement have grown spectacularly and there are now well over one million members of such non-Christian groups as Muslims, Hindus and Jews in the UK. Evangelical movements and sects like the Mormons have swept modern America into a religious ferment and now have considerable political influence as part of the New Right majority. Critics however see much of this revival as simply an expression of love of America rather than faith in God, packaged and sold to the American public like any other commercial product with little real religious meaning.

■ Fourthly, the whole underlying argument of secularisation rests on the idea of a decline from some golden age of religion in the past. However, historians have shown that even in the Victorian period religion was not as strong as it appeared. Whilst the middle classes may have seemed very puritanical and devout, the 1851 census showed only 40 per cent of the adult population regularly attended church. Possibly there has been no real decline; we simply never were a very religious society and so neither industrialisation nor rationalisation caused its decline.

The key problem with the secularisation thesis is that of adequately defining the term religion and finding a precise enough way of measuring religiosity – the strength of people's belief. Though writers like Glock and Stark (1965) have attempted to do this it is almost an impossible task because belief is such a subjective concept. Thus the very term secularisation is so vague and ill-defined that it is open to a wide variety of interpretations, some of which simply reflect a particular writer's own biases and opinions. David Martin (1969) has therefore argued for the removal of this term from the sociological dictionary. In many ways those involved in the secularisation debate often seem to be talking about different things and whilst it may well be argued that *organised* religion has declined, *individual* belief and need for spiritual meaning seem as strong as ever. Whatever conclusions this debate eventually reaches, Bryan Wilson's idea has helped stimulate one of the key debates in the sociology of religion of the past twenty years.

SEE ALSO

☐ Protestant ethic

SUGGESTED READING

Martin D. *A General Theory of Secularisation*, Blackwell, 1978 – a critique of Wilson.
Thompson I. *The Sociology of Religion*, Longman, 1986 – overview of the whole topic of the sociology of religion.
Wilson B. *Religion in a Secular Society*, Watts, 1966

FURTHER READING

Berger P. and Luckman T. 'The Sociology of Religion and Sociology of Knowledge' in Robertson R. ed. *The Sociology of Religion*, Penguin, 1969
Glock C.Y. and Stark R. *Religion and Society in Tension*, Rand McNally, 1965
Herberg W. *Protestant – Catholic – Jew*, Anchor Books, 1960
Martin D. *The Religious and the Secular*, Routledge & Kegan Paul, 1969

EXAMINATION QUESTIONS

1 'Western industrial societies are undergoing a process of secularisation.' Explain and discuss. (AEB June 1983 Paper 1)
2 Examine the view that although religious institutions have declined, religious beliefs remain. (AEB June 1988 Paper 1)
3 Does religion still have important functions in contemporary industrial societies? (Cambridge Local Examinations Syndicate June 1987)
4 'Conceptual confusion and competing evidence have made secularisation a contemporary myth.' Discuss. (London University June 1986)
5 'Though there is considerable evidence that participation in institutional religion has declined over the past century in most European countries, there is considerable disagreement over the interpretation of this process.' Explain and discuss. (AEB June 1982)
6 'The weight of statistical evidence suggests that Britain is now a secular society.' Examine this view. (AEB November 1989 Paper 2)

50

LOUIS WIRTH *and*
URBANISM

THE AUTHOR

Louis Wirth (1897–1952) was born in a rural village in Germany, the son of prosperous Jewish parents, but he emigrated to America when he was fourteen. Wirth graduated from the University of Chicago, eventually becoming' a professor there and a leading figure in the famous Chicago School of Social Science in the 1920s. Chicago in the early twentieth century was at the heart of America's urban revolution and a magnet for the millions of immigrants flooding into this 'promised land'. Under the leadership and inspiration of Albion Small, students of the Chicago School, like R.E. Park, Ernest Burgess, I. Thomas and Louis Wirth, became fascinated by this urban world – its apparent chaos, disorder, mosaic and ethnic communities and segregated neighbourhoods, its criminality and the sheer vitality of a seething mass of humanity in constant transition. Yet beneath such chaos, beneath such ebb and flow, lay some sort of natural order and the aim of the Chicago social scientists was to identify and explain these urban forces.

Louis Wirth's contribution was both theoretical and practical. He sought to reform urban society as well as explain it and was heavily involved in social work, housing, planning and race relations. His key focus was on group life and the essence of social order – consensus – how it arose, how it was maintained and how it collapsed.

His key works were:

- *The Ghetto* (1928) and
- *Urbanism as a Way of Life* (1938)

His influence was reflected in the generations of students he inspired and his Presidencies of both the American and International Sociological Associations.

THE IDEA

Wirth's idea of urbanism – of a distinctive *urban* way of life – was an attempt to identify and explain what exactly it is that makes life in a city or large town so very different to that in a village, suburb or coastal resort. Cities are both exciting and frightening places. The sheer pace of life, the traffic, the hustle and bustle, the bright lights, are both fascinating and exhilarating. But cities are also lonely places. Amid the swirling crowds you can feel very lonely and lost, angry and irritated. No one has time for anyone else, everyone seems cut off from each other as they struggle to survive in the urban 'rat race', warding off such predators as the loan shark, the city slicker and the urban cowboy. Such an alienating and artificial lifestyle seems to be a million miles away from the friendliness, sense of community, peace and quiet of country life; yet Americans in this period seemed to be swarming into these urban jungles in search of fame and fortune.

Whilst fellow students like Park and Burgess sought to explain urban life in terms of human ecology, a Darwinian-type theory of human struggle, adaptation and survival, Wirth developed a more cultural theory arguing that the three key influence on urban life are:

SIZE

By definition cities are large places containing thousands of people. This fact alone helps explain their impersonality, the highly transitory and segmental nature of urban relationships. People in the city are always on the move, rarely settle long enough to establish permanent friendships. They are in the city for a specific purpose, be it to make a purchase or for a business arrangement. They are 'on the make' so they don't have time for pleasantries. The city is a giant marketplace, a 'rat race' in which everyone is out to better themselves in the climb to the top and so they will either use or trample on others. It is easy, therefore, to feel a failure, rejected and powerless. The only way to cope and survive is to treat others in the same unsentimental way.

To cope with the sheer size of cities people split up into smaller communities based on a particular area or neighbourhood with others of similar background – the ethnic groups in the Chinatowns and Italian quarters of the inner city, the middle and working classes in the outer and inner suburbs. Such social segregation provides a sense of community, identity and security in the 'naked city' but can also lead to social conflict when one group feels that its territory (and its status) is about to be invaded.

DENSITY

Not only are cities full of people but they are physically packed tightly together. There is barely space to breathe and so life tends to be very tense and irritable. All manner of people now live in close proximity to each other and, inevitably, this increases the potential for social conflict, be it between rich and poor, ethnic groups or neighbouring territories.

HETEROGENEITY

The city attracts all types of people, from every ethnic group and from all types of background. It is the furnace at the heart of America's melting pot and such enormous variety of social groups is exacerbated by the intense division of labour and high degree of mobility of modern industrial society. Their differences outweigh their similarities as they all struggle for survival.

Thus, in his classic essay, *Urbanism as a Way of Life* (1938), Wirth proposed a minimum sociological definition of the city as 'a relatively large, dense and permanent settlement of sociologically heterogeneous individuals'. He went on to lay one of the foundations of the theory of an urban–rural continuum, the idea that where you live profoundly influences how you live, 'the city and the country may be regarded as two poles in reference to which, one or other of all human settlements tend to arrange themselves'. In other words, life in the city and the country are distinctly different because of their different environments and especially their differences in size, density and heterogeneity. However, Wirth also believed that eventually urbanism would become *the* way of life of modern society and would spread even to rural areas. Though he obviously feared that such a way of life was socially disruptive, a threat to society's moral values, sense of community and underlying consensus, he hoped that in time the cities of the 1920s would settle down and establish some sense of permanence.

THE IDEA IN ACTION

Urbanism and the urban–rural framework inspired a mass of community studies throughout the world over the next thirty years, detailing both urban and rural lifestyles as generations of sociologists joined this quest for community, this search for the 'good life' free of the pressures, violence and squalor of the city. However, it was these very studies that increasingly undermined Wirth's theory.

Wirth used Chicago as his social laboratory but, as Herbert Gans (1968) has argued, Chicago in the 1920s was hardly a typical city. It attracted a particularly large influx of immigrants (and criminals) and so appeared especially disorderly.

Wirth's argument that population size and density inevitably create psychological stress is counteracted by examples like Hong Kong where overcrowding is intense but disease and social disorganisation are low. Studies like Young and Wilmott's in East London (1962) and Herbert Gans' in Boston (1962) revealed the existence of 'urban villages': tight-knit communities in the heart of the urban sprawl. Equally, studies like Ray Pahl's of commuter villages in Hertfordshire (1965) and Oscar Lewis's in Mexico (1951) revealed aspects of urbanism – social conflict, class divisions, alienation – in the countryside.

As Gans and Pahl argued, neither urbanism nor a particular environment are the key influences on urban behaviour. People's social class and position in the family life cycle (whether they are young or old, single or married) have much more influence. For Marxist writers the source of all our urban problems is not the city itself but modern capitalism which generates class conflict, exploitation, alienation, urban decay and rioting. The city simply happens to be where most people live, where these divisions and problems are most intense and where the present class struggle is being fought out – on the streets. Amid the urban riots of the 1960s such radical theories soon became the basis of a new urban sociology that swept away the cultural and ecological theories of Wirth and the Chicago School.

Though now swept aside, Wirth's essay on urbanism still remains a classic, still has the strength of insight to possibly provide future food for thought once the dust of revolution has settled. Certainly he and the Chicago School have had a major influence on modern sociology.

SEE ALSO

☐ *Gemeinschaft–Gesellschaft*
☐ Human ecology
☐ Collective consumption
☐ Urban managerialism
☐ Housing classes, as extensions and alternatives to Wirth's idea.

SUGGESTED READING

Wirth L. 'Urbanism as a Way of Life' *American Journal of Sociology* Vol 44, 1938, pp 1–24, also in Pahl R. *Readings in Urban Sociology*, Pergamon, 1968

FURTHER READING

Gans H. *The Urban Villagers*, Free Press, 1962
Lewis O. *Life in a Mexican Village: Tepotzlan Revisited*, University of Illinois Press, 1951
Mann P. *An Approach to Urban Sociology*, Routledge & Kegan Paul, 1965
Pahl R. *Urbs in Rure*, Weidenfeld & Nicolson, 1965
Wirth L. *The Ghetto*, University of Chicago Press 1928
Young M. and Willmott P. *Family and Kinship in East London*, Penguin, 1962

EXAMINATION QUESTIONS

1 Examine the view that the urban way of life has certain distinctive and universal features. (AEB June 1988 Paper 2)
2 Is there a distinctive 'urban way of life'? (Oxford Delegacy May 1987)
3 How useful is the distinction made by sociologists between rural and urban communities? (Cambridge Local Examinations Syndicate June 1986)
4 Some sociologists have claimed that there is a distinctive 'urban way of life'.
  (a) Outline what are considered to be its main features.
  (b) Elaborate and evaluate recent assertions that it is no longer meaningful to talk of distinctively 'rural' and 'urban' ways of life. (AEB June 1982)
5 'People in urban areas have a different way of life from those living in rural areas.' Examine this view. (AEB June 1989 Paper 1)

BIBLIOGRAPHY

Aaronovitch, S. (1961) *The Ruling Class*, Lawrence & Wishart, London.
Adorno, T.W. *et al.* (1950) *The Authoritarian Personality*, Harper, New York.
Albrow, M.C. (1970) *Bureaucracy*, Macmillan, London.
Althusser, L. (1965) *For Marx*, Penguin, Harmondsworth.
  (1965) *Reading Capital*, New Left Books, London.
  (1969) *Lenin and Philosophy*, New Left Books, London.
  (1976) *Essays in Self-Criticism*, New Left Books, London.
Amin, S. (1976) *Unequal Development*, Harvester, London.
Anderson, R.J. and Sharrock, W.W. *Teaching Papers in Sociology*, Dept of Sociology, University of Manchester/Longman.
Aron, R. (1967) *Eighteen Lectures on Industrial Society*, Weidenfeld & Nicolson, London.

Barnes, B. (1982) *T.S. Kuhn*, Macmillan, London.
Barnet, F.J. and Müller, R.E. (1975) *Global Reach*, Jonathan Cape, London.
Barratt, M. (1980) *Women's Oppression Today*, New Left Books, London.
Becker, H.S. (1963) *Outsiders*, Free Press, New York.
Beechey, V. and Donald, J. (eds) (1985) *Subjectivity and Social Relations*, Open University Press, Milton Keynes.
Bell, D. (1960) *The End of Ideology*, Free Press, New York.
  (ed.) (1969) *Towards the Year 2000*, Houghton Mifflin, Boston.
  (1974) *The Coming of Post Industrial Societies*, Heinemann, London.
  (1981) *The Crisis in Economic Theory*, Basic Books, New York.
Bennett, J. and George, S. (1987) *The Hunger Machine*, Polity Press, Cambridge.
Benson, D. and Hughes, J. (1983) *The Perspective of Ethnomethodology*, Longman, London.
Berger, P. and Luckman, T. (1967) *The Social Construction of Reality*, Penguin, Harmondsworth.

(1969) 'The Sociology of Religion and Sociology of Knowledge' in Robertson R. (ed.) The Sociology of Religion, Penguin, Harmondsworth.

Bernstein, B.B. (1961) 'Social Class and Linguistic Development – A Theory of Social Learning' in Halsey et al. (1961) Education, Economy and Society, Free Press, New York.

(1971/1990) Class, Codes and Control, Vols 1–4, Routledge & Kegan Paul, London.

Betterton, R. (1987) Looking On, Pandora, London.

Birke, L. (1986) Women, Feminism and Biology, Wheatsheaf, Brighton.

Blau, P.M. (1963) The Dynamics of Bureaucracy, University of Chicago Press, Chicago.

Blauner, R. (1964) Alienation and Freedom, University of Chicago Press, Chicago.

Bocock, R. (1986) Hegemony, Tavistock, London.

Bottomore, T.B. (1965) Classes in Modern Society, Penguin, Harmondsworth.

(1966) Elites and Society, Penguin, Harmondsworth.

(1984) The Frankfurt School, Tavistock, London.

Bottomore, T.B. and Rubel, M. (eds) (1961) Karl Marx, Selected Writings, Penguin, Harmondsworth.

Bowles, S. and Gintis, H. (1976) Schooling in Capitalist America, Routledge & Kegan Paul, London.

Box, S. (1971) Deviance, Reality and Society, Rinehart & Winston, London.

Bradley, D. and Wilkie, R. (1974) The Concept of Organisations, Blackie & Sons Ltd, Glasgow.

Brandt, W. et al. (1980) North–South: A Programme For Survival, Pan, London.

Braverman, H. (1974) Labor and Monopoly Capital, Monthly Review Press, New York.

Brown, C.H. (1979) Understanding Society, John Murray, London.

Burgess, E. (1925) 'The Growth of the City' in R.E. Park and E. Burgess, The City, University of Chicago Press, Chicago.

Burns, E. (1966) Introduction To Marxism, Lawrence & Wishart, London.

Burns, T. (1986) Erving Goffman, Tavistock, London.

Burns, T. and Stalker, G.M. (1966) The Management of Innovation, Tavistock, London.

Callinicos, A. (1976) Althusser's Marxism, Pluto Press, London.

(1983) The Revolutionary Ideas of Karl Marx, Pluto Press, London.

Carew Hunt, R.N. (1950) *The Theory and Practice of Communism*, Penguin, Harmondsworth.
Carrigan, T. and Connell, B. and Lee, J. (1985) 'Towards a New Sociology of Masculinity' in *Theory and Society*, no. 14, pp. 551–604.
Carver, T. (1981) *Engels*, OUP, Oxford.
Castells, M. (1977) *The Urban Question*, Edward Arnold, London.
    (1978) *City, Class and Power*, Macmillan, London.
    (1983) *The City and the Grassroots*, Edward Arnold, London.
Chalmers, A.F. (1982) *What is This Thing Called Science?*, Open University Press, Milton Keynes.
Charver, J. (1982) *Feminism*, J.M. Dent, London.
Cicourel, A. (1964) *Method and Measurement in Sociology*, Free Press, New York.
    (1976) *The Social Organisation of Juvenile Justice*, Heinemann, London.
Clarke, E. and Lawson, T. (1985) *Gender: An Introduction*, University Tutorial Press, Slough.
Cockburn, C. (1977) *The Local State*, Pluto, London.
Cohen, S. (ed.) (1971) *Images of Deviance*, Penguin, Harmondsworth.
Community Development Project (1977) *Building the Ghetto*, CDP Interproject Editorial Team.
Comte, A. (1838) *The Positive Philosophy of Auguste Comte*, Bell, London [1896].
Craib, I. (1984) *Modern Social Theory*, Wheatsheaf, Brighton.
Crompton, R. and Jones, G. (1984) *White Collar Proletariat*, Macmillan, London.
Crothers, C. (1987) *Robert K. Merton*, Tavistock, London.
Crozier, M. (1964) *The Bureaucratic Phenomenon*, Tavistock, London.
Cuff, E.C. and Payne, G.C.F. (1979/1984) *Perspectives in Sociology*, George Allen & Unwin, London.

Dahl, R.A. (1961) *Who Governs?*, Yale University Press, New Haven.
Dahrendorf, R. (1959) *Class and Class Conflict in an Industrial Society*, Routledge & Kegan Paul, London.
    (1967) *Society and Democracy in Germany*, Weidenfeld & Nicolson, London.
    (1975) *The New Liberty*, Routledge & Kegan Paul, London.
    (1979) *Life Chances*, Routledge & Kegan Paul, London.
Davies, J. (1972) *The Evangelistic Bureaucrat*, Tavistock, London.
Davis, K. and Moore, W.E. (1967) 'Some Principles of Stratification' in Bendix, R. and Lipsett, S.M. (eds) *Class Status and Power*, Routledge & Kegan Paul, London.

Dearlove, J. and Saunders, P. (1984) *Introduction to British Politics*, Polity Press, Cambridge.

Delamont, S. (1980) *Sociology of Women*, Heinemann, London.

Ditton, J. (ed.) (1980) *The View From Goffman*, Macmillan, London.

Djilas, M. (1957) *The New Class*, Thames & Hudson, London.

Douglas, J.D. (1967) *The Social Meanings of Suicide*, Princeton University Press, Princeton.

Douglas, J.W.B. (1964) *The Home and the School*, MacGibbon & Kee, London.

Doyal, L. with Pennell, I. (1979) *The Political Economy of Health*, Pluto, London.

Dunleavy, P. (1980) *Urban Political Analysis*, Macmillan, London.

Durkheim, E. (1893) *The Division of Labour in Society*, Free Press, Glencoe [1960].

    (1895) *The Rules of Sociological Method*, Free Press, Glencoe [1958].

    (1897) *Suicide. A Study in Sociology*, Free Press, Glencoe [1951].

    (1912) *The Elementary Forms of Religious Life*, Allen & Unwin, London [1954].

Dye, T.R. (1970) *Who's Running America?*, Prentice Hall, Englewood Cliffs.

Eldridge, J. (1983) *C.Wright Mills*, Tavistock, London.

Engels, F. (1845) *The Condition of The Working Class in England*, Blackwell, Oxford.

    (1877/78) *Anti Dühring*, Foreign Languages Publishing House, Moscow [1959].

    (1884) *The Origins of the Family, Private Property and the State*, International Publishers, New York [1942].

Etzioni, A. (1964) *Modern Organisations*, Prentice-Hall, Englewood Cliffs.

Feyerabend, P. (1975) *Against Method*, New Left Books, London.

Fildes, S. (1985) 'Women and Society' in Haralambos, M. (ed.) *Developments in Sociology*, Vol. I pp. 109–139, Causeway Press, Ormskirk.

    (1988) 'Gender' in Haralambos, M. (ed.), *Developments in Sociology*, Vol. 4 pp. 111–136, Causeway Press, Ormskirk.

Firestone, S. (1972) *The Dialectic of Sex*, Paladin, London.

Foster-Carter, A. (1985) *The Sociology of Development*, Causeway Press, Ormskirk.

Frank, A.G. (1969) *Latin America: Underdevelopment or Revolution?*, Monthly Review Press, New York.

(1969) *Capitalism and Underdevelopment in Latin America*, Monthly Review Press, New York.

(1971) *Sociology of Development and Underdevelopment*, Monthly Review Press, New York

(1981) *Crisis in the Third World*, Heinemann, London.

Frisby, D. (1984) *Georg Simmel*, Tavistock, London.

Garfinkel, H. (1967) *Studies in Ethnomethodology*, Prentice Hall, Englewood Cliffs.

Garrett, S. (1987) *Gender*, Tavistock, London.

George, S. (1972) *How the Other Half Dies*, Penguin, Harmondsworth.

Gershuny, J. (1978) *After Industrial Society*, Macmillan, London.

Giddens, A. (1978) *Durkheim*, Fontana, Glasgow.

Glock, C.Y. and Stark, R. (1965) *Religion and Society in Tension*, Rand McNally, Chicago.

Goffman, E. (1956) *The Presentation of Self in Everyday Life*, Penguin, Harmondsworth.

(1961) *Asylums*, Penguin, Harmondsworth.

(1961) *Encounters*, Penguin, Harmondsworth.

(1964) *Stigma*, Prentice Hall, Englewood Cliffs.

(1970) *Strategic Interaction*, Blackwell, Oxford.

(1974) *Frame Analysis*, Harper, New York.

(1979) *Gender Advertisements*, Macmillan, London.

(1981) *Forms of Talk*, University of Pennsylvania Press, Philadelphia.

Goldberg, S. (1977) *The Inevitability of Patriarchy*, Temple Smith, London.

Goldthorpe, J.E. (1984) *The Sociology of the Third World*, CUP, Cambridge.

Goldthorpe, J.H. *et al.* (1980) *Social Mobility and Class Structures in Modern Britain*, Clarendon Press, Oxford.

Goldthorpe, J.H. and Lockwood D. *et al.* (1968) *The Affluent Worker*, CUP, Cambridge.

(1980) *Social Mobility and Class Structure in Modern Britain*, Clarendon Press, Oxford.

Gouldner, A.W. (1954) *Patterns of Industrial Bureaucracy*, Free Press, Glencoe.

Gove, W.R. (1975) *The Labelling of Deviance*, Sage, Beverley Hills.

Gramsci, A. (1971) *Selections From the Prison Notebooks*, New Left Books, New York.

Greer, G. (1971) *The Female Eunuch*, Paladin, London.

Habermas, J. (1963) *Theory and Practice*, Heinemann, London.
  (1968) *Knowledge and Human Interest*, Heinemann, London.
  (1970) *Towards a Rational Society*, Heinemann, London.
  (1973) *Legitimation Crisis*, Heinemann, London.
  (1979) *Communication and the Evolution of Society*, Heinemann, London.
  (1982) *The Theory of Communicative Action*, Suhrkamp, Frankfurt.
Haddon, R. (1970) 'A Minority in a Welfare State Society', *New Atlantis*, Vol. 2.
Hamilton, P. (1983) *Talcott Parsons*, Tavistock, London.
Hargreaves, D.H. *et al.* (1975) *Deviance in Classrooms*, Routledge & Kegan Paul, London.
Harrington, M. (1963) *The Other America: Poverty in the USA*, Penguin, Harmondsworth.
Harris, N. (1986) *The End of the Third World*, Penguin, Harmondsworth.
Harrison, P. (1981) *Inside the Third World*, Penguin, Harmondsworth.
Hayter, T. (1971) *Aid as Imperialism*, Penguin, Harmondsworth.
  (1981) *The Creation of World Poverty*, Pluto, London.
  (1985) *Aid: Rhetoric and Reality*, Pluto, London.
Herberg, W. (1960) *Protestant–Catholic–Jew*, Anchor Books, New York
Hewitt, C.J. (1974) 'Elites and the Distribution of Power in British Society' in Stanworth, P. and Giddens, A. *Elites and Power in British Society*, CUP, Cambridge.
Horkheimer, M. (1972) *Critical Theory*, Herder & Herder, New York.
Husserl, E. (1901) *Logical Investigations*, Routledge & Kegan Paul, London [1970].
  (1913) *Ideas for a Pure Phenomenology and Phenomenological Philosophy*, Macmillan, New York.
  (1936) *The Crisis of the European Sciences and Transcendental Phenomenology*, N.W. University Press, Illinois.

Illich, I. (1970) *Celebration of Awareness*, Calder & Boyars, London.
  (1973) *Deschooling Society*, Penguin, Harmondsworth.
  (1973) *Tools For Conviviality*, Calder & Boyars, London.
  (1975) *Medical Nemisis*, Calder & Boyars, London.
  (1977) *Disabling Professions*, M. Boyars, London.
  (1981) *Shadowing Work*, M. Boyars, London.
  (1983) *Gender*, M. Boyars, London.

Jencks, C. (1973) *Inequality*, Penguin, Harmondsworth.

Jessop, B. (1985) *Nicos Poulantzas*, Macmillan, London.

Joll, J. (1977) *Antonio Gramsci*, Fontana, London.

Jones, P. (1985) *Theory and Method in Sociology*, University Tutorial Press, Slough.

Karabel, J. and Halsey, A.H. (eds) (1977) *Power and Ideology in Education*, OUP, New York.

Keddie, N. (1973) *Tinker Tailor – The Myth of Cultural Deprivation*, Penguin, Harmondsworth.

Kellner, P. and Crowther Hunt, Lord (1980) *The Civil Servants: An Inquiry into Britain's Ruling Class*, Macdonald, London.

Kerr, C. *et al.* (1960) *Unions, Management and the Public,* Heinemann, London.

> (1962) *Industrialism and Industrial Man*, Heinemann, London.

> (1964) *Labor and Management in Industrial Society*, Anchor Books, New York.

> (1969) *Marshall, Marx and Modern Times*, Harvard University Press, Cambridge, Massachusetts.

> (1983) *The Future of Industrial Society: Convergence or Continued Diversity*, Harvard University Press, Cambridge, Massachusetts.

Kettler, D. (1986) *Karl Mannheim*, Tavistock, London.

Knights, D. *et al.* (eds) (1985) *Job Redesign*, cited in *Society Today/ New Society*, 8 November.

Kramarae, C. and Treichler, P. (1985) *A Feminist Dictionary*, Pandora, London.

Kuhn, T.S. (1962/1970) *The Structure of Scientific Revolutions*, Chicago University Press, Chicago.

> (1957) *The Copernican Revolution*, Harvard University Press, Cambridge.

> (1977) *The Essential Tension*, University of Chicago Press, Chicago.

> (1978) *Black Body Theory and the Quantum Discontinuity*, OUP, New York.

Laclau, E. (1977) *Politics and Ideology in Marxist Theory*, New Left Books, London.

Lane, D. (1970) *Politics and Society in the USSR*, Weidenfeld & Nicolson, London.

Lewis, O. (1951) *Life in a Mexican Village: Tepotzlan Restudied*, University of Illinois Press, Urbana.

> (1959) *Five Families: Mexican Case Studies in the Culture of Poverty*, Basic Books, New York.

> (1964) *Children of Sanchez*, Penguin, Harmondsworth.

(1968) *La Vida*, Secker & Warburg, London.

(1977) *Four Men, Four Women and Neighbours*, University of Illinois Press, Urbana.

Lipset, S.M., Trow, M. and Coleman, J. (1956) *Union Democracy*, Free Press, Glencoe.

Lloyd, B. Archer, J. (1982) *Sex and Gender*, Penguin, Harmondsworth.

Lockwood, D. (1958) *The Blackcoated Worker*, Allen & Unwin, London.

(1975) 'Sources of Variation in Working Class Images of Society' in Bulmer, M. (ed.) *Working Class Images of Society*, Routledge & Kegan Paul, London.

Lukes, S. (1974) *Power: A Radical View*, Macmillan, London.

(1972) *Emile Durkheim, His Life and Work*, Allen & Unwin, London.

Lund, P. (1978) *Ivan Illich and His Antics*, SLD, Denby Dale, England.

Maccoby, E.E. and Jacklin, C.N. (1974) *The Psychology of Sex Differences*, Stanford University Press, Stanford.

MacRae, D. (1974) *Weber*, Fontana, London.

Magee, B. (1973) *Popper*, Fontana, London.

Mann, P. (1965) *An Approach to Urban Sociology*, Routledge & Kegan Paul, London.

Mannheim, K. (1929) *Ideology and Utopia*, Routledge & Kegan Paul, London [1960]

(1940) *Man and Society in an Age of Reconstruction*, Routledge & Kegan Paul, London.

(1950) *Freedom, Power and Democratic Planning*, Routledge & Kegan Paul, London.

(1952) *Essays on the Sociology of Knowledge*, OUP, London.

Marcuse, H. (1954) *Reason and Revolution*, Humanities Press, New York.

(1955) *Eros* and *Civilization*, Beacon Press, Boston.

(1964) *One Dimensional Man*, Routledge & Kegan Paul, London.

Marshall, G. *et al.* (1988) *Social Class in Modern Britain*, Hutchinson, London.

Martin, D. (1978) *A General Theory of Secularisation*, Blackwell, Oxford.

(1969) *The Religious and the Secular*, Routledge & Kegan Paul, London.

Marx, K. (1973) *Gründrisse*, Penguin, Harmondsworth.

(1971) *A Critique of Political Economy*, Lawrence & Wishart, London.

(1970) *Das Kapital,* Lawrence & Wishart, London.

(1961) *Paris Manuscripts,* quoted in Bottomore and Rubel eds.

Marx, K. and Engels, F. (1956) *The Holy Family,* Progress Publishers.

(1965) *The German Ideology,* Lawrence & Wishart, London.

(1968) 'The Communist Manifesto', in *Selected Works,* Lawrence & Wishart, London.

Matthews, F.H. (1977) *Quest for an American Sociology: R.E. Park and the Chicago School,* cited in *Student Encyclopedia of Sociology,* Macmillan, London.

Matthews, M. (1978) *Privilege in the Soviet Union,* Allen & Unwin, London.

Mayes, P. (1986) *Gender,* Longman, London.

Mayo, E. (1932) *Human Problems of an Industrial Civilization,* Macmillan, London.

(1949) *Social Problems of an Industrial Civilization,* Routledge & Kegan Paul, London.

McClellan, D. (1973) *Karl Marx,* Macmillan, London.

(1975) *Marx,* Fontana, London.

(1977) *Engels,* Fontana, Glasgow.

McClelland, D. (1961) *The Achieving Society,* Princeton University Press, Princeton.

McKenzie, R. (1964) *British Political Parties,* Mercury Books, London.

Mead, G.H. (1934) *Mind, Self and Society,* Chicago University Press, Chicago.

(1938) *The Philosophy of the Act,* Chicago University Press, Chicago.

(1959) *The Philosophy of the Present,* Chicago University Press, Chicago.

Mead, M. (1950) *Male and Female,* Penguin, Harmondsworth.

Meisel, J. (ed.) (1965) *Pareto and Mosca,* Prentice Hall, Englewood Cliffs, New Jersey

Merton, R.K. (1938) *Science, Technology and Society in England,* Harper Row, New York [1970].

(1949) *Social Theory and Social Structure,* Free Press, New York

(1952) *A Reader in Bureaucracy,* Free Press, New York.

(1957) 'Bureaucratic Structure and Personality' in *Social Theory and Social Structure,* 2nd edn.

(1973) *The Sociology of Science,* University of Chicago Press University, Chicago.

Merton, R.K. and Nisbet R. (eds.) (1976) *Contemporary Social Problems,* 4th ed., Harcourt Brace Jovanovich, New York.

Meyer, A.G. (1965) *The Soviet Political System,* Random House, New York.

Michels, R. (1911) *Political Parties*, Free Press, New York.

Miliband, R. (1969) *The State in Capitalist Society*, Weidenfeld & Nicolson, London.

Miller, D.L. (1973) *George Herbert Mead*, University of Texas Press, Austin.

Millett, K. (1971) *Sexual Politics*, Abacus Books, London.

Mills, C.W. (1951) *White Collar*, OUP, Oxford.

    (1956) *The Power Elite*, OUP, Oxford.

    (1958) *The Causes of World War III*, Simon & Schuster, New York.

    (1959) *The Sociological Imagination*, OUP, New York.

    (1960) *Listen Yankee. The Revolution in Cuba*, McGraw-Hill, New York.

    (1962) *The Marxists*, Dell, New York.

Moore, R. and Rex, J. (1967) *Race Community and Conflict*, OUP, London.

    (1974) *Pitmen, Preachers and Politics*, CUP, Cambridge.

    (1975) *Racism and Black Resistance in Britain*, London.

    (1982) *The Social Impact of Oil – The Case of Peterhead*, Routledge & Kegan Paul, London.

Morgan, D.H. (1986) 'Gender' in Burgess, R. (ed.) *Key Variables in Social Investigation*, Routledge & Kegan Paul, London.

Morris, J. (1974) *Conundrum*, Faber, London.

Morris, M.B. (1977) *An Excursion into Creative Sociology*, Columbia University Press, New York.

Mosca, G. (1896) *The Ruling Class*, McGraw-Hill, New York.

Nelson, D. (1980) *F.W. Taylor and the Rise of Scientific Management*, University of Winconsin Press, Madison, Winconsin.

Nicholson, J. (1979) *A Question of Sex*, Fontana, London.

Oakley, A. (1972) *Sex, Gender and Society*, Sun Books, Melbourne.

    (1981) *Subject Women*, Penguin, Harmondsworth.

Pahl, R.E. (1965) *Urbs in Rure*, Weidenfeld & Nicolson, London.

    (1968) *Readings in Urban Sociology*, Pergamon, Oxford.

    (1975) *Whose City?*, Penguin, Harmondsworth.

    (1984) *Divisions of Labour*, Blackwell, Oxford.

Panitch, L. (1980) 'Recent Theorizations of Corporation', *British Journal of Sociology* Vol. 3 pp. 159–187.

Pareto, V. (1916) *Mind and Society*, Dover, New York.

Park, R.E. and E. Burgess (1921) *Introduction to the Science of Sociology*, University of Chicago Press, Chicago.

Parkin, F. (1982) *Max Weber*, Tavistock, London.

Parry, G. (1969) *Political Elites*, Allen & Unwin, London.

Parsons, T. (1939) *The Structure of Social Action*, McGraw-Hill, New York.

(1951) *The Social System*, Free Press, New York.

Parsons, T. and Shils, E.A. (eds) (1951) *Towards a General Theory of Action*, Harvard University Press, Cambridge, Massachusetts.

(1964) *Social Structure and Personality*, Free Press, New York.

(1966) *Societies: Evolutionary and Comparative Perspectives*, Prentice Hall, Englewood Cliffs, New Jersey.

(1967) *Sociological Theory and Modern Society*, Free Press, New York.

(1971) *The System of Modern Societies*, Free Press, New York,

(1977) *The Evolution of Societies*, Prentice Hall, Englewood Cliffs, New Jersey.

Peel, J.D.Y. (1971) *Herbert Spencer. The Evolution of a Sociologist*, Heinemann, London.

Pivcevic, E. (1970) *Husserl and Phenomenology*, Hutchinson, London.

Plummer K. (1975) *Sexual Stigma*, Routledge & Kegan Paul, London.

Popper, K. (1934) *The Logic of Scientific Discovery*, Hutchinson, London

(1945) *The Open Society and its Enemies*, Routledge & Kegan Paul, London.

(1957) *The Poverty of Historicism*, Routledge & Kegan Paul, London.

(1963) *Conjectures and Refutations, The Growth of Scientific Knowledge*, Routledge & Kegan Paul, London.

(1972) *Objective Knowledge: An Evolutionary Approach*, Clarendon Press, Oxford.

Poulantzas, N. (1973) *Political Power and Social Classes*, New Left Books, New York.

(1974) *Fascism and Dictatorship*, New Left Books, New York.

(1975) *Classes in Contemporary Capitalism*, New Left Books, New York.

(1978) *State Power and Socialism*, New Left Books, New York.

(1975) *The Crisis of Dictatorships*, New Left Books, New York.

Pryce, K. (1979) *Endless Pressure*, Penguin, Harmondsworth.

Pusey, M. (1987) *Jürgen Habermas*, Tavistock, London.

Ravetz, J.R. (1971) *Scientific Knowledge and its Social Problems*, OUP, Oxford.

Redfield, R. (1930) *Tepotzlan, A Mexican Village: A Study of Folk Life*, University of Chicago Press, Chicago.

Rex, J. and Moore, R. (1967) *Race, Community and Conflict*, OUP, London.
    (1970) *Race Relations in Sociological Theory*, Weidenfeld & Nicolson, London.
    (1973) *Race, Colonialism and the City*, Routledge & Kegan Paul, London.
Rex, J. and Tomlinson, S. (1979) *Colonial Immigrants in a British City*, Routledge & Kegan Paul, London.
Reynaud, E. (1981) *La Sainte Virilité*, quoted in *Achilles Heel*, nos 6 and 7, p. 62.
Rock, P. (1979) *The Making of Symbolic Interactionism*, Macmillan, London.
Rodney, W. (1972) *How Europe Underdeveloped Africa*, Bogle L'Overture, London.
Roethlisberger, F.J., Dickson W.J. and Wright H.A. (1939) *Management and the Worker*, Harvard University Press, Cambridge Massachusetts.
Rose, A. (1967) *The Power Structure*, OUP, New York.
Rosen, H. (1974) *Language and Class*, Fallingwall Press, Bristol.
Rosenthal, R. (1966) *Experimenter Effects*, Century Books, New York.
Rosenthal, R. and Jacobson, L. (1968) *Pygmalion in the Classroom*, Holt, Rinehart & Winston, New York.
Rostow, W.W. (1960) *The Stages of Economic Growth*, CUP, Cambridge.
Rowbotham, S. (1979) 'The Trouble with Patriarchy', *New Statesman*.
Ruis (1986) *Marx For Beginners*, Unwin Paperbacks, London.

Salaman, G. (1986) *Work*, Tavistock, London.
Saunders, P. (1979) *Urban Politics*, Penguin, Harmondsworth.
    (1981) *Social Theory and the Urban Question*, Hutchinson, London.
Saunders, P. and Dearlove, J. (1984) *Introduction to British Politics*, Blackwell, Oxford.
Scase, R. (ed.) (1977) *Industrial Society: Class, Cleavage and Control*, Allen & Unwin, London
Schumacher, E.E. (1973) *Small is Beautiful*, Abacus Books, London.
Schutz, A. (1972) *The Phenomenology of the Social World*, Heinemann, London.
Schutz, A. and Luckmann, T. (1974) *The Structures of the Lifeworld*, Heinemann, London.
Seager, J. and Olson, A. (1986) *Women in the World*, Pan Books, London.
Sedgemore, B. (1980) *Secret Constitution*, Hodder & Stoughton, London.

Seeman, M. (1959) 'On the Meaning of Alienation', *American Sociology Review*, Vol. 33, pp. 46–62
Segel (1987) *Is the Future Female?* Virago, London.
Selznick, P. (1966) *TVA and the Grassroots*, Harper, New York.
Sharpe, R. (1980) *Knowledge, Ideology and the Politics of Schooling*, Routledge & Kegan Paul, London.
Sharrock, W.W. and Anderson, R. (1986) *The Ethnomethodologists*, Tavistock, London.
Shipman, M.D. (1972) *The Limitations of Social Research*, Longman, London.
Simmel, G. (1892) *The Problems of the Philosophy of History*, Free Press, New York, [1977].
    (1900) *The Philosophy of Money*, Routledge & Kegan Paul, London [1978].
    (1950) *The Sociology of Georg Simmel*, Free Press, Glencoe, Illinois.
    (1955) *Conflict and the Web of Group Affiliations*, Free Press, New York.
Simon, R. (1986) *Introducing Marxism*, Fairleigh Press, Watford.
Slattery, M. (1985) *The ABC of Sociology*, Macmillan, London.
    (1985) *Urban Sociology*, Causeway Press, Ormskirk.
Smith, A. (1976) *The Body*, Penguin, Harmondsworth.
Souhami, D. (1986) *A Woman's Place*, Penguin, Harmondsworth.
Spencer, H. (1850) *Social Statics*, D. Appleton, New York.
    (1873) *The Study of Sociology*, King, London.
    (1873–1934) *Descriptive Sociology*, Williams & Norgate, London.
    (1876–96) *The Principles of Sociology*, Appleton, New York.
Stanworth, M. (1983) *Gender and Schooling*, Hutchinson, London.
Suttles, G. (1968) *The Social Order of the Slum*, Chicago University Press, Chicago.
Sztompka, P. (1986) *Robert K. Merton. An Intellectual Profile*, Macmillan, London.

Taylor, F.W. (1911) *Scientific Management*, Harper, New York [1964].
Thompson, I. (1986) *The Sociology of Religion*, Longman, London.
Thompson, K. (1982) *Emile Durkheim*, Tavistock, London.
Tiger, L. and Fox, R. (1972) *The Imperial Kingdom*, Secker & Warburg, London.
Tolson, A. (1977) *The Limits of Masculinity*, Tavistock, London.
Tönnies, F. (1887) *Community and Society*, Harper Row, New York [1951].
Touraine, A. (1971) *The Post Industrial Society*, Random House, New York.

Turner, B.S. (1985) 'Georg Simmel' in *Thinkers of the Twentieth Century*, Firethorn Press, London.
Turner, R. (ed.) *Ethnomethodology*, Penguin Harmondsworth.

Urry, J. and Wakeford J. (eds) (1973) *Power in Britain*, Heinemann, London.

Valentine, C. (1968) *Culture and Poverty*, University of Chicago Press, Chicago.

Warren, B. (1980) *Imperialism: Pioneer of Capitalism*, New Left Books, London.
Weber, M. (1905) *The Protestant Ethic and the Spirit of Capitalism*, Allen & Unwin, London [1930].
    (1922) *Economy and Society. An Outline of Intermediate Sociology*, Bedminister Press, New York [1968].
    (1949) *The Methodology of the Social Sciences*, Free Press, Glencoe.
    (1958) *The Religion of India*, Free Press, Glencoe.
    (1951) *The Religion of China*, Macmillan, New York.
    (1950) *General Economic History*, Collier, New York.
Webster, A. (1984) *An Introduction to the Sociology of Development*, Macmillan, London.
Weeks, J. (1986) *Sexuality*, Tavistock, London.
Williams, M. (ed.) (1986) *Society Today*, Macmillan, London.
Williams, R. (1973) *The Country and the City*, Chatto & Windus, New York.
Wilson, B. (1966) *Religion in a Secular Society*, Watts, London.
Winch, G. (ed.) (1983) 'Information Technology in Manufacturing Processes', cited in *Society Today/New Society* 8 November 1985.
Wirth, L. (1928) *The Ghetto,* University of Chicago Press, Chicago.
    (1938) 'Urbanism as a Way of Life', *American Journal of Sociology*, Vol. 44, pp. 1–24.
Worsley, P. (1964) *The Third World*, Weidenfeld & Nicolson, London.
    (1970) *Modern Sociology. Introductory Readings*, Penguin, Harmondsworth.
    (1982) *Marx and Marxism*, Tavistock, London.

Young, M. and Wilmott, P. (1962) *Family and Kinship in East London*, Penguin, Harmondsworth.

Zorbaugh, H.W. (1929) *The Goldcoast and the Slum*, University of Chicago Press, Chicago.